PAUL R. LUCAS

Valley of Discord

CHURCH AND SOCIETY ALONG THE

CONNECTICUT RIVER, 1636–1725

THE UNIVERSITY PRESS OF NEW ENGLAND

HANOVER, NEW HAMPSHIRE, 1976

Published with assistance from the Andrew W. Mellon Foundation

Printed in the United States of America

FOR MY PARENTS,

ROBERT L. & GRACE E. LUCAS

CONTENTS

PREFACE

THIS book grew out of fascination with a now familiar view of
the evolution of New England society in the colonial period.
Grossly oversimplified, this view labels the seventeenth century
as one when ideals and behavior conformed to a remarkable degree.
"Puritans," one historian comments, "could conceive of the good
society in no other terms than complete conformity based on common convictions."[1] Other writers suggest that New Englanders
not only possessed common convictions but constructed a society
reflecting them. Consensus was deemed necessary for social welfare, and Puritan society rested on such a consensus.[2]

Historians use certain key words and phrases to describe both
the rhetoric and reality of Puritan society: order, harmony, religiosity, sublimation of the individual to the good of the whole,
patriarchalism, zeal for communal perfection. The origins of these
cultural ideals are uncertain. Some writers emphasize radical Protestantism.[3] Others see reflections of English village life or, possibly, the common aspirations of most villagers in a pre-industrial
world.[4] Whatever the origins, historians agree that the American
environment had a corrosive effect upon English behavior and institutions. Rhetoric and social reality gradually separated as the
seventeenth century gave way to the eighteenth. Puritan New
England became "yankee" New England, and a new synthesis

of ideals and behavior began to emerge. Yankee society discarded
old values and fashioned different ones.[5]

My interest centers on the seventeenth century because the current view of Puritan New England differs so markedly from older
theories. Earlier writers saw a radical disjunction between ideals
and behavior from the beginning of settlement. Their accounts
emphasized conflict, not order or consensus. They explained conflict by noting contradictory and antagonistic values among early
English colonists. Consequently, in the pages of Brooks Adams,
James Truslow Adams, and others, Puritan bigots fought cham-
pions of tolerance and religious freedom; democrats struggled
with oligarchs and theocrats; whiggishly inclined Englishmen defended ancient liberties against the encroachments of petty despots.
The battles were endless.[6]

The discrepancy between new and old arguments encouraged
me to look more closely at some of the conclusions of the present.
The older arguments were too strong, their evidence too abundant, to be explained away or forgotten so quickly.[7] I chose to
look again at the growth and development of the congregational
church, since studies of New England in the seventeenth century
usually cast the church as the cornerstone of society, shaping and
reflecting its values and behavior. I chose Connecticut and the
Connecticut Valley because of the historians' traditional preoccupation with Massachusetts Bay.

My interest in the churches quickened when I sensed a second
area of disagreement between older and newer versions of New
England's story—one which has resulted also in a breach between
intellectual and social historians.[8] Older accounts charted society's
development through the conflict of rulers and ruled. Modern
treatments either deemphasize or disregard that conflict. Neverthe-
less, it has not disappeared, for it may be found in current arguments over who was most responsible for New England's early
development. Students of the Puritan "mind" credit the clergy and
secular leaders like John Winthrop, arguing that the values which
shaped behavior and institutional structure came from a small elite.

Social historians contend that cultural ideals reflected the common assumptions of all; that the thoughts and activities of the leadership —where they are even acknowledged—mirrored the thoughts of the group.

Readers will find that my sympathies lie as much with an older historiography as with current thinking. Not that I want to resurrect the specter of theocracy or applaud the triumphs of fledgling democrats; but I concur with the argument that ideas and behavior did not coincide in early New England, at least not to the degree that current historiography contends. Much of the problem stems from the conviction that Puritan New Englanders agreed on just about everything of consequence. We are blinded by the apparent homogeneity of their values. To borrow from the ecclesiastical parlance of the seventeenth century, we see them agreeing on "fundamentals" while occasionally arguing over "circumstantials." We tend to ignore what an older generation took for granted; that New England society was molded by ideas in conflict. Studying the evolution of society in the Connecticut Valley in the seventeenth century supports the wisdom of the past. Connecticut's Puritans recognized early and often that many of their cherished ideals were contradictory. They tried to reconcile differences but discovered that efforts to forge consensus only sharpened conflict. Their efforts bred factionalism and social discord. Dissension, in turn, modified ideals. The result was an institutional structure that never found stability.

Nowhere was instability more apparent than in the churches. The church system of Connecticut and the Connecticut Valley changed often in the seventeenth century. Moreover, its influence deteriorated as the century progressed, despite repeated attempts to strengthen its position. Its development was linked inextricably to the persistence of dissension among churchmen. Dissension, in turn, resulted from the continuing conflict of ecclesiastical ideals. While agreeing that the church ought to be society's cornerstone, initiating and securing a moral order, Puritans failed to agree on how it would be done or who would do it. At first they argued over the form and function of the church. That led them to a more explosive question: who would control the church apparatus? Eventually the Valley was torn by divisive social and ecclesiastical strife. As the century wore on, Puritans failed to resolve either their problems of church order or the dissension they produced. Worse, discord altered Puritan values, widening the parameters of ideological conflict. Those changes, in turn, transformed the character of dissension and made it a part of the church system itself.

Initially the churches were both shaped and governed by the ministers who grounded them more on an imported pattern of authority than on common assumptions about a "congregational" order. That pattern made the minister the undisputed spiritual and ecclesiastical leader of the congregation. It reflected the importance of the clergy in the birth and evolution of the Protestant Reformation. It was heightened by the sectarian nature of life among the nonconformist congregations in England and the persecution and contempt most experienced under James I and Charles I.

The ministerial architects of Connecticut tried to anchor church and society in the leadership of the few and the loving obedience of the many. Immediately, however, the ministers expressed contradictory theories of church order. Their arguments, and the politics they engendered, quickly undercut and destroyed the imported pattern of authority, allowing power to pass to the brethren. The brethren fashioned a different and distinctively colonial system of church order. That system, the Congregationalism which became New England's legacy, grew out of the laity's desire to end contention and curb social deterioration. It was rooted in the "power of the fraternity," a phrase that implied more than the old notion of the ultimate sovereignty of the saints in a "congregational" order. Rather, it denoted a church system shaped and governed by men and women who shared certain fundamental moral principles of behavior and who felt a commitment not only to live by those principles but to see their extension into the community. The brethren tried to mold the church into an agent for consensus and social control in the community by deemphasizing spirituality and demanding, instead, conformity to congregationally deter-mined standards of behavior. The church covenant became the fraternity's tool for disciplining itself; the half-way covenant its means to discipline the community.

Time and again the ministers retaliated, trying to reassert the authority they had fumbled away. As a consequence of debate among themselves and conflict with the brethren, some of their own cherished notions of the nature and function of the church began to change. The ministry adopted a more exalted conception of its own authority and linked it to an exaggerated definition of the hierarchical nature of the well-ordered society. By means both devious and direct the ministers tried to alter the evolution of Connecticut's churches, using as their intellectual guide the lessons of decades of strife as well as their continuing participation in the debates of English nonconformity. Colonial ministers remained attuned to English thinking and borrowed continuously and heav-ily throughout the seventeenth century. What they borrowed, however, proved critical. Faced with many possibilities the minis-ters adopted theories and practices promising a remedy for their plight. Thus although the colonial ministerial mind remained a satellite of English nonconformist thought, its components grew distorted by the vagaries of the colonial situation.

The collapse of clerical authority and the continuing struggle between laymen and clergy kept the church system in continual disarray, curbing its ability to carry out tasks assigned by breth-ren, ministers or society in general. The instability of the system infected the entire institutional structure of Connecticut and the Connecticut Valley. Mechanisms intended to curb dissension failed to perform. The locus of authority became as blurred in the civil realm as it was in the ecclesiastical. Consequently, Connecticut emerged not as the tightly knit, carefully structured, harmonious society so often described by New England's historians but as one troubled by drift, dissension, and a search for both order and purpose.

My analysis of the church system's evolution proceeds on separate yet related levels. On one level I dissect the system to find the mechanism or mechanisms inducing change. On a second level I show how the evolving church system both molded and reflected a changing society. Within this format the analysis of level one leads directly to level two. The evidence revealed that the system evolved through conflict. The actors, while not clearly differentiated at first, gradually separated into distinct groups: brethren and clergy. The issues separating them were of paramount importance: the nature of the church and, especially, the locus of authority. My characterization of society's evolution revolves around the same issues—form, purpose, and the locus of authority.

The organization of the book follows this pattern. Initially the church system reflected the thought and arguments of the clergy. Gradually, the area of debate expanded to include the laity, until, around 1670, brethren and clergy coalesced into separate factions struggling to mold the church system. This development created a difficult organizational problem: how to tell the separate stories of the protagonists without losing sight of the greater problem of the evolution of church and society. My solution was to focus on the areas of disagreement and conflict—and the changes in church order they produced—within the behavioral and ideological matrix produced by the divergent desires of laymen and clergy. The analysis of the lay mind emerged from a consideration of the pre-eminent shared behavioral characteristics of the brethren, while the analysis of the clerical mind developed, primarily, through and around the career of the Valley's most important and influential minister, Solomon Stoddard.

I have accumulated many debts since beginning my labors on *Valley of Discord*. I would like to offer special thanks to the staffs of the Minnesota Historical Society; the Massachusetts Historical Society; the Massachusetts Archives; the Connecticut Historical Society; the Connecticut State Library; the Forbes Library, Northampton, Massachusetts, and its former director, Mr. Lawrence Wikander; the American Antiquarian Society; the Boston Public

Library; and the Indiana University Library. I received much needed financial aid from the Graduate School of the University of Minnesota and from the Office of Research and Advanced Studies, Indiana University.

The book was begun under Darrett B. Rutman, now of the University of New Hampshire, and its strengths reflect, I hope, some of his toughmindedness and common sense. I owe much to friends and colleagues who read the book and offered helpful suggestions at various points in its evolution: Michael Zuckerman of the University of Pennsylvania; Robert Wiebe of Northwestern University; James T. Patterson, now of Brown University; Bernard Sheehan, Leo Solt, George Juergens, Robert Ferrell, and John V. Lombardi from my own university. My wife, Judy, has provided help and strength, and I remember fondly my old friends, Robert Scholz and Jon Butler, who helped me get started.

Portions of Chapters 1-3 and 7-9 appeared as articles in the *Journal of Presbyterian History* 50 (1972) and the *William and Mary Quarterly*, 3rd series, 30 (1973).

Bloomington, Indiana   P. R. L.
March 1975

VALLEY OF DISCORD

Church and Society along the

Connecticut River, 1636–1725

INTRODUCTION

THE first Englishmen in New England clustered in tiny settlements along the Atlantic coast. Soon a few of the more adventuresome looked inland and found more suitable conditions in the great valley of central New England carved by the majestic Connecticut River. Surrounded by hills covered with thick forests, the Connecticut Valley offered fertile soil, abundant fur-bearing animals, and a navigable waterway. The Dutch had trapped and traded along the river since Adriaen Block first explored its northward expanse in 1614. In the 1620s the Dutch acquired land at the mouth of the river, intent upon building a fort, and a few years later a Dutch party erected a small fort on the future site of Hartford.

In 1632 Edward Winslow of Plymouth studied the River and its Valley for purposes of trade and future settlement. He marked a spot, now Windsor, as the most likely place for a colony, and a year later another Plymouth group erected a small fort on his location. A struggle ensued between Dutch and English for control of the Valley and its resources. The English won handily, aided by a sizable group of English settlers from Massachusetts Bay who arrived in the Valley in 1635 and 1636, founding the towns of Windsor, Wethersfield, and Hartford. For the balance of the seventeenth century, Englishmen dissatisfied with opportunities along the coast often found something better along or adjacent to

3

the Connecticut River. It became the most prominent route for New England's westward expansion.[1]

"Connecticut" and the "Connecticut Valley," terms used interchangeably in this book, initially included the river towns of Hartford, Wethersfield, Windsor, and Springfield. For more than two decades expansion followed the Connecticut River and its tributaries, gradually spilling over into the Connecticut Valley of western Massachusetts. Settlement there began with Springfield's 1643 decision to join Massachusetts and was enhanced by the northward migration of Connecticut's religious dissenters in the 1650s.

The dominance of the river towns of Connecticut continued throughout the seventeenth century despite western Massachusetts' growth and Connecticut's movement beyond the confines of the Valley. The royal charter of 1662 gave Connecticut the towns of old New Haven Colony and vast stretches of wilderness east and west of the Valley. Between 1665 and 1700 those areas received settlers from southeastern Massachusetts as well as others who followed the smaller Thames and Housatonic rivers. Equally important were the proliferating settlements on the coast which by 1700 formed an almost continuous line of towns from the Massachusetts border to Long Island. Yet expansion never diminished the Valley's importance.[2]

Few readers will be familiar with the outlines of the early history of Connecticut or the Connecticut Valley because of the historian's concern for Massachusetts Bay. Connecticut is viewed as little more than an appendage of the Bay Colony in the seventeenth century and, in truth, the colonies were similar to a remarkable degree. Both Puritan, their early histories were marked by the same saintly glow. Both professed allegiance to a "congregational" church discipline and attempted to maintain doctrinal and ecclesiastical purity. They were settled by many of the same people, for a number of Connecticut's early inhabitants lived first in Massachusetts. Consequently, blood ties and friendships between inhabitants of the two colonies remained strong throughout the seventeenth century.

Connecticut, the younger colony, created an institutional structure similar to Massachusetts. The village pattern flourished along the Connecticut River, and the inhabitants followed agricultural pursuits, raising corn, wheat, rye, and other grains as well as horses, cattle, sheep, and swine. Methods of distributing and holding land were much the same. Town government resembled that of Massachusetts, with the town meeting serving as the focal point. Colonial governments were similar as well. Connecticut imitated the modified corporation government of the Bay with a governor, council of assistants or magistrates, and the elected representatives of the towns. All sat in a legislative body, the General Court. Judicial functions were handled by the governor and the assistants.[3]

There were, however, important differences between the two colonies. Connecticut never matched the Bay colony's growth. From the four towns and about 800 people of the mid-1630s, Connecticut grew steadily to thirty towns and 30,000 people in 1700, less than half of Massachusetts' population. Economically, Connecticut was an inferior unit. While Massachusetts grew quickly and was soon exporting many agricultural products through the port of Boston, Connecticut labored to climb above the level of subsistence agriculture. Hampered by the lack of a large commercial center or an important seaport, Connecticut's agricultural trade did not become significant until after midcentury, and then it was dominated by Boston merchants and Massachusetts shipping.[4] Reporting to the King's Council for Trade and Plantations in 1680, the Governor and Council of Connecticut admitted dependence upon Boston. Connecticut commodities went to diverse places like New York, the Indies, and Newfoundland, but Boston was the vehicle for that trade. In addition, most of Connecticut's manufactured goods came from England through Boston.

Commodities exported were from farm and forest. The 1680 report listed wheat, rye, peas, corn, beef, pork, barley, hemp, wool, flax, parry and tar, horses, deal boards, and pipe staves. In addition, Valley inhabitants raised their own tobacco, which exempted them from the Virginia trade. Still, the report argued, the colony's economy languished. Lacking men with capital there was little expansion of either industry or trade, and prospects for the future were uncertain.[5]

The correspondents painted a grim portrait. They did not mention, however, that in pre-1680 Connecticut economic ambition was held in check by a number of important factors. Some were institutional. The ministers railed against the dangers of economic greed, and laws existed to regulate the economy and punish the overly aggressive. The possession and disbursement of land was controlled by the towns and the General Court. The General Court, in creating a township, gave control of the land allotment to townsmen. They, in turn, gave land to applicants according to their social position, though they tried to make certain that all persons received some good land and some that was not so good. A social and economic hierarchy thus emerged from the beginning of settlement, and persons desirous of improving their lot encountered the watchful gaze of fellow townsmen and the General Court. It was not a situation likely to encourage social or economic mobility.

The fertility of the land and the abundance of the forests guaranteed everyone limited prosperity but little more. The fur trapping and trading which first lured whites to the Connecticut Valley quickly disappeared as a factor in economic growth. As a substitute, many farmers cleared forests and sold the lumber, but the amount of lumber to which any man had access was severely limited by law. The communal instincts of the founders, apparent in both the elaborate restrictions on individual activity and the subtle interweaving of institutional relationships at all levels of colonial life, discouraged individual initiative.[6]

Farmers found it difficult to enhance their prosperity. The seemingly limitless supply of land encouraged inefficient methods of agriculture, and that, in turn, made more land an imperative for increased wealth. But additional land was hard to get and even harder to farm. Town planning called for the inhabitants to live close to the center, with farming plots extending out from the core. As a result, persons able to obtain additional land usually found it to be far from their residence and thus difficult to cultivate. In addition, unalloted land was held in common by the townsmen, to be saved for coming generations or newcomers and withheld from would-be entrepreneurs. Land not controlled by a township remained with the General Court, and outright grants or sales of land to individuals were rare.[7]

Other factors proved even more detrimental to economic growth. One was the absence of currency and the subsequent dependence on barter. More important was the scarcity of labor. No newcomer wanted to work for another when land was plentiful, and farmers, consequently, were restricted to what they or their families could cultivate.[8] Still, neighboring Massachusetts experienced the same problems and overcame them fairly early, producing a sizable agricultural surplus which stimulated trade, shipping, and the early development of Boston as a commercial center. What happened to Connecticut? No definite answers exist but some possibilities should be mentioned. Hartford, the principal town of the Valley, was far from the coast and failed to provide the economic integration Boston thrust upon the Bay towns. Also, Connecticut's coast offered no harbor to match Boston's, so the Valley's trade either proceeded down the river and up the coast to Boston or overland to the same port. Both treks were difficult.[9]

Population and climate provided other answers. Despite the early attraction, colonists did not flock to the Valley in the first decades. The "Great Migration" into Massachusetts provided no equivalent bonanza for Connecticut. Subsequently, immigration slacked off to a trickle during the Protectorate and failed to increase until the mid-1660s. Climate proved a problem. Though the Valley offered land unmatched in Massachusetts, the Englishman quickly learned that through periodic flooding nature exacted a heavy tribute for the richness of the bottomland. Torrential spring rains or abundant snowfall in the upper Valley turned the normally placid Connecticut into a lake, inundating freshly planted crops and ending hopes for a rich harvest.[10] Some readers, possibly remembering Connecticut's Great Flood of 1936, will understand what the first colonists faced.

In the last decades of the seventeenth century, economic life in Connecticut and the Connecticut Valley began to change. Not that economic pursuits altered—most men still farmed the land and cleared the forests—but many of the institutional and non-institutional checks on economic growth began to subside. Population increase and land hunger provided part of the impetus; civil discord added the rest. People flocked into eastern Connecticut and the Valley from poor and overcrowded southeastern Massachusetts, demanding land. Older towns in and around the Valley watched their land supplies dwindle and sons move elsewhere seeking the main chance. The result was loss of control over the land-dispensing process by the Assembly and the towns, and the subsequent inability of either to control the economic or social order through land allotment. The corporate nature of the town and its communal motif began to deteriorate. Its demise coincided with the rise of a new economic type, the proprietor/land speculator engaged in land transaction for profit. Sometime after the Restoration of Charles II the General Court began granting land to individuals—proprietors—along the perimeters of existing towns. In the 1670s and '80s that trend became a boom, as proprietors and speculators began grabbing Indian titles vacated by Philip's War, often without any action or approval by the Assembly.

Suddenly it was possible to make a tidy fortune through land investment, and powerful factions emerged determined to use the institutional structure of town and colony to maximize economic self-interest. Land-hungry farmers, though still plagued by labor shortages, could buy land to increase production and profit. But lacking capital, how would they succeed? The answer was credit, a mania in eighteenth-century Connecticut. Credit came from speculators and traders eager to encourage the land boom, and farmers went into debt, then demanded currency to ease their situation. That demand led to the issuance of paper money and, of course, inflation.[11]

Connecticut's political development conformed to the general outlines of the growth of the economy. Before 1680 the government was plagued by political insecurity, a problem that discouraged economic growth and encouraged civil discord. The reasons for insecurity were several, but the most important was Connecticut's tenuous and legally dubious claim to the land in the Valley. Connecticut had no charter before 1662 and, hence, no clear title to the land claimed by its government and people. The settlers colonized illegally, squatting on ground contested by the Dutch, Plymouth, Massachusetts, and a host of English proprietors.

The best title belonged to an Englishman—Robert, Earl of Warwick. In 1632 he transferred part of his claim to Connecticut to a group of interested persons, though he gave them no power either to create a corporation or to form a government. In 1635 six of the grantees made an agreement with John Winthrop, Jr., to form a colony in Connecticut with Winthrop as governor. Winthrop, in turn, negotiated with representatives of the fledgling river towns. Eventually they struck a bargain: the Warwick grantees would recognize the validity of the Connecticut settlements, and in return Connecticut would acknowledge the legitimacy of the Warwick grantees' claim and would allow Winthrop, Jr., to become its governor. However, no provision was made for an independent government.[12]

Lacking any legal sanction, the river towns of Hartford, Wethersfield, and Windsor drafted and ratified the famous Fundamental Orders. Often called the fount of American democracy as well as our first written constitution, the Orders in fact represented a desperate attempt to create the appearance of legitimacy. The document reflected the corporation charter of the Massachusetts Bay Company, and the government that was created followed the precedents of neighboring Massachusetts. A General Court (including a governor, six magistrates, and four representatives from each of the towns) met twice a year and formulated the colony's laws. In addition, the magistrates and the governor sat together as a court of justice. Only in the source of governmental authority did the Orders depart radically from the Bay charter. Government for Connecticut grew out of a compact among the inhabitants of the towns instead of a document issued by the king to stockholders. Yet despite that departure, there is little evidence that the founders intended a great political experiment.[13]

For two and one half decades Connecticut lived with uncertainty, never knowing when its tenuous claim to the land or its illegal government would be disavowed. Those years proved to be among the most explosive in England's history, covering the Civil War, the Protectorate, and the first years of the Restoration. With the return of the Stuarts, Connecticut, frightened by what Charles II might do to a bastard Puritan colony, sought a charter through Winthrop, Jr. He obtained everything he desired. Brought home in 1662, Connecticut's charter legitimized the government and affirmed its claim to land already held. In addition, the charter extended the colony's boundaries beyond anyone's expectations. Tiny New Haven Colony was swallowed whole, as were vast stretches of wilderness, thus greatly enhancing Connecticut's prospects for future economic and population growth.

Connecticut's exultation, however, did not last. Within two years representatives of Charles II—a Royal Commission of four men—prowled New England looking for evidence to justify the end of charter government and the beginning of royal control. New England weathered Charles' initial attempts at empire building, saved by a disastrous Anglo-Dutch war and the subsequent demise of the king's chief adviser, Edward Hyde, Earl of Clarendon.

Connecticut looked to a happier future, but experienced only more frustration. First came a series of crop failures in the late 1660s and early '70s, brought about by some of the worst climatic conditions in the colony's brief history. Drought, flood, insects, violent storms, fires—all of the calamities nature could muster plagued the colonists. The government's helplessness did little to enhance its reputation for stability. Then came the greatest calamity of all, the great Indian uprising of 1675–76, named after Philip, the illustrious leader of the Wampanoags. Signs of an attack had appeared for a decade. In 1675, the Wampanoags attacked Swansea, Massachusetts, and soon many of New England's Indians had formed a loose alliance against the whites. The war spread to Connecticut when the powerful Nipmucks moved out of central Massachusetts into the Connecticut Valley. For a year Valley inhabitants fought to save lives and homes. Ultimately the Indians were routed and King Philip was murdered, but not before death, desolation, and economic ruin came to sections of Connecticut and the Connecticut Valley.[14]

The end of the war gave Connecticut little respite. Rumblings from England and the administration of Charles II again caused the colony to fear for its charter. In 1674 Edmund Andros, governor of New York, tried to obtain Connecticut's holdings west of the Connecticut River for the Duke of York. He went so far as to lead a naval force to Saybrook but retired when it became evident that Connecticut would fight before submitting. That inaugurated a decade of charges and countercharges, maneuvers and countermaneuvers, which ended with the issuance of writs of *quo warranto* against Connecticut in 1685. Engineered by Edward Randolph, agent for the Lords of Trade, the writs charged the colony with a number of violations of its charter. Within a year Connecticut had lost its independence and was part of the new Dominion of New England under the royal governorship of its old nemesis, Andros.

Connecticut tried to avoid submission. Finally, in 1687, Andros journeyed to Hartford from Boston to assume control, thinking that Connecticut would submit. Connecticut's leaders hid the charter, prompting the famous legend of the Charter Oak. Nonetheless, Andros took control and in the following two years authorized several unpopular measures designed to ensure loyalty and support among the King's Connecticut subjects. Then, with dramatic suddenness, the regimes of James II and Edmund Andros ended with the Glorious Revolution, and Connecticut resumed its old charter government.[15]

After 1689 much of the external pressure on Connecticut's government abated, but new and dangerous problems emerged from within colonial society. Those problems owed much to an economic order experiencing unparalleled expansion. Connecticut's General Assembly tried to cope with that expansion but failed; politics and government were transformed; and instability and factionalism became the most important characteristics of the colony's political life in the eighteenth century.

Connecticut's remarkable population growth between 1690 and 1730 resulted in a proliferation of towns and a demand for land. Especially serious in eastern Connecticut, the clamor for land was aimed at the General Assembly. Before Philip's War the Assembly had controlled town formation, or had at least tried to, but the war left most of the Indian lands of eastern Connecticut in the hands of colonial leaders. Altering its posture, the Assembly approved the claims of those leaders and allowed them to dispose of the lands as they saw fit.

The Indians in question had little idea of the extent of their lands, and the deeds to the whites reflected that ambiguity. Colonial speculators proved equally indifferent to precision, and soon the colony was in an uproar over disputed claims and titles. Factions formed around powerful leaders bent on pursuing their own speculative interests. The Winthrop family formed the core of a group comprising many of Connecticut's oldest families, while their opposition developed around an aggressive, opportunistic interloper from Norwich—James Fitch. Son of a minister and continually elected as a magistrate before 1708, Fitch assembled a group of malcontents with new and old grievances against the government of Connecticut. In addition he portrayed himself as a protector of popular rights, imparting to the whole controversy a political and constitutional tinge which suggested that Fitch's supporters were opponents of tyranny and arbitrary government. That stance also encouraged factionalism within the colony and the Assembly.

The courts and the General Assembly became the battlegrounds for the warring factions. Fitch's opponents tried to use the Assembly to thwart him, passing legislation designed to nullify his land claims and those of his supporters. The struggle led to the division of the Assembly into upper and lower houses in 1698: the upper house included the magistrates and the governor; the lower house comprised the deputies from the towns. The division tended to alter the course of factional strife, and within a short time upper and lower houses were competing for control of the reins of government.

Fitch's influence waned in the first decade of the eighteenth century, but his opposition to Connecticut's older families encouraged less powerful men to press their land claims under the ancient theory of "native right." The theory argued that royal charters conveyed only jurisdictional and governing rights to colonial governments, not title to land. The Indians owned the land and only they could sell it to whites. The leaders of the Assembly countered that all Indian purchases were subject to confirmation by the government, thus giving politicians the right to rule on the validity of those sales. The ensuing friction caused more factionalism and even led to mob action in some Connecticut towns after 1690—a phenomenon that grew more common in the first decades of the eighteenth century.

Factionalism led to corruption in politics. Land hunger and the speculative claims of powerful interests introduced a form of human behavior previously unknown in Connecticut. Most of the charges of corruption were leveled at Fitch and his supporters in New London County. Some were substantiated, others were not, but the whole affair left a sour taste in the mouths of Connecticut's inhabitants. Contentiousness, immoral behavior, and occasional mob action—all uncontrolled by the Assembly—caused respect for governmental authority to decline further, especially among those who believed that the government cared little for the common good but had become the instrument of powerful and conflicting interest groups. Factional strife died down in the late 1720s, then flared anew a decade or so later in the Great Awakening.[16]

The extent to which factionalism grew out of land speculation and economic expansion reflects an important facet of Connecticut's first century—namely, that political and economic developments apparently moved along paths that were both parallel and interdependent. As a result, the colony's early political and economic history divides into two distinct segments, with the line of demarcation falling somewhere between 1680 and 1690. Political insecurity and economic stagnation marked the first four and one half decades of settlement while rapid economic growth and political instability characterized the years after 1680.

Though these observations are intended only to provide background for the discussion of the churches which follows, it is important to note that when compared to the conclusions of this book, they suggest some intriguing questions about the possible interaction of politics, economics, and ecclesiastical affairs in early Connecticut. For example, although historians like to assume that a subsistence-level economy encouraged the maintenance of a communal order, harmony, and consensus, does not Connecticut's pre-1680 experience suggest the opposite? Could it be argued that the institutional and environmental checks on economic man in the Connecticut Valley caused commercially oriented Englishmen with a long history of contentious behavior to question the church system meant to form the core of their society and the leaders who shaped and directed it, producing social and ecclesiastical conflict in the process?

Assuming that economic sluggishness did encourage fissures in the colony's institutional structure, to what extent were those fissures widened by the insecurity of the colonial government before and after the Restoration of Charles II? As we shall see in subsequent chapters, at critical moments in the evolution of ecclesiastical factionalism the General Court attempted to curb disorder and failed. Did those failures reflect a government hampered by either an awareness of its own illegitimacy or by the specter of foreign intervention? Conversely, did the government of early Connecticut depend so heavily on the maintenance of consensus among its constituents that its legislative effectiveness declined sharply when that consensus was disrupted?

Or, in the years after 1680, what was the relationship between the institutionalization of political strife in the General Assembly, reflected in the growing constitutional debate between upper and lower houses, and a similar process taking place in the church system? On the surface the struggle for power in the Assembly differed little from the struggle between laymen and clergy in the churches. Even the rhetoric was similar. The overriding theme of the battles between laymen and clergy—popular control versus rule by an elite—appeared in Connecticut politics at about the same time. First it came from James Fitch, who championed the "popular" cause against an alleged oligarchy dominating the Assembly. Then it emerged among the representatives of the towns—the deputies—who used the theory of popular control in their fight with the assistants. Thus it was probably no accident that clergymen described their struggle with the brethren as a conspiracy of the mob against magistrates and ministers: the traditional symbols of authority in the good society.

Despite their importance these questions must await another book, for *Valley of Discord* is not a general history of Connecticut's first century. Rather, it is an attempt to shed light on the character of the social order through an analysis of the ecclesiastical system, because both church and society were influenced heavily by the initial and subsequent failures of churchmen to find a consensus on ideals or to make ideals and behavior conform. To understand those failures, however, it is first necessary to know something about the ideals and their history before 1636.

PURITANS, CONGREGATIONALISTS, AND
PRESBYTERIANS IN THE CONNECTICUT VALLEY

Terms like "Congregationalist" or "Presbyterian" provide endless confusion for students of early American history. Most want to give those terms the doctrinal definitions and denominational colorations of the present, forgetting that in the late sixteenth or seventeenth centuries they were imprecise terms with various definitions. Occasionally they were used only as epithets. Yet they are fundamental to the history of early New England, especially its ecclesiastical history; and their meanings, however imprecise, must be conveyed to the reader.[17]

The early inhabitants of the Valley believed in a congregational church order that was a product of Reformed thought modified by English experience. Yet those "congregationalists" imported as many questions as answers, as many problems as solutions. Contemporary historians often describe them as "searching" for a definition of Congregationalism, not simply applying a model constructed in England or on the Continent.[18] What do they mean? Mainly they refer to the ecclesiastical chaos that characterized the Reformed movement in the early seventeenth century. They also refer to attempts to find solutions for disciplinary problems unresolved by the early reformers. Two of those problems plagued the colonists of the Connecticut Valley and shaped the development of church and society. First, the founders sought agreement on the proper definition of church order and the correct relationship between the church and the world. Second, they agonized over who had final authority in matters of church order—ministers or brethren. Each problem produced a distressing number of contradictory solutions.

How did such confusion come about among people supposedly loyal to a congregational theory of church government? In opposing Catholicism, early European Protestants argued that the spiritual "keys" to earthly ecclesiastical authority passed from Christ to the brethren in the parish, thus establishing a premise for a congregational order. But lest they do away with the ministry or make it nothing more than a collection of superior laymen, the reformers gave the ministry a validity both independent of and dependent on the congregation. John Calvin argued that the office of the min-

ut that a portion of ministerial author-
ren through election. He and other
void a priesthood, created an ambiguous
ministers and brethren. Calvin suggested that
"mixed" government but failed to note which was

The Anabaptists, the so-called left wing of the Protestant Reformation, provided a different answer. Often persecuted, they were
motivated by hopes and expectations of the second coming of
Christ and adopted a church order reflecting that hope. They portrayed the church as a community of the elect voluntarily united
to prepare for the end. They denied the contention that the minister played any special role in church order or salvation and defined the ministry as nothing more than a few gifted laymen. The
congregation was the final authority for the Anabaptists.

Calvinists countered that the church was not a haven for the
elect but was the means of grace. The minister's role, determined
by God, was central to the purpose of the church because he, or
his preaching of the Word, formed the conduit for the passage of
grace to man from God. The church's mission was to go into the
world, not withdraw from it. However, Calvinists also emphasized
discipline as a function of the church and demanded outward con-
formance to the Law as a prerequisite for church membership and
admission to the Lord's Supper. As a result, Calvinists would not
throw open the doors of the church to all but tended to imitate
the Anabaptists in trying to separate wheat from chaff.[19]

The reformers' debates passed to England in the mid-sixteenth
century. The growth of the Church of England added a new
dimension, and Calvinists opposed it for a variety of reasons. First,
it placed the power of the keys in the hands of the bishops, not the
laity or the parish clergy. Second, it ignored discipline and opened
the church and its apparatus to all, compounding the error of
Catholicism. Third, it expressed and encouraged hostility to the
Calvinist emphasis on personal piety, holiness, and rigorous self-

discipline. Calvinist opponents to the Church eventually b
known as Puritans.

The evolution of church and society in late sixteenth-centu
England shaped Puritan thinking. Most Puritans were determine
to work for change within the institutional structure of the Church
of England. However, the Church's continuing failure to discipline its members, and the increasing power of the bishops, drove
Puritans to call for the establishment of semiautonomous, gathered
churches composed of the morally upright. At the same time they
increased demands for churches governed by a combination of laymen and clergy. Though holding to the notion of the brethren as
possessors of the "keys," the Puritans demanded rule by elder
through parish "presbyteries" and maintained the notion of a ministry with a God-ordained mission.

At the same time some Puritans grew restless with attempts at
reform and began to demand a break with the official church.
Those "separatists" tended to heed the Anabaptist call for purity,
asking for "covenanted" churches of the elect, formed voluntarily
to await and work for the Second Coming. That split proved
costly to early Puritans, for it divided their efforts and energies and
provided abundant ammunition for the attacks of enemies.[20]

Between 1590 and 1605 the early Puritan movement collapsed,
rooted out by the ambitious prosecution of Elizabeth's ecclesiastical hierarchy as well as the sullen hatred of James I.[21] Many
Puritans found refuge in the Netherlands, while others went
underground in England. The shock of exile created a bitter
legacy. Numerous Puritan clergy denounced England as corrupt
and labeled the Church as no true church, then embraced separatism and covenanted enclaves of saints. Others, unwilling to go
that far, narrowed their vision of the Church to an exclusiveness
unacceptable to a majority of English or continental reformers of
an earlier age. The debate over ministerial authority went on as
well. Some exiles endorsed an independent or semi-independent
ministry, while a few suggested the sovereignty of the brethren.
Most continued to hypothesize mixed government for an autono-

mous, gathered church and made no decision as to whether ministers or brethren ought to be supreme.[22]

In England the pietistic strain of the Puritans continued despite the lack of a public posture. Gradually in the last years of James I and the first of Charles I, constitutional crisis brought the Puritans to the fore once again. They raised the old standards, though ecclesiastical problems tended to pale before the struggle between king and Parliament. They also debated the old issues and proved to be no closer to solution. Instead, political polarization was followed by ecclesiastical polarization and as debate gave way to strife Puritans divided into Congregationalists (or Independents), Presbyterians, and a host of other political/ecclesiastical reforming bodies. But their arguments, however exaggerated by war and crisis, continued to reflect ancient disagreements among sixteenth-century Puritans.[23]

Early Puritanism was dominated by its clergy, and it is no surprise to find clergymen playing a central role in the migration to New England. Nor is it surprising to find considerable disagreement among those ministers over church order and ministerial authority, even though all professed to be adherents to the "congregational way." In the Connecticut Valley, determining the correct relationship between the church and the world caused great difficulty. The ministers argued over three conflicting viewpoints and eventually coalesced into factions. Ministerial authority generated less argument, although there continued to be much confusion and ambiguity. In theory most clergymen adopted a "presbyterian" position, admitting dual governance but placing considerable emphasis on the minister's independence.

In point of fact, however, the early ministers dominated the churches far beyond the most "presbyterian" view of ministerial power. The extent of that dominance reflected some nonecclesiastical factors. One was the peculiar relationship linking the brethren to the ministers of early New England. Many "flocks" had stayed together through trials and tribulations staggering to the imagination. Those struggles knit brethren and clergy together in a tight bond and fostered a sense of lay adulation and reverence for men like Thomas Hooker which exceeded the norms of ecclesiastical theory.

In addition, the piety and holiness which characterized English Puritan behavior represented what one observer has labeled the "gift" of ministers to laymen.[24] Thus by the 1630s and '40s Puritan laymen were conditioned to look to the clergy for guidance and sustenance in a manner that transcended the normal relationship between a clergyman and a parishioner. Finally, in exile and in England, the Puritan clergy of the early seventeenth century developed a sense of brotherhood which heightened their own feelings of self-esteem and self-worth in a way not reflected in their ecclesiastical theorizing. At the same time they found little public adulation in England. Instead, they were considered social inferiors, groveling for a living, caught in the maelstrom of a society dominated by a landed gentry.[25] In New England they sensed the imminent realization of some cherished dreams. Joining the pursuit for the godly commonwealth, they found their position and authority to be of great importance to the purposes of the state. In addition they were surrounded by adoring laymen, looking to them for comfort and direction. The temptations proved too great, and ministerial prerogative tended to evolve into ministerial arrogance.

Over a century the initial questions of order and authority produced not one answer but many, reflecting the Reformed tradition. Congregationalists with a small "c" became moderate, evangelical, and rigid Congregationalists. Ecclesiastical allegiances were shaped partly by traditional theory, partly by social realities. Among some clergymen the desire to dominate the brethren and control the church apparatus aided the growth of Presbyterianism of several varieties.[26] One form imitated its English counterpart by emphasizing ministerial dominance in the parish and a church composed of the morally upright. A second version came from Scotland, bringing with it a complicated governing hierarchy of ministerial bodies as well as a corporate, national church. Toward the end of the seventeenth century, however, the struggle with the laity blurred some of the traditional areas of conflict among Congregationalists and Presbyterians and led ministers of both persuasions to seek a source of ministerial authority independent of congregational election.

But the most striking development of colonial Puritanism was the creation and implementation of a lay version of Congregationalism in the late seventeenth century. The product of internal dissent and external pressure, lay Congregationalism attempted to strip the clergy of all but preaching and sacramental functions and to place decisive authority in matters of doctrine and discipline in the hands of the united brethren. As a consequence, the church became an engine for moral regeneration and the laity revealed a fervor for moral conduct unmatched in earlier days. More important, the laity took the initiative in shaping the goals and behavior of the church, a radical departure among heirs of the Reformed tradition. The result was a new version of congregational order: one created and nurtured in the wilds of New England.

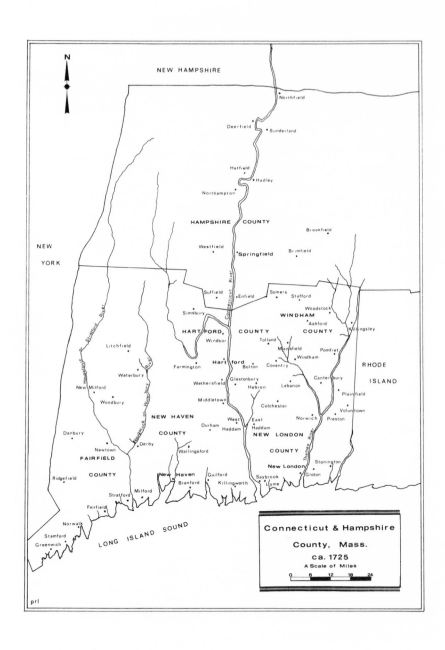

NEW HAMPSHIRE

Northfield

Deerfield •Sunderland

Hatfield

Northampton •Hadley

HAMPSHIRE   COUNTY

Brookfield

Westfield   Brimfield

Springfield

NEW
YORK

Suffield   Somers   Stafford

Enfield   Woodstock

Simsbury   WINDHAM

Ashford   Willingsley

HARTFORD   COUNTY   COUNTY

Windsor   Tolland

Litchfield   Mansfield   Pomfret   RHODE

Farmington   Bolton   ISLAND

Hartford   Coventry   Windham

Waterbury   Glastonbury   Canterbury

New Milford   Wethersfield   Hebron   Lebanon   Plainfield

Woodbury   Middletown   Voluntown

Colchester

NEW HAVEN   West   East   Norwich   Preston

Danbury   Durham   Haddam   Haddam

COUNTY   NEW LONDON

Newtown   Derby   Wallingsford   COUNTY

FAIRFIELD   New London   Stonington

Ridgefield   COUNTY   New Haven   Guilford   Saybrook   Groton

Stratford   Milford   Branford   Killingworth   Lyme

Fairfield

Norwalk

Stamford   LONG ISLAND SOUND

Greenwich

Connecticut River

Stratford R.

Housatonic R.

Naugatuck or Waterbury R.

Thames River

Connecticut & Hampshire

County, Mass.

ca. 1725

A Scale of Miles

0   6   12   18   24

prl

One

"THE DISCIPLYNE

OF THE CHURCHES,"

1636–1650

I N 1635 and 1636 Massachusetts unhappily watched the removal of a portion of its population to the banks of the Connecticut River. Whole congregations departed for the wilderness, led by ministers and laymen of great stature. The eagerness of the migrants was thinly veiled. Towns like Dorchester, Watertown, and Newtown seemed barren indeed in comparison with the lush, fertile beauty of the land in the great river valley. Although the trek was dangerous, the new location remote, and their title to the land nonexistent, the migrants showed hope rather than fear, optimism instead of dread. They seemed blinded by the promise of a new Eden.[1]

More than land brought them to the banks of the Connecticut. They were Puritans vitally concerned with religious faith and church order, and in those areas Massachusett's future appeared cloudy. The heresy of Antinomianism plagued the infant churches of the Bay colony, and the migrants to the Valley probably feared it would spread to their own ranks. Moreover, their brightest ecclesiastical luminary, Thomas Hooker, harbored dark suspicions about other attitudes and practices he detected among some of the clergy and laity of the Bay, suspicions he no doubt conveyed to his Newtown congregation. Specifically, Hooker feared that the churches of the Bay were rejecting evangelicalism and seeking to become islands of the elect instead of engines for conversion. Directing his ire toward his equally famous counterpart, John Cotton of Boston's First Church, Hooker attacked the growing practice of admitting to church membership only known regenerates satisfactorily relating an "experience" of conversion. Speaking to the problem in one of his last sermons before the Newtown or Cambridge church, Hooker argued against institutional rigidity and warned of the dangers of letting the gap between the church and the world grow too wide. "Although I knowe all must not be admytted," he admonished, "yet this may do much hurt, if one come amongst you of another minde, and they should joyne with him."[2]

Once in Connecticut the migrants quickly established the towns of Springfield, Hartford, Wethersfield, and Windsor, organized their churches, created the apparatus of town governments, and, in 1639, constructed a colonial government around the Fundamental Orders. They allocated lands for farming while holding some in common for future settlers, built their homes, and went about the business of daily living. Springfield soon returned to the jurisdiction of Massachusetts, but other settlers arrived to swell the ranks of the remaining towns. This led to further migrations and the establishment of new communities—like Middletown, on the banks of the Connecticut, and Farmington, to the east and along the shores of the smaller Farmington River. By 1662, the year Connecticut obtained a royal charter and shortly before its absorption of New Haven Colony, nine towns were included in the yearly rate, while several more were considered too small or too poor to be taxed. In addition, Connecticut families had founded towns on Long Island, several near the town of New Haven and several above Springfield in western Massachusetts. Growth was slow but steady.[3]

Connecticut's first inhabitants could not forget the pursuit of true religion which had driven them into the wilderness, nor could they ignore the necessity of protecting and nurturing their beliefs within the confines of churches. Gospel truths and church discipline went hand in hand, as they acknowledged in the Fundamental Orders of 1639. Providing for the establishment of religion, they agreed to "enter into Combination and Confederation together, to mayntayne and preserve the liberty and purity of the gospell of our Lord Jesus which we now professe, as also the disciplyne of the Churches, which according to the truth of the said gospell is now practised amongst us."[4]

A more complete and sophisticated analysis of the relationship of doctrine to discipline emerged a decade later in Thomas Hooker's classic defense of New England Congregationalism, *The Survey of the Summe of Church Discipline* (London, 1648). Smarting from the attacks of English Presbyterians as well as domestic critics, Hooker portrayed the founding of New England and her Congregationalism as the culmination of the Protestant Reformation. The Reformation, he argued, had proceeded in two distinct historical stages, both concerned with the recovery of primitive Christianity. The sixteenth century had witnessed the quest for pure doctrine. Once it had been completed, Protestants turned their interest and attention to discovering the gospel order that complemented Reformed doctrine. Several possibilities emerged from the study of the ancient texts, but Hooker endorsed only one: the Congregational way, he announced, was "the truth of the sayd Gospell." Persecuted in England and elsewhere, supporters of the true order were driven into New England, where Congregationalism became the "disciplyne of the Churches." New England's mission became quite clear. As enemies of Reformed thought made significant advances on the Continent and English Protestantism became a babel of confused and misleading voices, New Englanders would remain united in the belief that they would direct the Reformation's eventual triumph.[5]

Hooker provided an elaborate description of Congregationalism, tying it to the practices of the churches of Connecticut and New Haven colonies with the comment that "in all these I have leave to professe the joint judgment of all the Elders upon the river: of New-haven, Guilford, Milford, Stratford, Fairfield."[6] The "Church Visible," he wrote, "results out of that relation, which is betwixt the professors of the faith, when by voluntary consent they yield outward subjection to that government of Christs exerciseth by his word, spirit, and discipline, by his ordinances and officers over them who have yielded themselves subjects to his Headship and Supreme Authority."[7] Rejecting parish churches composed of godly and ungodly, Hooker noted that a Congregational order included only the faithful drawn out of the world and "gathered" into a church state to worship God, partake of the sacraments, and grow in Grace. "Voluntary consent" provided the key to church organization. "Visible Saints" able to demonstrate their sainthood were united by agreement or "covenant" under the "government" of Christ."[8]

The act of covenanting defined church government. Christ's ruling authority, the power of the "keys," passed to the brethren, making the church independent of clerical hierarchies or state control. Each church was equal, autonomous and nearly self-contained, though, to avoid the dangers of separatism, Hooker tempered his position with the recognition that the political power, the magistrate, could compel the church to execute the ordinances of Christ. Moreover, churches were linked in an informal alliance called "consociation." A fellowship of equals rather than a superior order, consociation existed to enable churches to obtain counsel or arbitration. Synods, however, possessed no authority other than that granted by individual churches and could not render binding decisions.[9]

"Autonomous" in the sense that each church was freed from meddling magistrates, bishops, or presbyteries, ruling authority in the church was balanced between elders and brethren. The brethren, through election, transferred some of their authority to the elders. They gave them the "united right of rule to be exercised over them." It was the clergyman's "outward calling by which they are warranted to act, and to put forth their abilities and ministerial authority over such a people."[10] Delegated spheres of authority resulted in which the elders were "superior in regard to Office, Rule, Act, and Exercise" while the fraternity was "superior" in matters of judgment (election, censure, admission, dismissal, etc.).[11]

The role of the minister created a few special problems for Congregationalism. Though a minister's call came from God, Hooker argued that he had no authority other than that conveyed by the congregation through election and could serve only that congregation. The brethren reserved the right to censure him for misconduct, just as his delegated authority represented a check upon the brethren. "Its true," Hooker wrote, "the Officer may by a Superior united right call them together, they cannot refuse. He may injoine them to hear, they may not withdraw. He may injoine them silence, if they shall speak disorderly or impertinently, he may dissolve the congregation and they must give way while he delivers the mind of Christ out of the Gospel."[12]

But though he tried to avoid it, Hooker could not escape completely the argument of Presbyterians and others that the minister's call implied a special position above and beyond the fraternity. Election, Hooker wrote, had an "instrumentall causall vertue under Christ, to give an outward call unto an Officer."[13] But there was also an inner call from God to the ministry that was independent of the brethren's election. Did that not give the minister special prerogatives, especially considering his importance in conversion as a preacher of the Word? Hooker said no; the call was inert, void of spiritual power until the brethren acted through election. That was not a satisfactory response, however, for the reality of the call placed the minister in a special category and, intentional or not, suggested a different meaning for Hooker's assertion that the pastor was "thus above the whole Church."[14]

Hooker confronted a dilemma, for the Reformed tradition offered different definitions of the ministerial function. Calvin suggested what one writer has labeled the "faithful shepherd." The minister was both pastor and prophet. He administered the sacraments and tended to the needs of the flock while he simultaneously announced the approaching kingdom. Hooker's view of the ministry reflected seventeenth-century English Puritanism's revision of Calvin. Some Puritan clergy exalted the prophetic, evangelical role of the minister and placed greater emphasis on conversion as "new birth" than had Calvin. They de-emphasized the slow, painful conversion which Calvin had related to church discipline and the sacraments, and focused instead on the minister's role as preacher of the Word. They envisioned the minister as a soul-winner, preaching and winning conversions and building churches of the elect.[15]

It was a position ideally suited to English nonconformity. Operating at odds with the pastorally oriented Anglican clergy, a minister with Hooker's mental and physical gifts could build a counter-congregation of the elect through efficacious preaching. In New England, however, where outs became ins, gospel preaching ran afoul of the institutional church much as it had in England. Confronted with churches of the faithful and the regenerate the minister seemed destined for the simple pastoral function of ministering to the needs of the members and administering the sacraments. Hooker resisted and continued to define the minister's role in the tradition of the evangelical preacher. At the same time he tried to accommodate gospel preaching with church order in a manner peculiar to the New England scene.[16]

Hooker was never completely happy as minister of the First Church of Christ in Hartford and probably often reflected on the excitement he had experienced rousing the faithful in the days before migration to New England. His definition of the pastoral function in the *Survey* revealed his continuing preoccupation with soul-winning through gospel preaching. The pastor, he wrote, was "to work upon the will and the affections, and by savoury, powerful and affectionate application of the truth delivered, to chase it into the heart, to woo and win the soul to the love and liking, the approbation and practice of the doctrine which is according to Godliness." He was "to lay open the loathsomme nature of sinne, and to let in the terrour of the Lord upon the conscience."[17]

Obviously Hooker relished fighting the faint heart or the impoverished soul but where were they among the faithful of early Hartford? They were his people. Most had followed him for years; and, while they needed help and encouragement, they were not the ones to whom he referred in his definition of the pastoral role. The church and the world were nearly one in Hartford in those first years, and Hooker, the evangelist, must have felt not exaltation but boredom. His special talents appeared useless. But he knew that would change. The restrictive posture of the church coupled with the continual arrivals of newcomers would soon drive a wedge between the church and the world. It was the task of the minister to soften the effects of that wedge.[18]

Hooker never believed that Congregationalism and evangelicalism could be combined, but he did think that they could be made compatible. He believed in a gathered, covenanted, autonomous group of visible saints. Still, he saw the problems inherent in churches based upon voluntarism and high standards of religiosity. How would subsequent generations meet those standards? Why could they be expected to seek membership? Hooker placed his faith in an evangelical ministry. The minister would have the dual role of maintaining the religiosity of the congregation while convincing unregenerates of the necessity of seeking Christ. A preparationist, Hooker anchored his conception of congregational order in the notion of preparation for salvation. It was the minister's responsibility to preside over the sinner's awakening, to lead him through preparatory work and through the doors of the church to the waiting arms of the fellowship.[19]

That evangelical bent and emphasis upon the Christian's quest explained much of Hooker's Congregationalism. For example, he upheld rigorous screening of new church members and opposed extending baptism to the children of "confederate" parents because he desired church purity.[20] Yet at the same time he opposed what he considered the overly restrictive practices of the Bay regarding new members, and urged the measuring stick of "rational charity"[21] in determining an applicant's qualifications. His mission was to find a middle way, a formula that would be severe enough to keep out the unworthy yet sufficiently flexible not to wound or deter the painful progress of the true Christian.

His thoughts on church government reflected the same logic. Regarding matters concerning only the congregation and internal discipline, he was content to let the fraternity decide. But in the arena of the pilgrim's progress the minister emerged supreme. Responsible, in part, for the sinner's awakening, the pastor led him to and through the portals of the church. The decision for admission was the minister's, based on extensive private conference. No one was better qualified, for only an experienced eye could detect the often faint signs of awakening. Hooker quizzed applicants extensively, probing their motives for particular conduct, hoping to detect the guidance of an unseen hand. Once satisfied, he communicated his decision, and his evidence, to the congregation for approval.[22]

Hooker's Congregationalism formed the basis for practice in Hartford until his death in 1647. Though, in theory, he assigned a considerable portion of ruling authority to the fraternity, his flock deferred to his wisdom and expertise on important questions of church government. Having followed him in two worlds, they seemed ill-disposed to question either his leadership or his actions. A strong bond linked the brethren to Hooker and to all the first-generation clergy in Connecticut, a bond that went beyond the stated relationships of church order. It was summarized, perhaps, by the response of Governor George Wyllys, a member of Hooker's congregation, to a 1644 letter from Massachusetts hinting that Hooker and the Hartford church were too lax in admitting new members. Wyllys' reply was confident, almost smug, in supporting Hooker's position and reflected many years of satisfaction with the performance of the famous evangelical. "This I am sure of," wrote Wyllys, "that with us none are admitted to partake of the seales of the covenant but such, and their seed, as in the judgement of charity have truth of grace. Which how comfortable it is, you will know when God shall be pleased to bring you to enjoy that mercy."[23]

The enthusiastic endorsement of George Wyllys typified the feelings of Connecticut's laity for first generation clergy, and in nearly every town churches were created according to ecclesiastical guidelines set down by a minister. Moreover, as in Hartford, the layman's reverence for particular individuals provided a latitude of clerical action and control which far exceeded any limits inherent in Congregational theory. Like Hooker, most ministers arrived in Connecticut with preconceived notions of church order, and the authority allowed them by their flocks provided a unique opportunity to put thought into practice. The result was ecclesiastical chaos.

Although they all emerged from the same English nonconformist tradition, first-generation clergymen brought to Connecticut a variety of definitions of a Congregational order. In the *Survey* Hooker argued that his evangelical posture enjoyed the approbation of all the elders along the river. Nothing was farther from the truth. Few shared his vision of an evangelical clergy or endorsed the church polity it entailed. Most saw nothing special in the preaching function; it was but one ordinance among many. Most resisted his exhortation to speak to the multitudes of unconverted. Instead, they defined their roles primarily as ministers to the faithful, presiding over the church and administering its sacraments.[24]

The shift in emphasis from a preaching to an institutional clergy was greatest among ministers often labeled "rigid" Congregationalists. They recognized both the inevitability and the desirability of a widening gap between elect and nonelect, regenerates and unregenerates. For them, the church meant a haven for the faithful whose primary function was the maintenance of purity. Not that the church or the clergy discouraged new members or rejected the evangelical function of seeking new members, but they argued that the primary function of both the church and clergy was to nurture the spiritual growth of those already in the fold. To that end adherents to the "rigid" posture advocated rigorous tests of admission, usually favoring a public recitation of conversion experience—including the time and place—to discourage hypocrites. Also, rigid Congregationalists placed greater emphasis upon the necessity of group pressure in guaranteeing the piety of an individual member, and to that end allowed the fraternity a more substantial role in church government. That was especially true in admitting new members where rigid Congregationalists favored a trial before the brethren and a majority decision on both the spiritual and temporal qualifications of the applicant.[25]

Rigid Congregationalism shaped the settlement and growth of the tiny coastal village of Guilford. A part of New Haven Colony for twenty years, Guilford was the creation of one man, Henry Whitefield, minister. Son of a lawyer, Whitefield rejected law for the ministry and spent twenty years in Ockham, Surrey, in a position both financially and spiritually rewarding. After a time he obtained an assistant, thus freeing him for his real interest, an itinerant ministry among the poor and needy of the area. During his travels he became acquainted with numerous ministers actively opposing the Church of England, and supposedly, on one such trip, he participated in a discussion with John Cotton and was converted to nonconformity.[26]

Through his work he developed a group of devoted followers, and as England became increasingly inhospitable to persons of his persuasion he resigned from his post and decided to take his flock to a new home. Subsequently, he made arrangements for their settlement on George Fenwick's patent between Saybrook and New Haven and in 1639 departed for the New World.[27]

Why Whitefield chose such an isolated spot became apparent after the creation of Guilford, for the inhabitants showed little interest in uniting with either Connecticut or New Haven. Whitefield apparently envisioned a separate colony, where he and his people could find freedom to pursue their goals. Failure to maintain political independence, however, did not alter their ecclesiastical goals, for in 1643 they formed their church with the pronouncement of the "mayne ends" of their settlement in New England, "Namely, that wee might settle and uphold all the ordinances of God in an explicit congregational way, with most purity, peace and liberty, for the benefit both of ourselves and our posterities after us."[28]

The insular nature of the "congregational way" was illustrated at the time the church was created, when no attempt was made to either seek the approval of other churches or invite outsiders to attend the ceremony. The formation of a church even resulted in the abolition of the existing town government, because the inhabitants believed that only verified saints ought to vote or hold governmental offices and verification was the function of the institutional church. Identification of saints for the church also meant the creation of a legitimate body politic from which could be chosen legitimate rulers.[29]

Whitefield, providing most of the theory behind the practices of the Guilford villagers, displayed his rigid Congregationalism in ardent attempts to use church polity to create a breach between elect and nonelect. No inhabitant received either church membership or civil privileges without a thorough examination by his peers. That examination amounted to a public trial in which an applicant presented evidence of a conversion experience as well as moral living, then underwent extensive questioning from the membership, and finally received a church vote. Despite that ordeal, few of the early inhabitants failed to qualify.

Within the church Whitefield's personality and ideals also held sway in determining the nature of church polity. The church possessed no "covenant" binding the members or elaborately defining institutional relationships. Instead, members subscribed to a simple confession of faith. Regarding government, Whitefield argued that although ruling authority was shared by brethren and clergy, decisive power lay with the brethren in most matters not directly connected to the spiritual function of the minister. Thus, except for a minister and a teacher, the Guilford church had no other officers.[30]

Behind the façade of a mixed government weighted toward the laity, however, loomed Whitefield's dominance over the affairs of the church. He continued as minister throughout the 1640s. Then, suddenly, he gave up his post and returned to England. Despite this loss, the rigid Congregationalism he espoused continued to guide the church's development, something the new minister, John Higginson, learned to his chagrin. The church refused to let ministers from neighboring churches participate in his ordination, arguing that as ministerial authority was derived from the congregation, only brethren could perform ordination. Higginson could not agree, and a brief controversy erupted which ended with the church holding to its position.

Higginson's relationship with his flock continued to be tainted with dissatisfaction over the minister's role in church government and the laity's unwillingness to give up ideas and practices associated with Whitefield's ministry. Higginson alluded to his predecessor's grip on the minds of church members when he wrote to Thomas Thatcher of Weymouth, Massachusetts, that he "thought the great design of Jesus Christ in this age is to set up his Kingdom in particular churches, and yet the great duty of such as are in church fellowship, is to conform themselves to those primitive patterns."[31]

Within the matrix of competing ecclesiastical systems lay a third position, moderate Congregationalism. Moderates sought to institutionalize evangelicalism, to allow the church to foster its own growth while relinquishing neither the theory nor the reality of the gathered church of visible saints. To accomplish that task, the moderates proposed a modified parish system in which membership and communion remained restricted to visible saints while church discipline and catechism were extended to nonmembers through such devices as baptism and pseudo-membership like that created by the later half-way covenant.

Moderate Congregationalism envisioned a church within a church. A central core would be composed only of full members, while surrounding them would be a group of children and adults subject to church watch and waiting for the opportunity to gain full privileges. The key to the church's ultimate success lay in two areas, ministerial authority and ease of admission. Moderate clergymen were not moderate in their demands for a dominant position in the ecclesiastical apparatus. Though recognizing that ministerial authority came from the fraternity, they argued that the pastor ought to be the arbiter of both doctrine and discipline. Moreover, most moderates supported the "broad way" in admitting new members. They argued that a confession of faith and a blameless life were ample for membership, hoping to ease the passage of applicants from pseudo to full membership.[32]

Samuel Stone, Hooker's colleague and "teacher" in the Hartford church between 1636 and 1663, championed the moderate cause in the Connecticut Valley. Born in Hertford, Hertfordshire, in 1602 and thus much younger than Hooker, Stone received the M.A. from Emmanuel College, Cambridge, in 1627. Three years later at Stisted, Essex, he was suspended for nonconformity and eventually migrated to Newtown with Hooker, as teacher of the church. He moved again with Hooker and his people in 1636 and spent eleven years as Hooker's subordinate in Hartford. Upon Hooker's death he took over his duties, though not his title, and served the church for sixteen additional years.[33] His ministry was as stormy and controversial as any in the annals of the period, mostly due to his ecclesiastical views.

Stone and Hooker differed, apparently, in more areas than they agreed in, but the differences did not emerge until after the latter's death. Hooker was an effective preacher; Stone was not. Hooker was affectionate, even tender, in dealing with people, while Stone was cold, stern, and occasionally arrogant.[34] But the most profound division came over church polity. Stone believed Hooker had allowed the brethren too much latitude in church government, and he attempted to make both doctrine and discipline ministerial concerns, allowing the brethren a voice only in admission and censures. It was Stone who was credited, justifiably, with the assertion that Congregationalism was a "speaking aristocracy" before a "silent democracy."[35] He applied his doctrine in the mid-1650s when he sought a free hand in selecting an associate. The ensuing uproar reverberated all over New England and Stone, labeled a "Presbyterian" by his detractors, nearly lost his position.

Stone also sought the modified parish of moderate Congregationalism by his early support of the principles that eventually resulted in the half-way covenant. Within three years of Hooker's death, Stone expressed public concern for persons who were the baptized children of full members but who could not or would not gain full membership for themselves. He urged, also, that their children should be baptized. Writing to Richard Mather of Dorchester in 1650, Stone announced that "unless there may be some conference of Elders, this year, in the Bay, that we may see some reason to the contrary, our churches will adventure to practice according to their judgment, i.e. to take in all such children as members."[36] Stone's statement proved premature, but he continued to push his case and was instrumental in gaining an endorsement from a meeting of Connecticut and Massachusetts clergy in Boston in 1657.

An equally significant departure from Hooker emerged in Stone's requirements for admission to the church. Stone believed that a candidate needed only evidence of a blameless life and an understanding of Christian doctrine, thus rejecting both the evangelical and rigid positions on visible sainthood. The key to his theory lay in what he meant by knowledge of Christian doctrine. For Hooker it had meant evidence of saving grace, no matter how tenuous, given to the minister in private conference and communicated by him to the brethren. Stone interpreted "knowledge" as nothing more than a simple, public profession of faith. "It may be convenient," he wrote to his congregation, "for such to make a Profession of the Principal Articles of the Creed to manifest their Knowledg: Without which they are, not Visible Saints."[37]

Stone's departures from Hooker represented a distinct church system designed to accomplish in an institutional sense what Hooker assigned to an evangelical preaching ministry, a constantly

expanding number of visible saints. Both differed from rigid Congregationalists in this regard, and neither expressed the latter's concern for "purity." By 1650 none of the three systems could claim
a majority of the churches or clergymen, largely because some of
the Valley's churches did not fit any of the categories. A few were
founded by laymen rather than clergy and revealed characteristics
not common elsewhere. Others were created by pastors of uncertain persuasion, men whose ecclesiastical views were poorly
defined.

Among churches conforming to none of the prevailing patterns
of Congregational order, New London's was among the most
unusual. Formed in 1646 the church gathered regularly for two
years before obtaining a minister, Richard Blynman, in 1648. By
that time, however, church polity was well-defined and Blynman,
though not satisfied, was forced to conform to the pattern laid
down by the members. In some respects that pattern resembled
Guilford and rigid Congregationalism. The brethren eschewed a
church covenant and adopted a very rigid and exclusive examination for prospective members, one demanding a recitation of the
"time and manner" of conversion before the fraternity. The applicant, having completed this narrative, answered questions from the
audience and then retired while the brethren contemplated a
decision.[38]

The brethren decided most issues involving discipline. But unlike Guilford, the power of the fraternity was not directed solely
toward the maintenance of church purity. On the contrary, New
Londoners adopted an unusual practice which, in its way, dissolved the gap between the church and the community and created
a parish. Nonmembers, though barred from the Lord's Table, were
allowed to participate in church discussions and to vote in all
matters not pertaining to the admission of new members. Church
affairs were normally discussed as part of the town meeting. When
the town's business was completed, the minister, Richard Blynman,
replaced the "moderator" as the presiding officer and ecclesiastical
matters were offered for consideration. No one was asked to leave,

remain silent or refrain from voting. Unfortunately, New London's records offer no explanation for this practice. Possibly it merely recognized the fact that few citizens were not members of the church and it was not worth the trouble of excluding them. Whatever the rationale, the extended fraternity of New London, while unique in the early years, provided an important precedent for other towns in the decades which followed.[39]

Windsor's experience was quite different. There, thanks to the erratic behavior of the first minister, John Warham, the discipline of the church changed frequently and, at one time or another, reflected all of the varieties of Congregationalism prevalent in Connecticut. Warham, though one of the first ministers to settle in New England, arrived with no apparent allegiance to any particular system of church order. He had gained some fame as a minister in Exeter then in 1630 was chosen to preside over a congregation of would-be immigrants in Plymouth when John White decided to remain in England. The group settled at Mattapan or Dorchester. A few years later a substantial number, including Warham, moved to Connecticut and founded Windsor.[40]

Although little is known of Warham's early views, while in Dorchester he revealed skepticism toward Congregationalism, endorsing a parish system instead of the gathered church of visible saints. In the early 1630s he became the center of a heated controversy over the nature of the visible church, a controversy that eventually necessitated arbitration by Samuel Fuller, the "physician" from Plymouth. Fuller later wrote to Governor William Bradford of Plymouth that he had "been at Mattapan, at the request of Mr. Warham. I had conference with them till I was weary. Mr. Warham holds that the visible church may consist of a mixed people, godly and openly ungodly, upon which point we had all our conference, to which, I trust, the Lord will give a blessing."[41]

In Windsor, Warham acted like a Presbyterian. Governing his church, he created a parish-like structure, refusing admission to few and baptizing all who desired it. He quickly drew the attention—and the ire—of Hooker, who conducted a personal campaign to convert him to evangelical Congregationalism. Only a few weeks before his death in 1647, Hooker appeared before the Windsor congregation, chastising them for failing to adopt a church covenant and restrict baptism to the children of church members. "Some say," Hooker counseled, "that a church covenant is but a conceit taken up of some—and that baptism should be dispensed but to children of the Church, they say it is but a conceit, to please some in a singular way; and so discourage from the truth as impossible ever to have comfort."[42]

Warham was susceptible to the influence of stronger personalities and, in the same year, he instigated some important changes in church discipline. A covenant was written and adopted; baptism was limited to the children of members, and membership was given only to visible saints. The new method of admitting members reflected Hooker's thinking. Each applicant became Warham's personal responsibility, and the test for admission involved a private conference with the minister and a recommendation conveyed to the waiting brethren.[43]

In the years immediately following Hooker's death few applicants sought admission to the Windsor church and, for the first time, a noticeable gap appeared between church members and nonmembers in the community. Warham, lacking either the personality or the preaching talents of the Hartford great, grew troubled by the obvious failure of the 1647 reforms. As a result he fell under the influence of Samuel Stone and began to think in terms of an extended congregation and moderate Congregationalism. In 1657, and probably with Stone's approval and aid, Warham's church adopted an early form of the half-way covenant, becoming the first Valley church to do so. Baptised nonmembers were brought under the umbrella of church discipline and offered the opportunity to have their own children baptized. Though a startling innovation for most of Connecticut's churches, the provisions for extended baptism differed little from the church's old, pre-1647 posture.[44]

Samuel Stone lived until 1663. Within a year of his death John Warham's ecclesiastical allegiance began to shift toward rigid Congregationalism. In 1664 he shocked his congregation by announcing the end of the half-way covenant. At about the same time he brought about a radical change in membership requirements by instituting a public profession or narration of conversion experience as the prime criterion for admission. Also, conforming to rigid Congregationalism, he transferred substantial power to the brethren by forcing each prospective member to appear before the fraternity and abide by a majority vote.[45]

Shortly thereafter a small number of families, recent arrivals from England, asked for admission to the Windsor church on the strength of their membership in the Church of England. Warham's response was a quick "no." He told them bluntly that the Church of England was not a true church and that, to join with the Windsor brethren, they would have to follow accepted procedure by providing a public narration of their conversion.[46]

By the mid-1650s Congregationalism in Connecticut revealed a bewildering array of contradictory beliefs and practices, much like the English nonconformity from which it grew. The gathered church was compromised by the fact that most of the early towns were founded by wandering congregations; hence few persons were excluded from membership. The covenant, long considered a prime facet of Congregationalism, was used sparingly. Purity of membership, usually reflected in stringent examinations for conversion experience, was questioned by evangelicals like Hooker and virtually ignored by moderates like Stone. The autonomy of the congregation suffered in the semitheocracy of early Guilford and the extended ecclesiastical franchise of New London. The authority of the brethren, supposedly the mark of a congregational order, was contradicted by the authority and prestige of first generation clergy. Even the ordinances were treated differently. Preaching, exalted by Hooker, was downgraded by Stone and Whitefield.

The common element in Connecticut Congregationalism was the power and prestige of the ministers. But considering their conflicting visions of the nature of the church and its role in the community, their authority posed grave problems for Connecticut's frail social order. Clerical division over doctrine and polity had contributed to social and political chaos in both Europe and England, and tiny Connecticut could ill afford to follow the same violent path. Neighboring Massachusetts, sensing the obvious dangers of ecclesiastical discord, managed to affect a compromise in the synod at Cambridge in 1646-48 and in the resulting Platform of discipline. The Platform received little notice in Connecticut. Hooker died before the synod completed its work, and his place was taken by Stone, who silently watched—and listened—and then returned to Hartford.[47]

This is not to say that the Connecticut clergy was insensitive to the dangers of dissension or reluctant to establish ecclesiastical uniformity. The brave words of the Fundamental Orders and the polemical arguments of Hooker's *Survey* documented the need for consensus. But Connecticut's ministers, few in number, shorn of Hooker's leadership and unable to show majority support for any ecclesiastical position, appeared reluctant to raise the question of whose order would prevail. But the problem would not be stilled. Like a harbinger of things to come, tiny Wethersfield exploded with ecclesiastical discord at the same time that Hooker penned his optimistic pronouncements in the *Survey*.

Founded in 1636, Wethersfield began with three distinct congregations and their ministers—Henry Smith, Richard Denton, and John Sherman. Within a year a fourth clergyman, Peter Prudden, appeared with a handful of followers. Half of the members of the first church were clergymen. Their presence and their visions of church order touched off a heated controversy over polity around 1639, a controversy that grew mightily when it spread to the disposition of land and the evident scarcity of choice home lots. Soon the town began to fall apart as small groups moved elsewhere. Denton, possibly a Presbyterian, returned to England. Sherman

and Prudden, rigid Congregationalists, took their people to Stratford, Saybrook, and New Haven, largely at the instigation of John
Davenport, New Haven's renowned minister. Davenport visited
Wethersfield shortly before the withdrawals began and blamed
the controversy on Henry Smith and his people, for they held
principles "not according to those of Connecticut."[48]

More withdrawals followed, until Smith and his followers were
the only ones remaining. Sometime after 1643 they started over,
forming a new church and trying to resurrect something from the
shambles of the battered community. They lived peacefully for
three or four years, until Smith's death in 1648. Then the ecclesiastical and economic problems that had turned neighbor against
neighbor emerged again, having survived even the separation of the
dissenters.[49] The pattern of disorder, separation, and more disorder
quickly spread to other towns along the Connecticut River and
proved the source of Connecticut's agony for generations to come.

Two

CONTENTION AND SEPARATION

THOMAS HOOKER'S death in 1647 not only ended the career of the Connecticut Valley's most distinguished and powerful clergyman but also silenced the leading exponent of evangelical Congregationalism. Samuel Stone, his colleague and a moderate, immediately became the Valley's most influential clerical voice, using his position to press the moderate cause. He was aided by John Warham's conversion to moderate Congregationalism and by the arrival, in 1649, of a young moderate, John Russell, as the new minister of the church in Wethersfield. The capture of those three important pulpits by the moderates gave them a majority and enabled them to begin a campaign designed to enhance and enlarge ministerial authority and to extend the boundaries and influence of the church in the community. That drive culminated in a Massachusetts/Connecticut synod's tentative endorsement of extended baptism in 1657 and in a series of violent church disputes which nearly destroyed several of the river towns, especially Hartford and Wethersfield.[1]

Samuel Stone began to agitate for ecclesiastical change in Hartford around 1650. His first proposal dealt with church membership as he tried to modify Hooker's formula to a simple profession of faith combined with evidence of good character. The church immediately divided with the opposition following one of the

church's and the colony's most imposing lay figures, elder William
Goodwin, long-time friend of both Stone and Hooker. Goodwin's
group, however, did more than simply defend Hooker's wisdom—
they also offered their own proposal, calling for a public relation
of the time and manner of conversion.[2]

The two sides remained stalemated until the church sought a
replacement for Hooker in 1655 or 1656 and Stone used the occasion to increase his own authority. Young Michael Wigglesworth
of Massachusetts was brought to Hartford and given a trial. He
was enthusiastically received by the church, and the membership
voted to offer him a permanent position. Stone, however, vetoed
the decision, arguing that it was the minister's prerogative to select
a colleague and that he had certain objections to Wigglesworth's
candidacy. Howls of anguish from the congregation, especially
the Goodwin group, were immediate. Some labeled Stone a "presbyterian" while others called for his immediate resignation. A
sizable group supported him because they agreed not so much with
his decision as with his right to make it.[3]

The furor became so great that the General Court intervened
and called for a council of neighboring ministers to arbitrate the
dispute. They did and found for the dissenters, urging Stone to
desist from the practices and doctrines his opponents considered
so objectionable. Stone and his supporters rejected the decision,
however, claiming their position had been ignored. Their charge
was lent credence by the fact that at least four influential members
of the General Court—Governor Webster, Deputy-Governor
Wells, and magistrates John Cullick and John Talcott—were members of the Hartford church and outspoken critics of Stone.[4]

Aside from the Wigglesworth matter, the specific questions considered by the council are not known. Apparently there were
other grievances against the Hartford minister as well. John Higginson of Guilford, one of the members of the council, testified
before a later council that it was Stone's intransigence and exalted
conception of his own authority that caused the situation and
frustrated all attempts to resolve it. Higginson noted that the first

council's duty was to either settle the controversy or allow the dissenters to withdraw from the church, and he felt it had found a solution in the censure of Stone. However, Stone's subsequent refusal to accept the decision, Higginson concluded, "hath bene the blameable cause of the continuance and increase and multiplying of those contentions and disorders that have bene since the Counsell . . . a wound to the congregational way."[5]

The contention in the Hartford church placed Stone in an intolerable situation. Personal vilification came not only from within his congregation but from "friends" like Higginson in other towns. Consequently, the aging minister resigned from his position and left for Boston, a broken and embittered man. Upon his arrival, several of his ministerial colleagues, including John Wilson, Richard Mather, Samuel Whiting, John Sherman, and John Norton, wrote to two of the leading dissenters, magistrate John Cullick and elder William Goodwin, asking for a summary of the issues involved as well as some inkling as to what could be done to resolve the tragic situation. At the same time several Bay churches wrote a letter to the Hartford church condemning it for allowing the dispute to continue and warning that the issues raised were so volatile that the disorder might spread to all of New England.[6]

The dissenters bitterly replied that they had no desire to stay in Hartford with or without Stone as their minister. Their letter emphasized that the dispute went much deeper than the mere personality of Samuel Stone. Cullick and Goodwin politely but firmly informed the Bay churches to mind their own business, adding that they wanted complete adherence to the council's decision or they wanted out. "No, Brethren," they concluded, "we know no rule warranting us to grant your request, neither doe you shew us any, if we understand your meaning; . . . we doe beseech and entreat you to yield to that councell that is already given: either in the first part of it which would be matter of great rejoicing and comfort to our hearts . . . or else that you would like tenderness towards us graunt us our dismission."[7]

While Stone remained in Boston the Connecticut General Court invited a number of Bay ministers, including the five letter-writers, to come to Hartford to find a solution. They arrived in early 1657 and were welcomed by the political and ecclesiastical leaders of Connecticut but not by the warring Hartford factions, who were united on at least one point: a visit by Massachusetts clergy was unwarranted and unnecessary.[8] Still, the visitors met with some success. They effected a compromise when they produced a letter from Stone in which he assumed personal responsibility for the entire affair. He had made serious errors in judgment, he admitted, and had he been wiser, he would not have blocked the vote on Wigglesworth but would "have been willing to have left the church (had they desired it) to their liberty in voting."[9]

Nonetheless, the question of Stone's resignation remained unsettled. By vote a majority of Hartford's members indicated a desire for his return, but Stone, who had so magnanimously accepted guilt in order to heal the rift, showed no such magnanimity where his future was concerned. He informed the church he would return only if all members agreed to certain propositions. Foremost, he wrote, the church must submit to every doctrine propounded by him. Second, the church was to give him full authority to find a colleague to fill Hooker's position. Finally, he cited his weariness with the situation and indicated a singular lack of enthusiasm about returning. "I am utterly unable to act those great and difficult matters of church government which must be attended with you: my judgment may also in some things be different from yours, which may be a cause of future breach."[10] After considerable debate the church accepted his terms, but with the stipulation that it be allowed some voice in matters of doctrine as well as a voice in the hiring of his associate:

> Proposition: The Church of Christ at Hartford doe bynde themselves in the presence of God to Samuel Stone their teacher, to submitt toe every doctrine which he shall propound to them, grounded upon the sacred Scriptures, and confirmed by such reasons from the work of God, that noe

man is able to gainsay. And Samuel Stone byndes himself to attend any reason which shall be presented toe him by any brother of the church or any man who shall offer himselfe to dispute with him, and thearby bring any of his doctrine in publique tryall.

Proposition: The church doe bynde themselves not toe offer toe induce or bring in any officer to joyn with Samuel Stone against his will and right reason, and without his consent and approbation.[11]

But after tentatively agreeing to Stone's resettlement, the dissenting brethren withdrew from the church as soon as Stone returned to his pulpit. That act created a furor in the General Court, for it threatened the very fabric of Valley society. Controversies were appearing in churches all over the area, and if dissenters were allowed to withdraw and leave their communities, churches and towns were in danger of imminent collapse. The Court reacted quickly to the new situation, demanding that representatives of the two sides in Hartford appear at the May 1658 Court session. In addition, laws were passed making the creation of new churches without the consent of the Court and neighboring congregations an illegal act and outlawing any "ministry or church administration . . . contrary to that dispensed by the settled and approved ministry."[12]

In May the Court met with the two factions but accomplished nothing. The stumbling block was Samuel Stone, who, in the words of Connecticut historian Benjamin Trumbull, viewed "the withdrawn brethren as in the hands of the church at Hartford, and the matters to be determined as not lying within any council of the General Court." At the same session Stone filed a petition against the dissenters, charging them with illegal withdrawal from communion and challenging one or two of their number to meet him in public debate.[13]

While those events progressed, many of the dissenters were in Wethersfield, residing with a similar group of dissenters in that community. In December 1657 they wrote to John Davenport and Governor Theophilus Eaton of New Haven, outlining their plight and asking for help. Their withdrawal, they wrote, resulted from the conditions Stone demanded of the church as the price for his return. They could not, they asserted, watch idly while Stone assumed full power in matters of doctrine and practice, and his demand that membership requirements be loosened was in opposition to everything they believed. "Wee have now sent you a coppie of Mr. Stone's letter," they went on, "wherein you will see the tearmes propounded of return, which wee cannott accept, in regard to the offences we have declared they lye but the truth is, wee have no small cause to feare that the Church will be filled quickly with such persons as we cannott close with in such a relation and way of indeared communion."[14]

Davenport and Eaton responded through a letter from the New Haven General Court to its counterpart in Connecticut. The letter avoided mentioning names but denounced those in Connecticut seeking "alterations in civil government and church discipline." The New Haven Court expressed fear and outrage at what was taking place in its sister colony and reminded Connecticut that its "civil polity and laws" were based "upon the divine word, and as the leaders and churches had gathered and received their discipline from the same they [New Haven] would exert themselves to preserve them inviolate."[15]

The thinly veiled threat from New Haven was ignored by the Connecticut Court, for more pressing matters demanded attention. The Hartford church was shattered and many members were living in Wethersfield. In desperation the Court turned again to Massachusetts, hoping that a resumption of the former council might yield a solution. For a change, Samuel Stone proved amenable and signified the church's approval, and an invitation was extended for the Bay ministers to return and form a council.[16]

The council seemed doomed to failure. Thirty-three of the Hartford dissenters were then preparing to join a migration of people from Wethersfield up the Connecticut River into western

Massachusetts. Included among the thirty-three were some of Hartford's—and Connecticut's—most distinguished residents: Elder William Goodwin, magistrate John Cullick, former governor Webster, and Thomas Hooker's son Samuel, later to be a minister at Farmington.[17] Nonetheless, a few of the dissenters remained in Hartford and the Court evidently felt that some kind of agreement was necessary. Similar issues were creating difficulties in other Connecticut churches, and a settlement in Hartford might serve as the basis for peace elsewhere. Moreover, the Court considered the actions of both the Hartford and Wethersfield dissenters an immeasurably dangerous precedent and wanted a declaration by an ecclesiastical tribunal to support its own position. To the Court's relief the Bay clergy accepted the invitation, although they demanded that the meetings be held in Boston. One trip to Connecticut was obviously enough.[18]

The council, consisting of the ministers of Boston, Cambridge, Charlestown, Ipswich, Dedham, and Sudbury, met from June 15 to August 19, 1659, and was attended by the representatives of the rival Hartford factions. The issues discussed were, evidently, many and varied. Benjamin Trumbull, writing from the perspective of documents no longer available, assessed the agenda in the following words:

> Nothing . . . is more evident from the questions propounded,
> which it appears were drawn by the very heads of the parties,
> and by the gentlemen chosen by the disaffected brethren,
> and rejected by the church, than that the whole controversy
> respected the qualifications for baptism, church membership,
> and the rights of the brotherhood.[19]

Yet when the council's decision was made public in October, none of those issues were mentioned. Instead the council confined its comments to the assignation of guilt for the failure of the compromise of 1657. Not surprisingly, the dissenters were blamed for the dissolution of the church. Their withdrawal, not Stone's "proposals," was cited as the reason for failure. In addition, the council

49

condemned the withdrawal as an illegal act, a position which no doubt comforted the Connecticut General Court.[20]

But the decision had little impact, for the dissenters were gone and even as the council members deliberated, similar disputes raged elsewhere. One of the worst occurred in nearby Wethersfield, where the bitterness and divisiveness of earlier years appeared again in the 1650s. As in Hartford, dissension swirled around the activities of a moderate, John Russell, and his attempts to alter the existing ecclesiastical system.

Hired in 1649, Russell experienced opposition from the beginning of his ministry. The nature and extent of his ecclesiastical reforms remain obscured, though apparently much of the bitterness toward him among church members and nonmembers related to his attempts to enlarge the ministerial prerogative. Like Stone, Russell's conception of his position seemed too "presbyterian" for a congregational church.

As in Hartford, the Wethersfield dissenters rallied behind a powerful and influential layman. Wethersfield's equivalent of William Goodwin proved to be Lt. John Hollister. Enemies for some time, Russell and Hollister created a public spectacle in 1656 when the minister dismissed Hollister from the church for alleged slanderous remarks by the latter. The dismissal, conducted without the consent or consideration of the brethren, brought an immediate crisis in the little community. Most of the church members supported Russell but Hollister, rallying all of the minister's enemies, appealed to the town meeting and won a resounding victory when the townsmen voted to censure their minister for failing to conform to Congregational principles. In addition, they cited numerous other issues wherein they disagreed with Russell and his followers, all involving abuses of ministerial authority.

Dissension continued until 1658, when Russell's group decided to leave Wethersfield for a site in western Massachusetts, farther up the Connecticut River. They were joined by the Hartford dissenters and a small contingent from Windsor, eventually founding the Massachusetts town of Hadley.[21] A few settled in neighboring

Northampton. Those remaining in Wethersfield, torn asunder by ecclesiastical division for the second time in as many decades, sadly attempted to organize another church and find a new minister.

As contention in Hartford and Wethersfield grew, revealing sizable local opposition to clerical innovation, Connecticut's moderate Congregationalists turned to the collective ministry and colonial government for support. As early as 1655 the moderates, led by Samuel Stone, appealed to the General Court for a synod of New England's churches to discuss the dangers of dissension, Connecticut's problems in that regard, and church government in general. Stone, aware of the growing sentiment in Massachusetts for reform, especially in baptismal practices, no doubt believed that what he could not achieve in Hartford on his own could be gained through synodical pronouncement with the aid of sympathetic colleagues in the Bay. The General Court, badly shaken by the seemingly insoluble problems of Hartford and Wethersfield, agreed and in 1656 sent a tentative agenda of twenty-one questions to the Courts of Massachusetts, Plymouth, and New Haven.

Plymouth did not bother to reply, but New Haven's return bristled with anger. Written by John Davenport, the letter mentioned the Connecticut church disputes and the strange doctrines prevalent in that region, and concluded with a ringing denunciation of the "innovations" proposed by the Connecticut Court. The notion of a synod was, Davenport wrote, a Presbyterian plot to undermine New England's adherence to Congregationalism. "We hear," he concluded, "the petitioners or others closing with them, are very confident they shall obtain alterations, both in civil government and in church discipline, and that some of them have procured or hired one, as their agent, to maintain in writing . . . that parishes in England consenting to and continuing their meetings to worship God, are true churches. And such persons coming over hither (without holding forth any work of faith, etc.) have a right to all our church privileges, and probably they expect their Deputy should employ himself and improve his interest to spread and press such paradoxes in the Massachusetts, yea at Synod meeting."[22]

Massachusetts consented to the synod but submitted its own list of questions for discussion.[23] Connecticut reluctantly accepted a modified agenda and in June 1657 the representatives of the two colonies met in Boston. After two weeks of debate the synod issued answers to twenty-one questions, chief among them an affirmation of support for the baptism of children of baptized parents—the heart of the later half-way covenant—and an extremely murky statement on membership requirements. The Connecticut clergy submitted the results to the General Court, which, after endorsing them, sent them on to the churches for consideration. The result was entirely unexpected. Instead of soothing the ruffled feelings of the laity, the proposals met strong opposition from both ministers and laymen and either intensified current disputes or caused dissension where none had previously existed.[24]

An example of the latter occurred in New London. Richard Blynman, the minister, attended the Boston meetings, talked at length with other clergy, and returned to New London opposed to enlarged baptism and convinced that his church was improperly constituted. In particular, he decided that the practice of letting all townsmen vote in church affairs was wrong and that the church should be a separate entity within the community, with its own government and a carefully restricted membership. At the first opportunity Blynman read the results of the synod to his congregation and announced his conviction that many of the practices of the church were in complete variance with other communities and ought to be altered.

His attack on traditional practice and his support of "rigid" Congregationalism drew outraged protests from many laymen. He was told that if he sought to implement his proposals, the town would refuse to pay his salary. That threat, in turn, infuriated Blynman, who informed his people of his intention to leave the community. The town then hastily met and urged him to stay, but Blynman was adamant in his refusal to alter his plans to reform church government and to make the church totally separate from the town. His sermons became thinly veiled attacks on those who opposed him. In one he argued that the New London church was much too lax in its membership requirements and was in danger of becoming polluted with unregenerates unless a greater effort was made to maintain "purity." In particular he mentioned as sources of impurity "men pressing to come into the church, children of the church pressing to come in without confession, children of the church challenging their right from their grand-father's covenant," and "the imperious members of other churches, in pressing the use of the ordinances."[25]

That statement struck a raw nerve among many listeners, and one member, Jonathan Brewster, a leader in both church and town, stood and denounced Blynman, arguing that the church's problems came not from others "but from ourselves." But Blynman was not to be denied, and at his instigation the church voted "to have noe publick communion with members of other churches, in either of the dealles, except dismissed to them," which meant that many people who were not members of the New London church but were members elsewhere were to be cast out until they obtained letters of dismissal from their old churches.[26]

A furor ensued in the town. Brewster, writing to John Winthrop, Jr., argued that Blynman acted in a "way episcopall and tiraniciall" and had alienated much of the town. The church, on the other hand, acted in a manner designed to "hinder the growth of church and town." Brewster, wanting to be "noe means to hinder the growth of Church and Town," had called a town meeting to discuss the action. Blynman attended and told the assembled townsmen that unless they conformed to his views, he would accept the invitation of another church to become its minister. The town refused, and Blynman subsequently departed.[27]

Elsewhere in Connecticut moderate Congregationalism was in deep trouble. Enlarged baptism generated no enthusiasm and was blocked in every church save one by either a stubborn minister, like Blynman, or an outraged congregation. The exception was Windsor where John Warham engineered its adoption in 1657. Stone in neighboring Hartford did not even present it for consideration in his already beleaguered church. Increased ministerial authority, the other moderate innovation, also lay moribund, and opposition to moderates was beginning to produce more general feelings of anticlericalism.

In desperation the moderates turned to the General Court for help, seeking either an endorsement or aid in resolving contention, or both. The Court responded as best it could by passing laws in 1658, for example, specifying a "legal" method for organizing new churches and forbidding dissident laymen from withdrawing from church fellowship without permission from the church.[28] The Court also sought to mediate some of the disputes. It entered the Hartford battle on several occasions and in 1659 went so far as to tell the two sides that unless they found a solution, the Court would preside over arbitration that would continue until the problem was solved.[29]

Despite legislation and mediation, however, the Court achieved little. Its laws were ignored and its good offices used by competing sides to achieve advantage. More and more it seemed that the Court would have to do what the clergy could not—create a platform of church government. While loath to assume that responsibility, the Court recognized the clergy's inability to act and recognized as well the necessity for a common discipline. Competing sides in all afflicted churches looked to the Court to put the stamp of legality on their position. Moreover, with the Restoration in England and the return of the Church of England, nonconformity was outlawed and pressure put on the New England colonies to make changes in church discipline. That pressure increased when a Royal Commission was dispatched to America in 1664.

The members of the Connecticut General Court—the General Assembly after 1662—were not without ecclesiastical loyalties. Most favored moderate Congregationalism, especially after some of the more influential members of both the Hartford church and the General Court left Connecticut in 1658 and 1659 after years of bitter struggle with Samuel Stone. The clearest evidence of the views of the majority of the Court members came in 1664 when, pressed by the churches and the Crown, the Court rendered an "opinion" on the correct procedure for admitting members to a church.

The opinion stemmed from the plight of the English families denied admission to the Windsor church by John Warham when they would not undergo an examination by the members. They retained a lawyer, William Pitkin, and petitioned the Assembly for aid. The Assembly considered the issue carefully, noting their prior membership in the Church of England. "Our grievance is," the families wrote, "that we and ours are not under the due care of an orthodox ministry, that will in a due manner administer to us those ordinances that we stand capable of, as the baptising of our children, our being admitted (as we according to Christ's order may be found to meet) to the Lord's Table, and a careful watch over us as we do well or ill, with all whatsoever benefits and advantages belong to us as members of Christ's visible church."[30]

In replying, the Assembly endorsed moderate Congregationalism. Though not specifically stating that English membership automatically entitled a person to membership in Connecticut, the decision recommended

> to the ministers and churches in this Colony to consider
> whither it be not their duty to enterteine all such persons,
> whoe are of an honest and godly conversation, having a com-
> petency of knowledg in the principles of religion, and shall
> desire to joyne with them in church fellowship, by an explicit
> covenant, and that they have their children baptized, and that
> all the children of the church be accepted and accounted real
> members of the church, and that the church exercise a due
> christian care and watch over them; and that when they are
> growne up, being examined by the officer in the presence of
> the church, it appeares, in the judgment of charity, they are
> duely qualified to perticipate in that great ordinance of the
> Lords Supper, by theire being able to examine themselves and
> discerne the Lords body, such persons to be admitted to full
> communion.[31]

The recommendation envisioned a parish-like structure, with membership criteria emphasizing personal morality and Christian knowledge as the heart of visible sanctity. Equally striking, the Court suggested "real" membership for all of the "children of the church," and placed the burden for their eventual admission on the church, not the applicant. Both proposals clearly and explicitly sought to extend the influence of the church in the community by enlarging membership rolls.

The Assembly then added a postscript, suggesting consideration and response by the churches before the next session in April 1665. The wording, peculiar even for trying times, indicated that the Assembly was testing public opinion before issuing the same message as legislation. The churches in their deliberations were asked pointedly to respond to the question "whither it be not the duty of the Assembly to order the churches to practice according to the premises, if they doe not practice without such an order."[32]

Two clergymen, Thomas Hanford of Norwalk and Adam Blakeman of Stratford, quickly wrote a lengthy and blistering rejoinder to the proposals as part of a critique of the Assembly's power to meddle in matters involving church discipline. Other opponents appeared as well, and when the April session arrived, the matter was quietly dropped and the Assembly refrained from further attempts to act as a synod. As for Windsor and the original petitioners, Warham maintained his stand and ignored the Assembly's deliberations and subsequent decision.

The Assembly's endorsement of moderate Congregationalism came much too late to help the besieged clergy. By 1662 the moderates were demoralized. Blocked at every turn, they did not even bother to attend the famous synod in Boston, which endorsed their position and created the half-way covenant. The synod's decision, like the Cambridge Platform before it, was hardly noticed in Connecticut. A year later the cause of the covenant and moderate Congregationalism suffered a mortal blow with the death of the powerful Samuel Stone and the inclusion within Connecticut's jurisdiction of the anti-covenant churches of old New Haven

Colony. Finally, in 1664, moderate Congregationalism capitulated when its remaining stalwart, John Warham of Windsor, announced to a startled congregation that he "had meete with such arguments against the practice concerning the baptising of members children . . . and could not go on in practice as he had done without scrupil of conscience . . . not that he intended to cast off the practice holy, but onely lay it for a time till he could better able to answer his present scruples."[33] Warham's decision, and moderate Congregationalism's stinging rebuke, did not end Connecticut's travail, however, for the seeds of contention sown by the moderates found fertile soil throughout the Connecticut Valley.

Three

A WIDENING CHASM

THE collapse of the moderate Congregationalist leadership did not end clerical attempts to reshape Connecticut's church discipline. Instead, it aided the development of more radical programs, especially Presbyterianism. Present in the colony since the late 1650's, Presbyterianism maintained a low profile because of colony law and because of the drive by the moderates for control of the churches. With the death of Samuel Stone and the quick defeat of the half-way covenant, Presbyterianism emerged in some strength and began its own struggle for dominance or, at the least, legal status. The resulting furor not only increased the intensity of debate and dissension in Connecticut's towns and churches but altered some of the clergy's most cherished notions.

Connecticut's Presbyterianism grew from several sources. The arrival of harried nonconformists from England, forced to flee by the Restoration, accounted for some lay and clerical support for Presbyterianism just as it produced the Pitkin Anglicans in Hartford. Yet, of known Presbyterian clergy in Connecticut at the time —men like Gershom Bulkeley of New London, John Haynes of Hartford, and John Woodbridge, Jr., of Killingworth—most were recent graduates of Harvard.[1] That Harvard of the late 1650's and early 1660's and the Boston area in general were places of political and religious turmoil is well known. That they might have been centers of Presbyterian sentiment is less certain. However, at least one alleged Connecticut Valley Presbyterian, Solomon Stoddard of upriver Northampton, graduated from Harvard at approximately the same time. His commonplace book of his Harvard years included a 1664 inventory of his personal library. Missing were some of the standard works of English and New England Congregationalism, while conspicuous was *The Due Right of Presbyteries* and several other volumes by the Scottish Presbyterian, Samuel Rutherford.[2] Likely as not English and Scottish Presbyterianism, though vastly different, interested the questioning minds of prospective ministers at Harvard.

But the greatest stimulus to the growth of Presbyterianism lay in the dilemma of the Congregational clergyman in Connecticut. The authority and prestige of first-generation clergy like Hooker— the source of clerical initiative—was gone, replaced by anticlericalism. Moreover, traditional methods of problem-solving, such as by councils and synods, had proven insufficient. Even the General Court appeared unable to stem the rising tide of dissension and unrest. Little wonder then that ministers had tired of the vagaries of Congregationalist government and had sought the restoration of lost authority and order outside the individual congregation in the promise of Presbyterian rule by synod and elder. If congregational election impeded the work of the minister, then a new source of clerical authority would have to be found and imposed.

In addition, many moderate Congregationalists appeared Presbyterian-like in their ecclesiastical views, so much so that before 1660 the term "Presbyterian" was often used to deride the moderates. The epithet identified any cleric or layman who opposed a public or private narrative of conversion experience as a prerequisite for membership and favored admitting a person of high moral character who made a simple profession of faith. It also identified persons who supported extending the limits of baptism, or saw limited power in church councils, or upheld the minister's right to ultimate authority in matters of doctrine and discipline. Thus Samuel Stone of Hartford, Hooker's friend and colleague, was called a Presbyterian because he upheld the ministerial prerogative in certain areas of doctrine and discipline and because he opposed an attempt by some of the brethren to force all applicants for membership to give a public profession of their religious experience, including the "time and manner" of their conversion before the congregation. John Russell of Wethersfield was labeled a Presbyterian because he excommunicated a member of his church without a church trial and in other ways promoted a lofty conception of ministerial authority. Yet neither man was a Presbyterian, for neither rejected the Congregationalist doctrines of the gathered church, the brethren as the primary source of ministerial authority, or the dual sovereignty of clergy and laymen in church government.[3]

Though they remained a minority, Connecticut's Presbyterians exercised power disproportionate to their numbers. Their ecclesiastical views, while reflecting both English and Scottish models, generally followed the English pattern. They embraced a parish-like church organization and rule by elder, but preferred congregational autonomy to the Scottish web of interchurch government. John Haynes of Hartford and John Woodbridge, Jr., of Killingworth were among the leading exponents. Scottish Presbyterianism, complete with a national church and a complicated hierarchical structure of church government, established a foothold but exerted a very minor influence. It had able spokesmen like Gershom Bulkeley of New London and Wethersfield but few other supporters.[4]

Presbyterians usually appeared in towns already torn by strife, probably because ministerial candidates were scarce and few young men wanted to inherit the problems of a divided congregation and community. Gershom Bulkeley arrived in New London in 1661, replacing the discredited Richard Blynman. The church, weakened by years of contention, took Bulkeley because he was the only candidate interested in the job. The members knew of his Presbyterianism and, in no mood for another clergyman exalting the ministerial prerogative, tried to bind him to an agreement that he would eschew proselytizing. Bulkeley consented for a time, but church and minister were soon at loggerheads and, by mutual consent, Bulkeley left the community in 1665 or 1666.[5]

Bulkeley moved on to battle-weary Wethersfield where, after several years of indoctrination, he successfully formed a Presbyterian church. The irony probably amused John Russell of Hadley, harried from the community a decade earlier for proposing changes in polity, but there was little amusement in Wethersfield. The removal of Russell and his followers had nearly destroyed the town, and subsequent attempts to organize a new church ended in failure. A succession of ministers came, then left. Few remained longer than a year. John Cotton's son, John Jr., was one of the first young men hired, but he stayed only a few months. A young Presbyterian, John Haynes, arrived in 1663 eager to rebuild the church, but he left after a short while to fill Samuel Stone's vacant and prestigious post in nearby Hartford. And so it went until the town contacted Bulkeley, who no doubt exacted a promise that the townsmen would at least give his Presbyterianism a fair hearing. Now desperate, the town agreed.[6]

Few Presbyterians, however, achieved Bulkeley's success. Most served as catalysts for further social and ecclesiastical turmoil, thus weakening an already shaky institutional structure. Windsor provided an example of the impact of Presbyterianism on a contentious community. After John Warham's decision to end the halfway covenant in 1664, the church and town divided, and a bitter period of controversy followed. Warham, too old and sick to perform his pastoral duties, suggested the hiring of a younger man. After much bickering, the community settled on Nathaniel Chauncey, product of a well-known Massachusetts family. Chauncey favored the covenant, and in 1667 it was restored.[7]

But the contention was not ended. Soon after Chauncey's settlement a substantial minority withdrew from fellowship and tried to hire a minister. The dissenters petitioned the General Court for approval (which was given) and soon settled on a young Presbyterian named Benjamin Woodbridge, brother of John at Killing-

worth and son of another well-known Presbyterian, John of Newbury, Massachusetts.[8] The town of Windsor voted to allow
Woodbridge to lecture on the Sabbath and Thursdays of alternate
weeks. He and his followers immediately petitioned the Court for
the right to form a separate church, that the minister "might have
freedom for a quiet and perfect settlement amongst us."[9] That
meant Presbyterianism.

Whether allegiance to Presbyterianism caused the original break
with the church is not known, but by the time of the petition the
dissenters had apparently united around the views of their new
minister. "We have offered Candid and christian Termes of Com-
pliance with those that stand as our opposites," they wrote, "and
have yielded so far as we judge, either Peace will command us, or
Truth will permit us. Even to walking according to their owne
principles. Whereby we grieve that we have some occasion to
thinke, that tis not so much our perswasions as our Names that are
so offensive."[10] And what were their "names"? To John Davenport they were the "looser and worser party"; to Simon Bradstreet
of New London they were the "Presbyterian party."[11]

The worst Presbyterian-Congregationalist fight erupted in Hartford. In 1660 the church and the minister, Samuel Stone, made an
attempt to mollify lingering dissenters within the congregation by
hiring John Whiting, a moderate Congregationalist and former
resident of the community, as Hooker's replacement.[12] Then
Stone died in 1663, and his place was taken by the Presbyterian
John Haynes. Immediately the church became embroiled in a new
controversy. Haynes attempted to go beyond the half-way covenant by offering baptism to adopted children and servants born in
the house of an employer or master. A significant number of Hartford's members opposed both the extension of baptism and the
minister's right to take any action without first consulting the
congregation. Commenting on the new dispute in a 1666 letter to
John Winthrop, Jr., John Davenport of New Haven called it an
uprising of the "Presbyterian faction" in the church. Referring to
Haynes' innovations, he noted that Hooker "would have decryed

the baptizing of Adopted children, by their adoptants right most
of all, the baptizing of servants borne in the house, or bought with
monie . . . But he is at rest and the people their are woefully
divided, and the better sorte are exceedingly grieved, while the
looser and worser party insult, hoping that it will be as they would
have it, viz., that the plantacions shall be brought into a parish-
way."[13] The dispute quickly extended beyond the question of
baptism to include all the old issues that had divided the church in
the 1650's.

The bitterness of the new struggle deepened through the activities of the two ministers. Whiting gained public notice in 1666
when he refused admission to the still homeless Pitkin Anglicans.
They approached the Hartford church in the same manner they
had approached Windsor two years before, asking for admission
on the basis of membership in the Church of England.[14] Though
the General Assembly had ruled in their favor, they were again
denied. Whiting met with William Pitkin in November 1666 and
discussed the group's interest in membership. Later, Whiting wrote
that "my answer was I did desire to know upon what account they
desired that communion. Whether upon account of any union they
should have by joining to it." Pitkin replied that "they did desire
it upon account of a union they had already (being in covenant or
church members) but if anything further were required by rule
they would attend it. Whereunto I [Whiting] returned answer
that I knew no such union they had to the Church of Hartford as
to entitle them to communion in all the ordinances of Christ, but
however that I would consider of their motion and give them
further answer in some convenient time."[15] Whiting, of course,
refused their petition; the issue went to the General Court; and
the Hartford minister drew a stinging rebuke.

The quietest settlement of Presbyterianism occurred in the tiny
village of Killingworth, where the community's first minister, John
Woodbridge, Jr., created a Presbyterian church in the late 1660's.
Woodbridge, writing to the noted English Presbyterian Richard
Baxter in 1669 and 1671, assessed the strength of Connecticut's

Presbyterians. He reported exuberantly that they were numerous and more "full in their practice" than anywhere in New England. He cited no figures regarding Presbyterian laity, but he felt that Presbyterianism had made numerous inroads among the colony's twenty-two clergymen and had led to the creation of two bona fide Presbyterian churches, his own and Bulkeley's in Wethersfield.[16] He might have added that Presbyterians were near victory in Hartford and Windsor as well.

The demise of moderate Congregationalism, the rise of Presbyterianism, and the steadily increasing social and ecclesiastical discord in the towns produced a dramatic shift in thinking among Connecticut's clerical and political leaders in the mid-1660's. The rapidly deteriorating position of the minister—and rising anticlericalism—led many ecclesiastical and governmental figures to think what had once been unthinkable: that ministerial authority ought to be legally rooted in something other than election by a particular congregation. In that reevaluation Presbyterians like Gershom Bulkeley and Congregationalists like Joseph Fitch were equally conspicuous. Furthermore, the failure of moderate Congregationalism—a movement supported by the Court and symbolized by the still-born half-way covenant—and the success of Presbyterianism suggested to many the need for a new approach to Connecticut's confused and chaotic ecclesiastical system. No one suggested suppressing the Presbyterians. The Assembly's ineffectiveness in dealing with local disputes was well known, and a concerted attack upon Presbyterians would have only encouraged further strife. Instead, prevailing sentiment turned toward an ecclesiastical system based on compromise and consent rather than coercion and fiat—a system created by a synod of Connecticut's churches.

Support for a Connecticut synod—one that would simultaneously solve the problem of ministerial authority and devise a platform of church government—emerged sometime between the Assembly's 1664 statement on church membership and the summer months of 1666. In the latter year the Assembly turned anew to the strife in the towns and churches of the colony. A new charter secured, the recalcitrant Dutch driven from New Amsterdam, New Haven's towns peacefully settled under Connecticut's banner, and Charles II's feared Royal Commission having completed its business and its snooping, the Assembly felt free to give its attention to local conflict. As a prelude to further action it issued an order demanding an end to all debate and dissension pending a public announcement on the controversial questions.[17]

The order was generally ignored, but the Assembly, undaunted, issued a call for a general synod during its October meetings. Most clergymen responded affirmatively, and a set of questions was drafted for debate. Simultaneously, an invitation went to the Court and clergy of Massachusetts, but the Bay Court suspiciously asked for a summary of matters to be discussed. As though anticipating that reply, the Connecticut Court quickly altered its invitation to a request that a select group of Bay clergy attend as observers, not participants.[18]

The coolness between Massachusetts and Connecticut underscored the fact that despite common origins, traditions, and problems, the political boundaries separating them had never seemed more important. The distrust and apprehension that drove Hooker and others into the wilderness continued in the attitudes of both sides, despite the temporary harmony produced by the 1657 synod. Mutual suspicion reflected the politics of the two colonies. It also reflected their dealings with each other, the Crown, the Dutch, and the Indians, as well as a host of other areas where narrow self-interest usually precluded the delineation and pursuit of common goals.

Despite the old and oft-heard refrain of "New England's" churches, each colony possessed a critical, jaundiced view of the other's ecclesiastical establishment. The Bay Colony reacted typically by expressing skepticism, caution, and fear of Connecticut's request for a synod. Though bothered by some of the same problems, Massachusetts' institutional structure seemed more stable, and both colonies acknowledged that fact. Massachusetts knew dissension, anticlericalism, and fragmentation but not on the scale of her neighbor. The leaders of the Bay approached Connecticut like a group inquiring into the health of a neighbor victimized by the plague. There was sympathy, but it was subsumed by fear of contagion. Connecticut anticipated that attitude and dealt with it, asserting in the process the determination to solve local problems and end the agony of contention through a separate ecclesiastical constitution.

The Connecticut Assembly went about its grim business. Issuing a public call for a synod, it reflected the gravity of Connecticut's turmoil as well as the existence of a new menace to public order. The synod could "consider of some way or means to bring those Ecclesiastical matters that are in difference in the severall Plantations, to an issue." Until that time, the Assembly declared solemnly, "the churches and people in this Jurisdiction" were ordered to "suspend all matters controversial and the practice of them not formerly received and practiced in the Churches here."[19] The latter spoke directly to all Presbyterians.

The "matters controversial" were not delineated, but an attached list of seventeen questions for discussion read like a litany of Connecticut woes. Included were the plight of the ministry and the proper relationship of ministers and brethren; the rights, if any, of towns to dictate ecclesiastical polity to churches; the limits of baptism; the requirements for membership; the power of synods; and so on until the reader came to Proposition Seventeen. Proposition Seventeen asked, "Whether it be not justifiable by the Word of God that Civil Authority indulge Congregational and Presbyterian Churches, and their discipline?"[20] Toleration for Presbyterians! No wonder Massachusetts had asked for a copy of the agenda before responding to the invitation.

The synod convened in Hartford in the spring of 1667, but despite optimistic pronouncements by both Assembly and clergy it began very badly. Some rigid Congregationalists objected to the term "synod," and the title quickly changed to an "assembly of ministers." More ill will resulted when only teachers and ministers were admitted to the deliberations, thus lending credence to the fears of some Congregationalists that they were participating in the creation of a Presbyterian establishment. The seventeen proposals were offered for consideration. For weeks the elders debated, harangued, and attempted to fix blame for the clergy's—and Connecticut's—dismal condition. Gradually the spirit of compromise dissipated in the heat of battle, until the meetings adjourned with the announcement that a second attempt would be made in October.[21]

The October meetings proved equally futile. The competing sides debated for weeks, agreeing on nothing. Then, suddenly, John Warham, John Whiting, and Samuel Hooker of Farmington, fearing that the Presbyterians were gaining strength and were about to create their own platform, asked that the meeting be thrown open to include the Massachusetts "observers" in attendance. The other members refused, and many of the Congregationalists left without considering toleration for Presbyterians. The synod ended abruptly.[22]

The church disputes started anew, aided by the vitriolic exchanges of the clergy during the synod. The General Assembly, angered by the clergy's failure to act and frightened by the possible social consequences of the continuing turmoil, appointed a select committee of clergymen to recommend any solution, including toleration. The council of four ministers—Gershom Bulkeley, Samuel Wakeman, Joseph Fitch, and Joseph Eliot—met in May 1669 and quickly recommended toleration for Presbyterians as one solution for Connecticut's woes. The Assembly acted immediately, passing a law granting toleration for all persons "approved according to lawe, orthodox and sound in the fundamentalls of Christian religion."[23]

Although toleration for Presbyterians represented an important milestone in Connecticut's and New England's ecclesiastical history, its practical effect was minimal. Sharing the same fate as earlier official attempts to produce harmony, toleration gained little notice in those communities hardest hit by Presbyterian-Congregationalist squabbling. Feuding continued until time, fatigue, and the natural course of events produced a solution.

In Hartford the warring factions parted company in 1670, when the Congregationalists, mostly moderates, withdrew and formed Hartford Second Church. In a rare display of public candor the new church created a covenant explaining many of its differences with First Church. Its grievances lay in First Church's departure from the "congregational way" as it was "formerly settled, professed and practised, under the guidance of the first leaders of this church of Hartford." That practice, the covenant continued, embodied complete local autonomy, purity of membership, and the power of the fraternity. It also included the half-way covenant.[24]

The reaction of First Church is not known. A fourteen-year gap appears in the history of the church, broken only by the assumption of the ministry by a young Presbyterian named Timothy Woodbridge. Yet Woodbridge, destined to become a leader of Connecticut and New England's Presbyterians, did not preside over a Presbyterian church. First Church, in 1684, revealed a congregational discipline grounded in the concept of a gathered church ruled by the membership. Perhaps Haynes and his followers tried Presbyterianism, then discontinued it for reasons unknown. Or perhaps some Congregationalist dissidents remained behind, blocking the designs of the Presbyterians until the latter grew weary of the struggle. Whatever resulted, it had little to do with official toleration.[25]

In Windsor toleration came too late to have much effect on the troubled community. The Presbyterians under Benjamin Woodbridge already possessed a separate church, and the two groups lived together in an uneasy truce. While toleration gave the new church legitimacy, it had little to do with its eventual fate. Money proved to be a more important factor. The town grew tired of its new creation and refused to support Second Church as liberally as it supported First.[26] Second's membership dwindled, and its financial problems became acute. Finally, around 1677, the church made one final plea to the town for additional financial support and, when refused, asked First Church for permission to return to the fold. The town immediately sought a council of neighboring ministers to oversee the reunification. The ministers met and proposed that Second and First Churches simply combine their membership with as little rancor as possible.[27] First Church, however, objected loudly, sensing an opportunity to humiliate its enemies. It demanded that each member of Second Church undergo a public examination concerning his or her fitness for membership, giving the time and manner of conversion.[28]

Second Church refused, and again the community lapsed into bitter turmoil. The town meeting was impotent, unable to decide between the two churches and their views. Several more ministerial councils were assembled and disbanded with little success. Finally, the town intervened and fired the two ministers, Chauncey and Woodbridge, assuming that the clergymen had become symbols of resistance on each side and that a new minister might serve as a quieting force and lead to reunification. First Church apparently cared little about Chauncey, but the loss of Woodbridge completed the demoralization of Second and effectively destroyed Presbyterianism in Windsor as well. Dissension continued, but it no longer involved the members of the new church. Thoroughly beaten, they silently waited their fate while First Church and the town meeting squabbled over who was to decide the manner whereby Second and First Churches would be rejoined.[29]

Connecticut Presbyterianism seemed to be declining as quickly as it had appeared, at least among the laity. Gershom Bulkeley left Wethersfield, and the Presbyterian experiment in that community quickly ended. John Woodbridge, hating Killingworth and tired of conversing only with "Oakes and Indians,"[30] left at the first opportunity, and Presbyterianism went with him. By 1675 not a single town boasted a Presbyterian church, though the number of Presbyterian clergy was about the same. Yet despite its short-lived successes, Presbyterianism had some long-term effects. Though its influence on church practice dissipated, it had a profound influence on the Assembly and the clergy. It forced both groups to seek a common ecclesiastical constitution, and it caused many ministers to ask for an independent source of ministerial authority. Eventually, it prompted magistrates and ministers to accept limited toleration, an act of desperation which punctuated the hopelessness of Connecticut's political and ecclesiastical elite and the apparent disintegration of her institutional structure. Presbyterianism both symbolized and contributed to the continuation and expansion of Connecticut's discord.

Four

CHURCH, TOWN, AND THE
HALF-WAY COVENANT

A M O N G the questions listed for debate by the Synod of 1667 was the half-way covenant, moderate Congregationalism's innovation turned epitaph. The covenant, created by the Synod of 1662, established a special category of church membership for unregenerates baptised in infancy. They were barred from the Lord's Supper and denied voting privileges but permitted to have their children baptised. At the time of the 1667 synod's spring meetings no Connecticut church employed the covenant, though a number continued to argue its merits. Moreover, in the decade since its suggestion in 1657 and five years since its creation, only one Connecticut church, Windsor First, had given it a trial.[1] Nonetheless, the ministers at Hartford put it on their agenda and argued its merits. They could do little more.

Lacking either endorsement from the Connecticut ministry or support from a majority of church members the half-way covenant's future seemed as bleak as its recent past. Yet in the four years following the Hartford synod Connecticut's churches reversed themselves to the point that by 1671 a majority had adopted either the covenant or a local variation.[2] The catalyst for the sudden and dramatic reappraisal of the covenant came from outside the churches. The instigators proved to be nonmembers operating through the apparatus of the town meeting, and their activities revealed still another facet of Connecticut's ecclesiastical turmoil.

Dissension between churches and towns erupted in the mid-1650s. Ironically, as the power of the clergy slipped to the brethren, the authority of both was challenged by the town meeting. Moreover, by 1667 many towns were winning, and the autonomous, self-governing nature of the congregational church lay breached in some communities, imperiled in others. The clergy at the Hartford synod knew of those developments and made church-town relations one of its most important items of business.

The clergy knew of a more recent development as well; the half-way covenant was finding new friends among nonmembers. Showing little interest in the theological questions swirling around extended baptism or satellite membership, the unchurched used the covenant as a lever to expand their challenge to the autonomy, exclusiveness, and authority of the church. Consequently, the more a minister or a majority of members, or both, belittled the covenant, the more nonmembers demanded the town meeting impose it. The attitudes of the unchurched provided considerable impetus for the 1667 Synod to find a solution for turmoil resulting from towns trying to exercise ecclesiastical authority. The clergy's failure consigned the problem to settlement through strife. Between for the 1667 synod to find a solution for turmoil resulting from victory became the rejuvenated half-way covenant.

Church-town strife grew out of the original institutional makeup of the towns, especially from the restrictive membership policies adopted by many churches. Most of the early towns were founded by wandering congregations, which meant that few persons were initially excluded from church membership. Correspondingly, little attention was given to precise definitions of the respective areas of authority of churches and towns, since each served the same clientele. Gradually, however, the zeal for visible sanctity drove wedges into the communities. Nonmembers became more numerous, and churches and towns developed different constituencies.[3]

A second dimension exacerbated the growing estrangement between churches and towns: economic discontent. The Connecticut River Valley and the smaller valleys harboring tributary streams possessed some excellent land and much that was not. Thus, as in Wethersfield, population growth produced dissension over land allocation, and that often merged with ecclesiastical difficulties to deepen feelings of bitterness and frustration.

The isolation of the church, however, provided the immediate catalyst for turmoil. It was not entirely unexpected. Among the first clergy all but the most rigid Congregationalists brooded over the possible social consequences of a too-wide rift between the church and the world. The excluded helped pay the minister's salary and attended his services, though they had no voice in either his hiring or firing. They contributed to building and maintaining the meetinghouse, though they were barred from participating in either the worldly business or the spiritual blessings of the church.[4] They might, it was feared, develop into a vocal minority, or even majority, demanding change.

In the mid-1650s fear became fact. Connecticut's unchurched reacted to real or threatened ministerial innovation with the same interest and anxiety as full members. Soon, however, their interest turned to anger and they began to demand a voice in church government. It started in Wethersfield. When John Russell dismissed John Hollister for slander in 1656 the latter angrily denounced the minister for failing to present the case to the church.[5] But instead of seeking a trial, Hollister turned to interested nonmembers and found many willing to argue his case. Between 1656 and 1658 the town divided over the issue, with a majority supporting Hollister, although most church members remained loyal to Russell. The town even sent Hollister to serve as a deputy in the General Court in 1657. In August 1658 fifty persons petitioned to find a new minister. The fifty—composed of Hollister, nine church members, and forty nonmembers—charged Russell with "a grievous oath acknowledged by himself to be ambiguous . . . and sinful." They felt, they concluded, no further obligations toward him because he had "given so great a scandal to the Gospel of our Lord Jesus Christ."[6] Despite Hollister's presence, the Court refused the petitioners' request, urged the divided town to reunite, and asked Russell to "speak more plainly for the future."[7]

But the division of the town continued, and Russell and his supporters began to make preparations to leave. In December 1658 the town meeting took up the problem. Hollister, whose supporters outnumbered Russell's by a two-to-one margin, carried the day. The town voted that it no longer had a minister and established a committee to find a new one. Shortly thereafter, Russell and all but five members of the church joined dissident church members from Windsor and Hartford in a trek up the Connecticut River.[8]

It would be reassuring, perhaps, to think that Russell's group left Wethersfield for the good of the community but neither side showed any concern for the welfare of church or town. Nor can it be said that the dispute centered solely on the problems of John Hollister. Hollister symbolized a much deeper rift in Wethersfield, one that antedated his dismissal. Nonmembers, obviously incensed at the church and its minister, rushed to his defense then tried to manipulate both the apparatus of town government and that of the colony to obtain Russell's removal. They were successful, for Russell and his followers were harried out of the community, and the battered theory of the autonomous, self-governing congregation went with them.[9]

The Wethersfield dispute could not have ended in withdrawal had not Connecticut's General Court proved so powerless. The Court attempted to be both conciliatory and stern and neither approach worked. The warring factions in Wethersfield ignored a Court attempt to act as peacemaker in August 1658, just as they had ignored an earlier attempt at toughness. In March of 1658 the Court, sensing that the churches in Hartford and Wethersfield were disintegrating, made it illegal for church members to withdraw and form separate bodies without the prior approval of neighboring churches and the Court.[10] However, that failed to keep either Hartford's or Wethersfield's dissidents from moving to western Massachusetts a year later.

As Russell's group was either about to leave or was already on its way, the Court, pressured by Hollister, finally censured Russell for his dismissal of Hollister several years before.[11] A meaningless gesture, it was matched in October 1659 by the Court's pious notation of "the long and tedious differences and troubles that have been and are still continuing twixt Mr. Russell and several members of the Wethersfield church" and its suggestion that "messengers" from Hartford and Windsor look into the matter.[12] But that was not the end. In 1661, long after Russell's departure, the Court decided that his group had left Wethersfield without "allowance or approbation from this Court or the Magistrates . . . or the Churches within this jurisdiction or the neighboring Churches."[13]

The General Court's inept handling of the Wethersfield affair coupled with the obvious willingness of inhabitants to ignore Court orders guaranteed the spread of dissension and quickly made church-town disputes one of the colony's most vexing problems. At the height of the Hollister-Russell feud, for example, Richard Blynman made his ill-fated decision to reform the polity of New London's church by separating church members and nonmembers and, especially by ending the practice of allowing nonmembers a voice in church business.[14] That prompted a controversy as danger-ous as Wethersfield's. New London represented one of the few communities where nonmembers were included in church affairs and the nonelect fought hard to preserve what their colleagues else-where sought. They united against the minister, using the town meeting as their forum. Most church members sided with Blyn-man and the drama moved to a tragic though predictable conclu-sion. Nonmembers retained a voice in church government, Blyn-man was ousted from his position, and the harmony between mem-bers and nonmembers which had marked earlier years ended abruptly.[15]

The successful defense thrown up by New London's un-

churched, coupled with the victory of nonmembers in Wethersfield, caused church-town struggles to gain intensity in the late
1650's and early 1660's. Around 1660 the infant community of
Middletown nearly collapsed when its aged minister, Nathaniel
Stow, proposed an innovation in discipline. A majority of the
inhabitants immediately turned against him, and a furious controversy ensued, with the town meeting conspicuous in the fight
against the minister. Finally, the General Court intervened and
dismissed Stow "on account of the evil temper of the people towards him."[16] Too old for another position and too poor to move
elsewhere, Stow appealed to the victorious town for a pension and
was refused. Nothing further appears in the records. A similar fate
befell young Samuel Wakeman of Fairfield a few years later. He,
too, supported an unpopular ecclesiastical position and provided
the catalyst for an uprising of townsmen against the church which
led to the minister's ouster by the town meeting.[17]

Gradually, after 1662, dissension between members and nonmembers lost its parochial and sporadic character and centered on
the half-way covenant, an issue well suited for such strife. Another
ministerial innovation, it was foundering before the opposition of
stubborn ministers and congregations. Nonmembers, eager to
weaken the bastion of the autonomous church, adopted the covenant and used it to broaden and dilute ecclesiastical authority and
narrow the distance between the church and the community.
Their numbers and influence proved sufficient to alter the covenant's destiny in Connecticut. As the formerly stymied lay and
clerical adherents of extended baptism received the potent support of the unregenerates, the covenant gradually developed sufficient momentum to carry it over all opposition in a number of
towns in the colony.[18] The struggles often lasted for several years,
but many of the coalitions achieved success between 1667 and
1671.

One of the first churches to embrace the covenant after 1667
was Windsor's First Church. John Warham's decision to abandon

the covenant in 1664 had immediately divided the church into two groups. His supporters far outnumbered his opponents, however, and nothing could be done to reverse his decision. In the interim the issue spread to the town, where sentiment was overwhelmingly against the minister and the majority of the church. Warham stood firm, but pressure and abuse from the town was intense. Then he made his request for an associate and possible successor. Learning of his illness and his request, the town demanded a voice in the selection of a new minister. The church refused, and the town split wide open. A stream of candidates visited the community, but none sufficed. Finally, anti-Warham forces settled on Nathaniel Chauncey, brother of the minister of Stratford.

The debate over Chauncey, a supporter of the covenant, served as a test of strength between not only pro and anti-Warham factions but also church and town. So much bitterness was generated in the once placid community that the General Assembly intervened in an attempt to restore order, charging the citizens to vote immediately on Chauncey's candidacy. But who would vote, church or town? The Assembly, pressured from all sides, reached a decision in October 1667, ordering the "Towne of Windsor" to gather the following Monday and for "all the freemen and householders within the limit of the said town and Massacco" to "bring in their votes [for or against Chauncey] to Mr. Henry Wolcott." The victorious town won again when Chauncey carried easily, 86 to 52, and completed the humiliation of Warham and the church when Chauncey ordered, as his first act, the restoration of the half-way covenant.[19]

Neighboring First Church of Hartford adopted the covenant at about the same time, and the role of the town, though less dramatic than in Windsor, proved decisive. Samuel Stone sparked controversy in his church almost continuously from 1653 to 1663, despite the withdrawal of many of his detractors in 1658. One of the sources of irritation was his determination to select a successor for Hooker without consulting the laity. Under attack for his position, he withdrew from the church in the mid-1650's for self-imposed exile in Boston. A condition for resettlement, which he demanded and received, was the right to select a colleague. He took his time, and in 1660 chose John Whiting, a former Hartford resident and a young man who was very popular among Stone's opponents.[20]

Stone's death in 1663 necessitated the selection of another minister. According to the precedent established a few years earlier, the decision ought to have been made by Whiting, but, inexplicably, the town intervened and conducted its own search for a new minister. With the church in an uproar, the town soon settled on another native son, John Haynes, the Presbyterian minister in Wethersfield.[21]

Haynes's presence in Hartford produced a rift with Whiting, a staunch Congregationalist. Within a few months the two ministers were bitter opponents and church and town divided in support of one or the other. Then Haynes proposed his innovations in church polity, including the distorted version of the half-way covenant. He explained his thinking and tried to implement extended baptism in 1666 but was blocked by the Whiting group, which brought in John Warham in a vain attempt to engage Haynes in debate.[22]

Whether Whiting's people opposed the half-way covenant or just Haynes's Presbyterian version is not known, but their continued opposition kept the covenant out of the discipline of the church until around 1668. Dissension went on, however, despite Haynes's victory. The two factions had become implacable enemies, and their bickering continued until the Whiting group withdrew and formed a separate church in 1670.[23]

Though the role of the town in Hartford's church affairs was less conspicuous than in Windsor, nonmembers secured a substantial portion of ecclesiastical power in the selection of Haynes and aided the progress of the covenant as well, though they promoted a dangerous schism in the community in the process. Similar events occurred in Stratford, another of the early adherents to the covenant.Dissension erupted in 1665 with the death of the first minister, Adam Blackman. Ill for some time, Blackman had recommended Israel Chauncey as his successor. At the time of his death the church had just begun deliberations over the covenant, and subsequent consideration of Chauncey, an outspoken opponent of half-way status, also provided an early test of the covenant. Chauncey was approved and hired by a comfortable margin, and the covenant was rejected a short time later.[24]

Within a few months Stratford's population grew with the arrival of a number of English immigrants who asked for admission to the church. The members refused, arguing that though the newcomers were "independents" and professed to be church members elsewhere, they were suspected of supporting the half-way covenant. The newcomers responded that the church could not deny their request without first allowing their qualifications to be examined by Chauncey. Haughtily, the church members responded that theirs was a "closed society" bound only by tradition and that the right of examination lay with the church, not the minister. "And Whereas you apprehend you have equal right with ourselves in all the ordinances of Christ in this place," the members affirmed, "these may certifie you at the present that we are of a different apprehension from you in that matter."[25]

The newcomers persisted by petitioning the town for permission to form another church. Sensing an opportunity to exploit the controversy, the town quickly granted the newcomers' request. Soon a separate congregation began to meet, its ranks swelled by inhabitants formerly kept out of First Church, as well as by a small contingent from First Church still angry over the selection of Chauncey and the defeat of the covenant. The dissenters, again aided by the town, obtained the services of a young minister, Peter Bulkeley, but Bulkeley remained only a short time before giving way to another young clergyman, Zachariah Walker. Walker's credentials included support for the half-way covenant.[26]

Sometime in 1668 or 1669 the dissenters endorsed the covenant. Meanwhile, the town meeting, exercising considerable control over Walker's congregation, sought to humiliate Chauncey's followers by demanding that the two groups share the same meeting-house. Moreover, in the order of services, the town allowed the dissenters to meet first, thus forcing the members of First Church to wait outside until Walker completed his services. One Sunday in early 1669 Walker's group met for over three hours, forcing Chauncey and his followers to huddle together near the door in the chill of early spring. Incensed, the members of First Church removed to the home of one of their leaders, where they vowed that, the town notwithstanding, the dissenters would never use the meetinghouse again. The following Sunday, when Walker's congregation assembled at the meetinghouse, they found it boarded up and the door nailed shut. They, too, retired to a member's home to plot strategy.

The problem eventually went to the Connecticut General Assembly, with the dissenters demanding the right to use the meetinghouse and the old church petitioning to deny them that right. The Assembly's response was to call a council of ministers, but the old church refused to submit to a council, arguing that the dispute involved only the use of the meetinghouse, not ecclesiastical differences. There the matter rested until September 1669, when First Church sent a curious message to Walker's congregation asking that, if some ecclesiastical differences did separate them, why should they not submit those grievances to a council of ministers then meeting in New London? The dissenters agreed, but the journey to New London proved fruitless.

Finally, after years of argument, Connecticut's governor, John Winthrop, Jr., personally intervened by suggesting that the dissenters—Second Church after 1670—move elsewhere. His advice was taken and, in 1673, Walker moved his congregation, and the half-way covenant, to Woodbury.[27] The loss of Second Church meant defeat for town government and victory for First Church but, considering the years of dissension and schism and the loss of so many inhabitants in the end, the victory was hollow.[28]

Disputes between churches and towns ignored the boundary separating Massachusetts and Connecticut, appearing in the Connecticut-oriented river towns of western Massachusetts. Northampton, populated largely by former Connecticut residents, many of whom were refugees from the strife in Hartford and Wethersfield, adopted the covenant at about the same time as Hartford, Windsor and Stratford—in 1668. As in the Connecticut towns, the success and timing of the covenant in Northampton was due to dissension resulting from a widening gulf between inhabitants and church members.

Founded in 1654, Northampton placed few if any restrictions upon participation in town affairs. At first the town meeting met weekly and each adult male received a voice in the proceedings. Gradually, however, the system proved cumbersome. Much governing responsibility gravitated to elected officials, and the frequency of town meetings fell to one or two every three months. But even as the locus of authority shifted, the town meeting remained open to all who cared to participate.

The same general equality pervaded early religious gatherings. Unable to obtain a minister, the town began holding weekly services in the meetinghouse in 1655. All were welcome, and the meetings were led by laymen who preached and offered devotions. The arrangement, though disappointing to those longing for a minister and the sacraments, proved satisfactory until the arrival of a minister in 1658.[29]

The early emphasis upon equality in politics and religion nearly proved the town's undoing in 1658, when a great controversy erupted. A minority of the inhabitants led by Edward Elmer revealed a variety of grievances against the town, ranging from land allotment to the nature of the weekly religious services to the conduct of town government. Their dissatisfaction mounted until they made an attempt to elect their own slate of selectmen. They failed, though they claimed they had won, and the whole matter eventually ended in futile litigation.[30]

When a ministerial candidate, Eleazer Mather of Dorchester, arrived for a trial in late 1658 or early 1659, dissension quickly engulfed the new minister. Mather agreed to settle in Northampton only if allowed to bring seven or eight families with him and only if the town agreed to provide them with some of its best land. Elmer's small group expressed opposition, especially when it was decided that each inhabitant would contribute a portion of his own land to the newcomers. Elmer and two others refused. The two eventually relented but Elmer held firm, finally selling the land in question for a tidy profit. That angered the selectmen and the town meeting. Elmer was ordered to "give a satisfying account" of the money or face prosecution.[31]

Though it was obvious that the town was divided by Mather's stand, the majority wanted a minister badly enough to accede to almost any request no matter how painful. That spirit tended to diminish when Mather, supported by the Dorchester faithful, indicated that no one would be admitted to the church who could not satisfactorily describe his or her conversion experience to the minister and the membership. Thus the church, when organized formally in 1661, included few more than the Dorchester people. Nor did the situation improve much in the years following. By 1669, the year of Mather's death, the church still embraced fewer than half of the community's adults.[32]

Mather's popularity slipped considerably in 1661. Within two years disenchantment turned to opposition when he blocked the desires of some members and many nonmembers to adopt the halfway covenant. No doubt aware of the difficulties the town had experienced years before in its search for a minister, Mather gave it the choice of either having the covenant or himself. He would not compromise. Not wanting to lose its minister, the town grumbled but gave in.[33]

Between 1663 and 1669 many proponents of the covenant took refuge in the town meeting, and bickering between church and town remained constant. Mather, perhaps exhausted by the pressure, became ill in 1667 and, like John Warham, relinquished many of his pastoral duties. So great was the dislike for the man[34] that even as he lay ill, covenant supporters forced a vote before the church. Lacking Mather's leadership, covenant opposition collapsed and Northampton instituted a self-styled "reformation" of polity in 1668 and 1669. The reformation, which represented an attempt to expand church discipline and baptism into the community without violating the concept of regenerate membership so zealously guarded by Mather's former supporters, created a special "state of education" which pushed the covenant far beyond the intentions of the 1662 synod. The "state of education" was designed to include all persons baptized in the church but not admitted to full membership. Placed in that position, they were considered neophytes to be catechized, watched, observed, and encouraged until such time as they could qualify for full membership.[35]

The reformation of 1668 and 1669 fell far short of reinstituting the equality of the old community church, but it did signify an important victory for the town over the Mather faction in the church. The town then went even further by demanding and receiving the right to search for Mather's successor. As a result, when a committee went to Boston in 1669 to interview candidates, it went as representatives of the town, not the church. Moreover, the man it selected held ecclesiastical views about as far removed from Mather's as anyone in New England at the time. That man was the young Solomon Stoddard.[36]

By 1671 Connecticut's and the Connecticut Valley's virulent disputes were subsiding but the fruits of two decades of bitterness, schism, withdrawal, and anticlericalism were only beginning to be recognized. Pressured by events they could not control and only half understood, Connecticut's inhabitants accepted a painful restructuring of institutions within their communities and the colony. In the process town government emerged as the most powerful local institution—perhaps the most powerful colonial institution—adding a share of ecclesiastical authority to its control of civil affairs.[37] Non-church members and probably the economically underprivileged as well, gained a kind of parity with their wealthier and more powerful brethren by giving form and substance to the apparatus of the town meeting.[38] Colonial government—the General Assembly—proved unable to shape the development of either churches or towns. But the most numerous of the changes were ecclesiastical. Connecticut witnessed an ecclesiastical revolution in which the Congregational churches of the founders were modified to an extent foreseen by no one. The collapse of the clergy and the attacks of the nonmembers produced a dilution of ruling authority so complete that virtually everyone had a voice in church government. Moreover, dissension destroyed the autonomy of the church just as it weakened its exclusiveness by extending discipline and baptism into the community, creating a parish-like system of church order almost by accident. Finally, the successes of the Presbyterians and the limited toleration they achieved—combined with the ineffectiveness of the Congregationalist clergy and the General Assembly—laid to rest any pretensions of Congregationalism as Connecticut's only church system. Moreover, it was apparent that the colony's church system, however labeled, could not be protected from either internal dissension or external attack, and that those once labeled by Hooker as of "another mind" would find a home along the Connecticut River.

Connecticut's inability to enforce consensus or handle dissension was the most striking product of social and ecclesiastical strife. In the first years church discipline—and consensus—lay rooted in the authority and power of the minister. When the ministers fell from power, taking their magisterial colleagues with them, little remained to control or channel popular energies. Synods, councils, legislation: all became ineffectual. The town meeting proved to be a vehicle for promoting dissension, not a forum for resolving disagreements. Only separation, the Puritan Englishman's last resort, saved many of the communities—and possibly the colony—from dissolution. But Wethersfield and Hartford demonstrated that separation provided only a temporary solution. It removed people but it did not remove issues. It silenced dissenters but not dissension. Connecticut's decades of turmoil produced winners and losers but not order, and that realization dominated the thinking of the clergy and laymen in the decades that followed.

"THE RIGHT WAY TO ESCAPE

DESERVED RUINE," 1670–1700

T H E disastrous Synod of 1667 and its aftermath marked a dramatic turning point in the evolution of the Connecticut ministry. Long sustained by knowledge of its prestige and power and drawn by the pull of competing ecclesiastical allegiances, the ministry found itself powerless, enmeshed in an ecclesiastical system not of its making. The ministers sensed the irony of the situation. A few, like Gershom Bulkeley, turned to other pursuits. Most demanded an explanation, hoping to formulate a plan to right a world turned upside down.

Events had loosened their ties to the churches, and the ministers spoke their thoughts to one another as never before, seeking common ground. Ministerial authority and leadership provided the foundation for the well-ordered society; they agreed on that. Ministerial authority had to be revitalized or Connecticut faced calamitous days; they agreed on that as well. But why had they fallen so quickly and so far? Responding, they talked and wrote of a great conspiracy against the good society. Soon they were convinced of it. Dissension had not just happened. Rather it represented a carefully planned plot to destroy the ministry and the godly commonwealth. The restoration of lost authority took on added significance. The ministers fought to preserve a way of life, a divinely sanctioned social order. Duty told them to root out and expose the conspirators for they would save Connecticut in the process.

Reflecting on the tragic course of events in Connecticut's churches and towns, the ministers found the conspirators in plain view. The conduct of the people, especially the brethren, had been barbarous. Many had rebuked established authority, both civil and ecclesiastical, and risked anarchy in the process. They showed contempt for one another when, supposedly, brotherly love and affection were the cornerstones of New England society. Moreover, they exhibited a total disregard for the common good of the community and pursued selfish private interests even when their actions threatened the very existence of society.

Th clergy had a word to describe such behavior—worldliness—and it opposed all the values of the Christian commonwealth. Order, harmony, respect for properly constituted authority, pursuit of the common good—those were the virtues of the right-ordered society, the virtues upon which New England society had been founded. Obviously a new spirit existed among the people, and it was that spirit, not ecclesiastical discipline, which provided the impetus for the people's discontent. The clergy's analysis, as well as that of the General Assembly, had been in error, for no abstract principles of church government motivated the brethren. They were in revolt against the most fundamental values of the society, and if allowed to succeed the society would crumble.

The realization of that fact both comforted and frightened the ministers, for it explained their sudden fall from a position of respect and authority. It was meant to happen. The people had lashed out at all forms of authority but had focused on the ministers. They were accessible and an obvious symbol of the status quo. They were the promoters of the common good in the community, the preachers of subservience of private interest to the good of the whole. Trying to maintain those standards during the disputes, they were punished for their efforts. The ministers sacrificed their interests, their beliefs, and, in some cases, their livelihoods, in an attempt to restore peace. But their flocks revealed no such selflessness. No respect was given the ministerial position, no reverence accorded its learning or wisdom, no fear shown for the power it represented. The minister's authority was undermined and overturned; the values they supported were trampled; and all in the name of private interest. To a lesser extent, civil authority shared the same fate.

The ministers concluded that the crux of the conspiracy was a quest for power. The colonists rejected both the holy purpose of their errand into the wilderness and the authority supporting it. They demanded control and direction of their own affairs. The clergy interpreted that development as a sign of God's abandonment of his people. New Englanders were once God's chosen, sent into the wilderness to live according to universal principles just as the Israelites had tried to do. But Israel had failed and now New England followed suit.[1]

The evidence of worldliness—preoccupation with private interests, rejection of authority, absence of brotherly love and affection—so prevalent in the church struggles represented both a cause and a sign of God's displeasure with his people. Moreover, the ministers found other indications of divine wrath. The Connecticut Valley experienced extended periods of drought, unusually severe storms, and a succession of dismal harvests in the late 1660's and early 1670's. In addition violent outbreaks of influenza and typhoid took many lives, including those of clergy and other public figures. Finally, New England confronted the terrible Indian War of 1675–76 when much of the Connecticut Valley was ravaged or threatened by King Philip's warriors. All of those events convinced the clergy that New England had declined from the noble purposes of the founders and had incurred the wrath of God as a result.[2] A majority of the divines tried to close ranks. Many attempted to play down their well-known ecclesiastical and doctrinal divisions while they sought to exhort and guide the people back to the proper path. At the same time, the ministers fought to regain authority and respect.

The ministers employed the only mechanism available—the

pulpit—to press their views. Sermons became vehicles for inflam-
matory warnings of impending doom, and in a short time the
jeremiad came to be universally employed. Whenever a minister
spoke at a public gathering, the people could expect their sins to
be recounted and God's wrath foretold.[3]

One of the earliest reforming sermons came from James Fitch of
Norwich before an election day gathering in Hartford in 1673.[4]
Citing the controversies in the churches and towns as evidence of
God's displeasure, he reminded his listeners of their mission in the
wilderness and of their covenant with God. In that covenant New
England promised obedience to God's will in return for protection
from internal and external dangers. Social tranquility, Fitch argued,
signified God's contentment. Discord and disunity meant that the
people had broken the covenant. The hatred and bitterness engendered by the church struggles evidenced God's displeasure;
and subsequent famine, disease, and storms were products of divine
wrath.

Fitch cited Hartford, Windsor, and New Haven as three great
churches where controversies continued unabated. Consistent with
the clergy's new approach to the nature of the dissension, he
pointed to men's "private interests" as the source of conflict. It
was not so much the fact that men disagreed which brought
tragedy, but the spirit in which they did so; for they argued not
from a sense of the welfare of the whole or from a spirit of
brotherly love and affection, but from a desire for private gain at
public expense. The "sidings and party-taking Interests" of the
people were at fault, and such interests, he warned, had to be
destroyed. In concluding, he urged the people to search their hearts
for other signs of apostasy. "The Doctrine calleth for Self-Examination; Let us Examine ourselves, and commune with our hearts
. . . we live in perilous dayes, are some Storms blown over worse
than those may soon come upon New England, will the Lord be
a Pillar of Fire round about New England."[5]

The "pillar of fire" visited the Valley sooner than even Fitch
anticipated. The ministry interpreted King Philip's War as God's

revenge. In December 1675 "reforming synods" met in Hartford and New Haven to find the reasons for God's "controversy" with the Valley and to determine what should be done to placate the Almighty.[6] Responding with the same analysis propounded by James Fitch in 1673, the clergy absolved itself of blame and placed it instead on the shoulders of the laity. Worldliness was the source of evil, and contention in the churches symbolized the new spirit. No one mentioned Presbyterian or Congregationalist doctrines as sources of division. Rather, the clergy emphasized the pursuit of private interest and the rejection of duly constituted authority. New England's sin, it concluded, was "the root actually and nextly of all the other sins . . . Apostasie from the true Religion. We have fallen away from our heritage."[7]

The "apostasy" meant a decline of piety, a general and conscious neglect of religious duties. In citing the sins of omission of the people, the clergy mentioned neglect of secret prayer and self-examination, laxity in family duties like morning prayer, few private christian meetings, nonattendance at public worship, non-participation in the sacraments, and the failure of some to "take hold of the covenant." The ministers sensed a deteriorating family unit and placed most of the blame on the laxity of heads of households. "How can it be," the clerics asked, "that a master of a family, who liveth in neglect of Family duties, should prove a true Friend to the purity . . . of religion in Church, or to a true pious Government in the Common Wealth?"[8] The nonperformance of pietistic acts released a hundred baser instincts. Sensuality, pride, lust, greed, and self-interest became the "bitter fruit of Apostasie."[9]

Despite obvious concern for a bloody Indian war and its causes, the ministers remained obsessed with the conflagrations in the churches and communities which, in their minds, had led God to unleash the heathen. They could not forget the specter of events in Hartford, Windsor, Wethersfield and a host of other towns. Thus, as they spoke of the "sensuality" of the people and the pursuance of private interests at the expense of public weal, they looked beyond the Indian uprising to the revolt of the brethren.

Laymen had utilized ministerial arguments over church discipline to strip the divines of the authority and prestige they demanded and deserved. The ministers bluntly reminded laymen that the "greatness" of the first generation rested on its willingness to follow its leaders. Conversely, the apostasy of the present generation lay in its desire to overturn the old system by ignoring the advice and commands of leaders. The synods of 1675 issued a sharp rebuke to the laity's quest for power.

But the ministers did more than dispense admonitions and rebukes. Confronted with a social revolution they put ecclesiastical differences aside and effected a unified stance for the first time in their history. That unity, in turn, allowed them to design a plan to counter the tactics of the laity. Assuming that behavior reflected spirituality and that the obstreperousness of the laity grew from the absence of the Spirit, they moved to instigate a great spiritual awakening through the institutional church and the sacraments.[10] Departing from New England tradition, they placed unusual emphasis upon the sacraments as the primary means of spiritual growth. They issued an evangelical appeal to both members and nonmembers. Members were urged to come to the Lord's Table. Backsliders—those under a work of the Spirit who failed to experience spiritual growth—received assurance of the efficacy of communion. Nonmembers demanded even greater attention, especially the baptized but unconverted. Their prominence in recent conflagrations assured the clergy's interest. The ministers bemoaned the multitudes "who neglect the Sacrament of the Lord's Supper, and can content themselves to be Baptized, or to have their Children baptized, but are insensible of the need of the Lord's Supper."[11] Composed of two groups—those who were lazy and those who were overly scrupulous—they were ordered to live by their baptismal covenant, reject sin, prove themselves followers of Christ, and prepare for the Table.

But winning souls for Christ reflected only one dimension of the ministers' awakening. Sacramentally induced piety promised to shore up the fragmented institutional church, making it an engine for conversion. From baptism, "a sacrament of entrance into Covenant with Christ," the unregenerate would proceed in an orderly fashion through conversion to the Lord's Supper, a "Sacrament of our continuance in Covenant and Communion with Christ and his Church."[12] Once among the elect, the saint would grow in grace through continued participation in the Supper. All of that was meant to resurrect and sustain ministerial authority. The church militant would revolve around the minister, for in heightening the importance of the sacraments the clergy magnified its own importance beyond anything previously envisioned.

The ministers drew from several sources in preparing their spiritual awakening. They owed much to moderate Congregationalism, though in elevating the sacraments they went beyond even the dreams of Samuel Stone. They owed something to Presbyterianism as well for the participants in the 1675 synods operated more as ministers of Christ than representatives of particular churches. They borrowed extensively from midcentury debates among English nonconformists, adopting the theory and practice of sacramentally induced piety from the arguments of a host of overseas colleagues.[13] They were not slavish disciples, however, for they picked and chose from among available alternatives according to their perception of social realities. Sensitivity to a changing order, anticlericalism, and spiritual deadness ultimately determined the method of attack.

The ministers pressed their reformation in a variety of ways. The synods urged every church to celebrate communion as often as possible. A few ministers endorsed the extension of baptism to professing Christians without specific church ties, thus going beyond the intent of the 1662 synod. Most suggested continuous pressure upon regenerates and unregenerates through sermons and private consultation. Still others suggested renewed emphasis upon educating youth in the principles of a Christian faith; to that end James Fitch of Norwich produced a catechism based on the synod's discussions.[14]

The synods also endorsed mass renewals of baptismal covenants by the children of each church as a logical means for the baptized but unregenerate to "take hold" of their covenant obligations. In the year of the synods, 1675, James Fitch's Norwich church enacted a covenant whereby baptized persons renewed their covenant obligations. It specified that children would be catechised and disciplined until they achieved full communion, and the Lord's Supper would be celebrated at least once every six weeks.[15] Similar covenants appeared throughout Connecticut and the Connecticut Valley in ensuing years, incuding one adopted by Hartford First in 1695 and endorsed by one hundred ninety-two children of the church. Intended for both members and nonmembers, that covenant called for some to accept the promise of grace offered by the Lord's Supper while it asked others to reapply themselves to the dictates of the baptismal covenant. All agreed to "freely give up ourselves to the Lord to walke in communion with him in the ordinances appointed by his holy word."[16]

The clergy asked for the aid of the civil government. On each election day in the years following 1675 a minister appeared before the General Assembly and spoke of a shared responsibility for the welfare of the people. In times of crisis, the argument noted, the ministers could not provoke a reformation unaided. Speaking in 1686, John Whiting of Hartford's Second Church repeated the litany. The ruler should reward good and punish evil. "This is the design and duty of Rulers. The sword of civil power is put into their hand by divine appointment, as to reward them that do well, so to wound evil doers . . . In matters of righteousness, Their work is large; In general, a faithful endeavour to do every man right without favour or fear."[17] Whiting warned the magistracy to avoid the popular tendency toward self-interest. Though its natural allies in God's work, the ministry remained wary of its colleagues, knowing full well that many of the laymen who dominated the congregations also sat in positions of power in local and colonial government.

But events proved the General Assembly as sensitive as the ministry to alarming currents in church and society. The Assembly, like the clergy, recalled deep involvement in the church struggles of midcentury and stinging rebukes from recalcitrant citizens. The Assembly remembered how warring factions frequently used its good offices to pursue selfish aims. Assembly members knew of the inability of either clergy or magistrates to contain the passions of controversy and remembered numerous occasions when they had watched helplessly as dissident laymen mocked civil law by withdrawing from churches or towns.[18] Consequently, the Connecticut Assembly welcomed the reforming synods of 1675 and endorsed their findings.

The Assembly responded to ministerial pressure as best it could. Since most of the ills enumerated lay outside its jurisdiction, it continued along the course charted during the 1650's and 1660's. It reminded the people of the ill omens contained in natural disasters like storms, floods, droughts, and insects. It dwelt on the spiritual significance of Indian attacks, disease, and a host of other social irritants. It proclaimed fast days and days of humiliation to focus attention on popular abuses, and occasionally passed laws to remedy specific problems. The zenith of Assembly interest in Connecticut's "decay" came in May 1680, when it debated the condition of churches and society in Connecticut and the Connecticut Valley, reviewed the signs of God's wrath toward his people, and asked what could be done to lessen His anger. The conclusions deviated little from those of the 1675 synods. Whereas the ministry found the source of God's anger in the neglect of Christian duties, the Assembly found it in a general "decay of love to God and one to another." Assemblymen echoed the clergy's contention that ecclesiastical dissension resulted from a fundamental moral breakdown, not competing systems of church polity. The General Assembly then published its solemn judgment:

This Court seriously considering the dispensation of Divine Providence towards our nation in generall and ourselves in particular, and the decay of love to God and one to another appearing in those divisions that in some places doe yet con-

tinue, with the abounding of sin amongst us . . . threatening
divine anger against us, as ready to fall upon us in the present
face of affayres, and in the unseasonableness of the weather,
the overflowings of the watters in sundry places . . . all which
calls upon us aloud to humble ourselves before the Lord for
what is provoking amongst us; and this Court accordingly
doe appoynt the 3d Wednesday in June next to be observed
throughout this collony a day of publique humiliation and
prayer . . .[19]

Ordering a day of humiliation proved the limit of the Assembly's
involvement in reforming the manners and morals of the people.
It added a few specific recommendations, but they amounted to
little more than suggestions that the ministry catechize youth on
the Sabbath and hold weekly lectures.[20]

Still, the Assembly's consideration of civil and ecclesiastical disorders was significant in that it revealed a new and altered perspective on the nature of the disputes. In recommending toleration
for Presbyterians only a decade before, the Assembly had agreed
with the ministry that disciplinary questions had sparked the lay
revolt. Then the clergy had altered its position by announcing that
the uprisings were aimed at all legitimate authority and the social
values buttressing that authority. The clergy had labeled the struggle a quest for power, and the Assembly's reassessment now produced the same conclusion. Moreover, Assembly followed clergy
by portraying the lay conspiracy as evidence of a general moral
collapse. Unfortunately, Assembly members could produce few
concrete solutions, save to wish their clerical brethren success in
their attempts to promote a spiritual awakening.

As the 1670's gave way to the 80's and 90's the early optimism
of many of Connecticut's clergymen began to wane, yielding to
dark feelings that efforts to effect a spiritual reformation were ending in failure. The flurry of activity in the 70's—the synods, the
covenant renewals, the emphasis on the sacraments and sacramentally induced piety, the preaching, the teaching, the concern of the

civil government, the "reforming" laws—all were characterized in the 80's and 90's as not having produced the expected conversions or heightened spirituality. Delivering the election-day sermon in Hartford in 1685, Samuel Wakeman of Fairfield revealed the despair of many ministers with his title, "Sound Repentence. The Right Way to Escape Deserved Ruine."[21] Wakeman reminded his listeners of their special status with God—the covenant—and of the conditional nature of that status. "If they will be his People he will be their God," he announced. "If they will own him he will own them: if they will continue with him he will continue with them, but if they will none of him he will none of them; if they cast off him he will cast off them. 2 Chron. 15.2."[22] God would not ignore the covenant unless his people failed to fulfill its conditions. And that, Wakeman warned, was exactly what was happening. The people sinned by "unworthy entertainments of the glorious Gospel of the blessed God: our receiving of the grace of God in vain, the neglect of that great salvation . . ."[23] In short, the hearts of the people no longer received the great truths of the gospel. Piety gave way to formalism. New England emerged a land of hypocrites, performing the externals of religion while hearts lay dormant. "Men are gone off in their judgments," Wakeman lamented. They "stand not so clearly and fixedly perswaded in their own minds of the necessity and importance of such attendancies, and begin to take up an opinion that there needs not so much ado that all this is not of that absolute necessity but that it will be a tolerable thing, at least to abate somewhat of it."[24]

Speaking for many of his colleagues, Wakeman sadly noted that religion now meant little more than the appearance of piety. Men showed no concern for their souls, no sensitivity to the need for grace or the dangers of perdition. They wallowed in selfish concern for private interests. They clung to the belief that a façade of piety would bring admission to heaven. "Where is the rule for daily secret Prayer, meditation, self-examination?" Wakeman questioned. "Or where is the rule that a man must every day read a Chapter or two to his Family; yet the Judgments are secretly, insensibly wrought off from laying the weight and stress upon these things, as to the constant, diligent, accurate thorough attendance of them."[25]

But none of that was new. It echoed synodical findings of a decade earlier. What *was* new in Wakeman's argument was the frustration, the feeling that the people continued to ignore their peril and clerical attempts to lead them away from it. "How many wayes, and for how long a time hath God manifeste his displeasure against us? Hath not the sword gone through the Land, hath not sore diseases had their annual return upon us; yea, of late both Summer and Winter abode with us to the taking of many from us? and how sadly hath God of late years smitten us in all the labours of our hands by blasting, mildews, catter pillars, worms, tares, floods and droughts."[26] Weren't magistrates and ministers dying in unprecedented numbers? How much evidence was needed to convince people of God's anger?

Wakeman spoke of an awful symptom of divine wrath and ministerial impotence, declining church membership. Not emphasized previously by either the synods of 1675, the Assembly, or by the clergy in its calls for reforms, Wakeman referred to it as a universally accepted fact. "Once," he asserted, "our Sion had multitudes converted to God." Now, he continued, converts were few. Wakeman interpreted this as a sure sign that holy ordinances lacked divine power. Men were "forsaken of his sometimes working power and vertue towards the souls of his own, they are not affected, humbled, quickened, raised, warmed, conforted by them, as sometimes they do not prosper, thrive flourish and bring forth fruit under them as heretofore . . . and can we have a sadder token of gods withdrawing and estranging himself from us than his failing his Ordinances of the wonted influences of his spirit, both as to conversion and Edification."[27]

Wakeman's emphasis on declining church membership and anemic ordinances received support in John Whiting's election-day sermon a year later (1686). Whiting, of Hartford's Second Church, condemned the entire populace, then reminisced about an earlier age when all aspects of colonial life were qualitatively superior to the present. "Shall I say," he remarked bitterly, "it was better every way. We had better peace and plenty, better health and harvests, in former than later years; it was better for soul and body, better in spirituals, less Sin; and better in temporals, less sorrow."[28]

The ministers remained obsessed with social and spiritual decay and the conviction that their authority and prestige continued to wane. Consequently, it became commonplace in the reforming sermons, particularly in the annual election sermon, for the ministers to cajole listeners to reform manners and morals and to plead for obedience to persons in authority. John Whiting's 1686 election sermon ended with an exhortation to ministers, people, and magistrates—the normal practice. Speaking of the clergy he said, "The Lord hath made us Watchmen, to watch for souls, as those that must give account. And therein our work is, to receive the work at his mouth, and give warning from him to deliver his mind and message plainly . . . To awaken men from sin, and warn them to a Saviour, by both Doctrine and Conversation, to lead in the way to heaven."[29] His recitation was directed to the "people" as a reminder of the exalted function of the minister. It represented a plea to the laity to reflect on the ministerial role and offer the deference due the Lord's "Watchmen." It contained a reminder that ministers were selected to lead while others were intended to follow, just as "Obedience to Magistrates is a moral duty that all men should mind, yet many need to be reminded of it."[30]

The crisis of authority which initiated and sustained the clergy's analysis of the ills of Connecticut society and which underlay its calls for reform through spiritual rebirth received eloquent testimony a decade after Whiting's appearance before the Assembly. The occasion was election day 1697, and the speaker was the young minister from New London, Gurdon Saltonstall. Saltonstall, unborn when Connecticut's churches divided in the 1650's and 60's, delivered a sermon as germane to those years as to his time. Though a citizen of Connecticut for only a short time, Saltonstall presented an abstract discussion of the nature of civil authority, the duties

of the magistrate, the rights and responsibilities of the people, and
the end of civil government in the colony. He emphasized the
representative character of the political institutions of Connecticut
and the people's power and glory under them. But his narrative
contained a recurring theme: one not entirely consistent with
statements about popular power. That theme involved the peculiar
purpose that had brought settlers to the country. "You [the As-
sembly] have the Care and Charge of a People whom God hath
by special favor taken to be his own Peculiar," he told the assembled throng, "and such a Trust as this ought to be strenuously
and faithfully discharged. The Lord our God hath by signal Pro-
tections, and a stretched out Arm, made these (once dark) corners
of the earth a place of comfortable Entertainment to a Remnant
of his faithful Servants, and their Seed: Here he hath intrusted us
with the choise Mercies of his Word and Ordinances: we have had
them and enjoyed them, in safety from all the endeavours of such,
as with an envious eye and vexed Soul, have beheld what God hath
been doing for us."[31] The mission, Saltonstall continued, required
a virtuous and intelligent population. It required a commitment by
all to the common good over private interests and a recognition
that the journey of God's chosen into the wilderness remained
an occasion of cosmic importance not only for the present age but
for future generations as well. It also entailed a great burden. If
New England failed to create and perpetuate a society reflecting
God's will, man would lose the last opportunity to purify himself
and his institutions and create a new Eden.

Having outlined the basic responsibilities of New England's inhabitants, Saltonstall repeated a refrain familiar in Connecticut
and the Connecticut Valley: that people should choose virtuous
rulers and follow their judgments as long as they did not attempt
to thwart God's will. "God hath designed the Civil Government
of his People," Saltonstall lectured, "to concenter with Ecclesiastical Administrations and (though by different Mediums) they are
both levelled at the same end; the maintaining of Piety, and promoting of a covenant walk . . . This is the work that belongs to

you in your Publick Capacities; and it calls for your Wisdom and Justice, and Zeal and Holiness; if you would be found thus ruling with God, and faithful with his Saints."[32] In that manner Saltonstall restated the clergy's case for reformation. The people of the Connecticut Valley and New England lived in the New World to show the Old that man could live in harmony with the Will of God. Their "mission" required the subservience of the individual to the noble purposes of the whole. Success could and would come only through respect, reverence and submission to rightly constituted authority—civil *and* ecclesiastical.

The analysis completed, Saltonstall informed his listeners that despite decades of warning from God, the authority of ministers and magistrates was neither respected nor followed. Private interests held sway in church and commonwealth. "Oh how justly may the Lord complain of us, that we are become the degenerate Plant of a strange Vine unto him? Where is that Zeal for God and his ways that high Esteem of Gospel Priviledges: that faithful improvement of Sacred Ordinances, that Care and Concernment for the Advancing of the Kingdom of Christ? which things were once our praise."[33] The people, Saltonstall warned, ignored their mission, rebuked the fine examples of their ancestors, turned from the virtuous life, and now faced the wrath of God's vengeance. "Hath not the Lord himself been coming near to Judgment?" Saltonstall asked. "It is obvious that God hath a Controversy with us, and He is wrath with his Inheritance . . . yet if we consider the bloodshed, and ruinous Devastations in some Places of this Land, together with the languishing State of the whole Country at this Day, we may also take up the Psalmists complaint."[34]

Revealing the anger and frustration of the clergy, Saltonstall exempted his colleagues from the customary closing exhortations. Instead, he addressed all of his remarks to the civil rulers and to the people. He demanded wisdom and justice from the rulers, enumerating the ways in which they could aid in the reformation of the land. He repeated that good rulers came only from a good people and that he wasted words if he urged magistrates to be virtuous when their electors were not. He pleaded with the people to elect good rulers and, above all, to return to their holy mission by reinstituting the proper attitude toward civil and ecclesiastical authority. He assured them that magistrates and ministers had God's approval to interpret the common good. He told them also that God expected them to forsake private interests, to reject factionalism, and to respect and submit to properly constituted authority in the pursuance of New England's peculiar destiny. "Speak no evil of Dignities; Abhor that Unchristian way of Detraction, Backbiting and Slander. If they are God's Viceregents, certainly it must be a Crying Sin and Shame for us thus to treat them. Do our Enemies charge us, that his is the way wherein we have been used to requite those that with greatest Pains, have travailed for the Publick Good?"[35] Saltonstall spoke of civil authority, but his words applied to the plight of the clergy as well.

Yet, while Saltonstall's sermon offered an analysis both eloquent and succinct, its importance lay, partially, in what was left unsaid. Its tone suggested that the sacramentally induced spiritual awakening had failed. It suggested also that attempts to mute internal conflicts over church discipline had accomplished little. Saltonstall's sermon provided abundant evidence of the continued impotence of the clergy and the prevalence of worldliness.[36] In the churches the perpetuation of the "power of the fraternity" appeared to be the single goal of the laity, and woe to the minister whose purposes failed to conform to the wishes of the brethren. Examples of the clergy's involuntary subordination to the laity existed in abundance. The records of the General Assembly contained numerous complaints from ministers concerning nonpayment of salaries. Many of their problems stemmed from simple attempts to exercise leadership over their congregations, attempts which alienated portions of the membership and brought punishment. Several clergymen shared the tragic fates of Nathaniel Chauncey and Benjamin Woodbridge, ministers to the warring factions in Windsor in earlier years. Fired by the town because it was thought they symbolized the issues separating the people, they spent years trying to collect the salaries their congregations neglected to pay them.[37] Their stories, and others, became all too familiar examples of Connecticut's continuing ecclesiastical divisions and the clergy's failure to achieve mastery.

THE SEARCH FOR A NEW
MORAL ORDER, 1665–1700

M A N Y of the laymen of Connecticut and the Connecticut Valley shared the clergy's fear of chaos and social disintegration, despite charges and accusations to the contrary. They proved equally sensitive to rapid social change and echoed the ministry's recitation of the debilitating effects of three decades of social and ecclesiastical disorder. The brethren linked change and disorder and, like the ministers, concluded that dissension had caused Connecticut society to break from its moorings. As a solution many began to appeal to the old virtues of consensus and peace as necessities for the godly commonwealth. At the same time they sought an antidote for the apparent sickness of some ancient guarantors of social cohesion: the General Assembly, the town meeting, and the clergy.

Most of all, sizable numbers of laymen sensed the institutional church's failure to provide a basis for moral order in Connecticut. Imitating the ministers the brethren saw the influence of the church as central to the good society. They also knew that Connecticut's churches were in shambles. Factionalism and separation had effectively curtailed their roles in the community. Church membership lagged everywhere, especially in towns hardest hit by strife. Windsor First, for example, ripped by two decades of partisanship, averaged only 1.5 new members per year between 1639 and 1677, a figure more than offset by deaths and withdrawals.[1] Laymen, like the clergy, assumed logically that while church members fought with one another and membership declined, society suffered as well.

Floods, Indian wars, sickness, and other calamities had the same effect on the brethren as on the clergy. God's anger became only too evident in the 1660's and 70's, and the times demanded immediate action. Consequently, in churches all over Connecticut and the Connecticut Valley reform-minded brethren began to work to heal the wounds inflicted on their congregations and communities by years and even decades of strife. Their immediate goal was to close ranks, to create a united brethren which would use its new authority to alter both the order and the mission of the church. Their long-range goal was to create a program to ensure peace in the congregation and morality in the community. Their efforts began in towns like Northampton in the late 1660's and Norwich in the early 70's, and spread steadily until they covered the breadth and width of Connecticut and the Connecticut Valley by the 90's. Consistent with the localism of the past, the nature and extent of reform varied considerably from town to town, and church to church. Still, the assumptions which underlay reform, as well as the devices used to achieve it, were much the same in every locale. In some ways they differed little from the means and ends of the clergy. In other important areas, however, reforming brethren and ministers differed fundamentally.

First, while the clergy called for order through spirituality, the brethren demanded controls on behavior. Not that they ignored the practice of piety or rejected the necessity of conversion; they simply did not share the clergy's belief that spiritual quickening promised social order. Laymen searched for institutional mechanisms to guide men's action. They looked for devices to forge and maintain consensus. Second, the clerical reformation sought the restoration of ministerial authority, while the lay reformation institutionalized the power of the fraternity. Both movements intended to stabilize the institutional church and breathe new life into its operations in the community. One, however, lacked the power to achieve its objectives, while the other lacked the unity.

Brethren and clergy also employed different tactics. Ministers looked primarily to the sacraments and secondarily to devices like the reforming covenant to produce piety. The brethren employed three mechanisms to control behavior: the church covenant, the half-way covenant, and a revised membership examination emphasizing conduct, not religious experience. The reforming brethren drafted and ratified new church covenants, exalting the power and unity of the fraternity and promising obedience to its principles. They intended to establish consensus and also provide the means for handling future dissent. Dissent could not be outlawed, but it could be controlled when all members agreed to live by ideals considered final and above question. The half-way covenant provided the means to extend the principles of peace and consensus into the community. Half-way members became neophytes awaiting admission. Their trials involved not spirituality but the willingness and ability to live by the standards of the membership. Finally, an altered definition of the "visible saint" tied the reforms together. Those found worthy of the principles of the church covenant—whether half-way members or newcomers to the town —were admitted only after a serious and often lengthy public and private examination of past behavior.[2]

How did ministers and brethren react to the reforming crusades of the other group? On the surface they seemed cordial enough. Reforming covenants, so prevalent in the late seventeenth century, often contained the tactics and goals of both sides, as though brethren and clergy operated in conjunction. The covenants normally contained pledges to promote piety and attend the sacraments, reflecting the minister's influence. They also affirmed the power of the fraternity and enunciated the laity's desire to live in peace according to common standards of behavior.[3]

Behind that façade lay considerable tension and hostility. The brethren tended to ignore clerical appeals for spiritual awakening, just as they thwarted attempts to exalt ministerial power. Ministers opposed the laity's reformation in all its facets, though they agreed with the need to forge a consensus and improve behavior. They tried to undercut the unity of the membership. Many opposed the half-way covenant even as they urged persons to "take hold" of their baptismal covenant. Most clergymen bitterly resisted attempts to change the basis for membership from spirituality to behavior. Above all—and as their jeremiads suggested—the ministers grew furious over the layman's desire to substitute conduct for conversion in defining the church's mission. "Worldliness," the word used by the ministers to describe the progress of evil in Connecticut, referred directly to the lay reformation. Time and again the ministers spoke of the reforming brethren's erroneous belief that works, not faith, offered the key to salvation. It was not simply rhetoric. Rather it reflected the intensity of the fraternity's campaign to influence behavior just as it spelled out the extent of the clergy's opposition.[4]

While hostility between brethren and clergy increased, friction between church members and nonmembers lessened. The reasons were several. First, the reforming brethren made few attempts to challenge the powers won by the town meetings in earlier years. On the contrary, in many communities the brethren tried to forge alliances with town meetings by portraying ministerial arrogance as a danger to the authority of both. Second, and more important, the programs offered by reforming brethren attracted the support of townsmen because they promised to resolve some of the old grievances of nonmembers against the churches. Thus in many communities brethren and townsmen worked together to implement the half-way covenant and narrow the gap between the church and the community.

The lay reformation revolved around an altered rationale of the nature and purpose of the church covenant. Probably the best-known mechanism of Puritan ecclesiastical order, the covenant is usually considered synonymous with Puritanism and Congregationalism, conjuring up images of pious immigrants pledging their obedience to a document revealing the saints' duties to God and to fellow men. Supposedly it provided form and substance for the

regenerate community of saints—the pure church—just as it outlined the principles of peace for both church and community. The
covenant created the parameters of consensus while it controlled
behavior. Much of the conventional wisdom about the significance
of the covenant reflects the early apologists of New England
Congregationalism. Writing in the *Survey of the Summe of Church
Discipline*, Thomas Hooker portrayed the covenant as the heart
of a Congregational order, fulfilling both spiritual and social functions. "Every Spirituall or Ecclesiasticall corporation," he wrote,
"receives its being from a spirituall combination."[5] For the Congregationalist, that combination was the covenant, the vehicle whereby saints came together in a church state to worship God and
enjoy his ordinances. "Mutual covenanting and confederating of
the Saints in the fellowship of the faith according to the order of
the Gospel," he emphasized, "is that which gives constitution and
being to a visible Church."[6]

But there was more. The covenant set the standards of behavior
for the group and gave it the power to command obedience. "The
sum in short is this," Hooker continued. "By mutual ingagement
each to the other, such persons stand bound in such a state and
condition to Answer to the terms of it [the covenant], and to
walk in such waies, as may attain the end thereof." "This ingagement," he continued, "gives each power over another, and main-
tains and holds up communion each with other, which cannot but
be attended, according to the termes of the agreement." Thus, he
concluded, the covenant was meant to be

> the cement which soders them all, that soul as it were, that
> acts all the parts and particular persons so interested in such a
> way, for there is no man constrained to enter into such a con-
> dition, unless he will: and he that will enter, must also willing-
> ly binde and ingage himself to each member of that society to
> promote the good of the whole, or else a member actually he
> is not.[7]

"The good of the whole," consensus, peace: those were the values defining the social utility of the church covenant. Behind them lay a group which prescribed the terms of the moral life and then enforced those terms.

Theory and practice, however, ran afoul in early Connecticut, for the brethren lacked both the initiative and the ecclesiastical authority to make the covenant function as the vehicle for peace. The covenant was no less a ministerial device than the public examination of prospective members. Whatever power it exerted over behavior was derivative of the authority and prestige of the minister. The Hookers, Warhams, and Stones, not mutual confederation, provided the "cement which soders them all" in the towns along the Connecticut River. So long as their authority went unquestioned, the peace of the group continued.

Clerical dominance led to much confusion over the nature and purpose of the covenant. Hooker drew a sharp distinction between explicit and implicit covenants, arguing that while both were satisfactory the former was the Congregational way. The implicit covenant applied to English parishes where "without verball profession thereof" the people "walk in such a society, according to such rules of government, which are exercised amongst them, and so submit themselves thereunto."[8] An explicit covenant included an "open expression and profession of this ingagement in the face of the Assembly, which persons by mutuall consent undertake in the waies of Christ." Of the two, Hooker continued, "Its most according to the compleatnesse of the rule, and for the better being of the Church, that there be an explicit covenant." Why? Because the members were more likely to avoid "cavilling and starting aside from the tenure and terms of the covenant" and "their hearts stand under a stronger tye, and are more quickened and provoked to do that, which they have before God and the congregation, ingaged themselves to doe."[9] In short, an explicit covenant guaranteed peace and moral behavior.

But the explicit covenant failed to gain universal acceptance in early Connecticut because many clerical architects of discipline did not share Hooker's vision of Congregational order. In addition, the disputes of midcentury destroyed the efficacy of the explicit covenant by nullifying the authority of the ministry which lay behind it. By the mid-1660's nothing remained to guarantee consensus, order or proper behavior in the congregation except the new "power of the fraternity" and that was hopelessly fragmented by factionalism. Lay control appeared destined to end in the tyranny of the majority.

It did not. At the same time the clergy planned its campaign to curb worldliness and restore ministerial authority, reforming brethren constructed programs designed to make lay authority the operating principle of church order. From the late 1660's to the end of the seventeenth century, laymen throughout Connecticut and the Connecticut Valley struggled to ensure peace and counter the debilitating effects of decades of conflict, a rapidly deteriorating social order and renewed ministerial attack. They tried to close ranks and forge the outlines of a new consensus based on common standards of behavior. They attempted to express and enforce that consensus in explicit covenants which would enable the brethren—the fraternity—to take control of the parish-like church system produced by dissension and mold it into an engine of reformation, an engine designed to elevate the behavior of members and nonmembers alike.[10]

Their campaign resulted in a new definition of Congregational order—one might term it lay Congregationalism—created without the aid of clergy or the pronouncements of synods or political bodies. Predicated on a group-determined and group-enforced consensus, it met the alleged social crisis by repairing the structure of the institutional church and using it in a concerted effort to reinforce public and private morality. Among its many consequences, lay Congregationalism further enraged the clergy because it tended to de-emphasize spirituality, placing works above faith, while it frustrated clerical attempts to resurrect ministerial authority.

The reforming brethren moved from factionalism to consensus easily in some locales, painfully in others. In Northampton the movement to reestablish peace ended a decade of strife, and First Church emerged as a pioneer because of its reformation. The brethren met solemnly in late 1668 and early 1669 to admit their failure to attend to the needs of many within and without the church, calling it "this day of our reformation."[11] Eleazer Mather, their pastor, lay near death and was no longer able to preside over the church, though he had drafted a confession of faith which was later adopted.

Meetings dragged on for several months while the members sought to reach accord on the principles of church order and behavior which would guide them in the future. At last they agreed on a new and enlarged church covenant, adopted the half-way covenant and made several special provisions for persons not covered by half-way status. The result represented a valiant attempt to close the doors to future dissension by cloaking the church and the community in a code of behavior having the consent of all, or at least all of the members of the church.

The reforming covenant represented the heart of the church's labor. A remarkable document covering several pages of cramped though legible scrawl, it was two to three times the length of the first church covenant written seven years earlier—Eleazer Mather's covenant. It began by "Disclaiming all Confidence of, or any worthinesse in ourselves to be in Covenant with God," then bound the signers to "promise and Covenant to keep and seek all the Commandments of God, and to walk in obedience, learning and doing all whatsoever the Lord hath, or hereafter shall reveale and make known to us to be his mind and will."[12] Then, more pointedly, the members spoke to the bane of their existence—contention—and agreed to give up old ways and seek peace and harmony:

> We further promise and engage tearfully and conscienciously to avoid all strife, contention, evil surmizing, perverse disputings, whisperings, envy, schisms, pernicious opinions contrary to sound doctrine, and whatsoever all may find to weaken union . . . disturb peace interrupt communion, together with all the causes and occasions of them, but con-

stantly . . . to seek after the things that make for peace, and
the things wherewith we may edify one another, ministering
one to another . . . by frequent exhortations, constant watch-
fullness and seasonable admonition . . . till we grow up into
a perfect majesty in Christ's name.[13]

The covenant recited a lengthy list of duties and obligations of
the members toward each other, toward others, and especially,
toward the children of the community, and noted "our sinfull
neglects and faylings" in that regard. Much was made of the need
to lead exemplary lives for the edification of the young. "We parents, fathers and mothers," the covenant continued, "will teach
and command our children to know, fear and love the Lord . . .
endeavouring ourselves to be in behavior . . . patterns an example
of sobriety . . . and holiness."[14] Even the elders, against whom so
much rancor had been generated, were included in the pledge of
loving affection, though a cryptic note was attached that obedience
continued to hinge on their following the ways of Christ.

The covenant concluded with a stirring affirmation of hope and
renewed zeal:

These things we all promise as before the Lord . . . we are
humbly bold to insist that . . . miscarriages and comings short,
contrary to the settlements and resolutions of our hearts, shall
not make void this Covenant. And whereas not through weakness shall this fail, but with trust and hope through Grace
in . . . Christ our Redeemer for pardon, acceptance, and healing for his namesake. Now, because of all this we make a . . .
covenant in the behalft of ourselves and our little ones, con-
firmed and assent to the same this day, and unfayntedly engage ourselves, and our hearts, and subscribe our names
thereunto.[15]

Northampton's reforming covenant bound the signers to a new
consensus. Making specific reference to the contention of recent
years, the brethren agreed to abide by high standards of moral
conduct in the future, vowing never against to let either church

or community fall into such desperate straits. Above all, the members vowed to mold the church into an educational institution, paying special attention to the moral education of children in the church and children of the community. Using an argument with a timeless ring the members reminded one another that the success of their experiment depended, for the most part, on their ability to inculcate the values of the moral community in their "little ones."

The reformation humiliated Eleazer Mather. Its architects used the occasion of the minister's illness to reconstruct the polity of the church. The reforms represented almost total rejection of Mather's leadership and ecclesiology. Moreover, the reformation crippled the ministerial prerogative, making it forever subordinate to the expressed concerns of the fraternity. The reformation did not, however, cause further friction between church and town. On the contrary, by accepting the town meeting's aid and intervention in the struggle over the half-way covenant, the reforming brethren took a large step toward forming a permanent bond between church members and nonmembers.

Northampton's achievements set the tone for lay reform for three decades. Implicitly anticlerical, the reforming covenants adopted all over Connecticut and the Connecticut Valley exalted the power and unity of the fraternity, limited or nullified the independence of the minister, and focused the attention of all on the maintenance of peace through proper behavior. They announced, blatantly, that the era of ministerial dominance and leadership had ended.

Meanwhile, the clergy launched its own reformation. The laity did not reject the ministry's plea for sacramentally induced piety and spiritual rebirth, just its demand for ruling authority. Moreover, the brethren made spirituality secondary to behavior and moral order. They defined evangelicalism as the moral conquest of the community by the fraternity's rules of proper behavior, not as a new manifestation of spiritual enthusiasm. Thus the separate campaigns of ministry and laity and the friction they produced often appeared in the reforming covenants, and it became clear that clergy and laity possessed differing ideas about the covenant's intent.

After the synods of 1675 most reforming covenants included specific references to renewing baptismal obligations, catechising children in the principles of Christianity, and increasing the frequency of the celebration of the Lord's Supper; all reforms reflecting the clergy's desire for spiritual awakening. But evangelical piety, as such, was never the central purpose of any covenant. Indeed, each one extolled the fraternity's power and unity, pledged the church to live by accepted standards of conduct, and called for the eradication of specific abuses endangering the peace of the group. Even the language used to describe the covenants varied between clergy and laity. The ministers spoke of covenant "renewals," but the resulting documents rarely employed that term except in reference to baptismal obligations. Obviously written by laymen, the covenants implied uniqueness, as though the fraternity had come together for the first time to enunciate its problems, define its goals, and produce acceptable and workable standards of behavior.

The mixture of clerical and lay means and ends and the dominance of the brethren may be found in two of the reforming covenants discussed in the preceding chapter. The Norwich covenant, for example, included much more than references to baptismal obligations, the efficacy of the Supper, or the need for spiritual awakening. In language and purpose it imitated Northampton's reforming covenant. The document listed the sins of omission and commission plaguing the church, especially contention and factionalism, and called for the unification of the brethren in a pledge of peace and moral behavior. The tone of the covenant clearly placed the need for moral reformation above that of spiritual awakening, and to that end the brethren agreed to place extraordinary emphasis on the church as a mechanism for moral education. Errant brethren were to be immediately called to account, not for punishment as much as reorientation. Children were to be "catechised" concerning the meaning of proper behavior in Norwich and were to be examined continually until they joined the church.[16]

The same evidence may be found in the Hartford covenant of 1695. That document called for a renewal of baptismal obligations as well as sensitivity to the ordinances but drew a sharp distinction between the need for spiritual enlightenment and the necessity of controlling certain behavioral problems plaguing both church and town. The brethren explained that "drunkenness and fornication" absorbed their youth. To remedy the obvious dangers to the peace of the community, one hundred and ninety-two "children," some of whom were already members in full communion, pledged obedience to the principles of peace and order governing the church.[17]

While Northampton and Norwich drafted provisions for moral behavior, some communities found that the search for consensus led to further division. The most tragic situation continued to be the dispute in Windsor. Discussed briefly in Chapter 3, above, the dispute merits further attention. The town of Windsor tried to support two congregations, one Congregationalist and one Presbyterian. Gradually the economic straits of the 1670's forced the townsmen to reconsider their support for the newer and smaller church. First Church met in a new meetinghouse, Second in an older structure. By 1676 both buildings needed repair, but the town could find funds only for the newer one. Second Church, chronically short of financial resources since its inception and now forced to meet in a dilapidated and unsafe building, spent the ensuing year discussing its future. Convinced that outside aid would not appear, the members sadly voted to disband and seek readmission to First Church. Hearing their application, the General Assembly quickly called for a ministerial council to draft a plan for reunification. That plan, made public in 1677, called for the united churches to adopt the "order of First Church, which we understand to be the congregationall way of church order."[18] The formula specified that:

those members of the second congregation who were of the
first congregation, return to their former station therein either
in full communion or otherwise. And that all such members
of the second congregation (whether formerly of the first
church or not) being persons of competency of Knowledg
and unblameable life, be also entertained to full communion
with first church.[19]

If anyone objected to persons offered for membership, the applicants in question were to be examined by members of the
council, not by the members of First Church. Also, it was suggested that Nathaniel Chauncey continue as minister of First
Church "acting according to the professed congregationall principles as above exprest." Benjamin Woodbridge, minister of Second Church, was to be allowed to preach from time to time in
the hope that the two ministers would reconcile their views and
serve the church together.[20]

Second Church agreed but First Church did not. The General
Assembly intervened immediately, demanding to know why the
old church refused. Was it simply obstinacy or had thirteen years
of strife made factionalism a way of life for the brethren? The
church's carefully worded reply dismissed both possibilities. Sensing imminent victory the church demanded a settlement on its
terms, according to its principles and nothing less. The ministerial
council, the members wrote, had urged reunification under the
terms of the synods of 1648 and 62, but the suggested formula
violated both of those synods, especially the former. The church
would not or could not "admit persons to church fellowship without inquiry into or haveing matter of satisfaction presented respecting their fitness for communion."[21] In short, the church demanded an admission of error from former brethren and a public
trial in which the dissidents would agree to submit to the principles, both ecclesiastical and moral, which they had formerly
snubbed. It was the power of the fraternity in its most ruthless
form, made doubly unpalatable for Assembly, clergy, and errant

members of Second Church by the fact that First Church also demanded the immediate dismissal of both ministers and the selection of a single replacement.[22] The ministers, Chauncey and Woodbridge, would serve as scapegoats.

While the church's behavior surprised both Assembly and clergy, its reasoning probably left them dumbfounded. It was as though a decade and a half of strife had not occurred. Instead of brethren, or town, challenging the authority of clergy and other duly constituted officials, it was now clergy and Assembly challenging the ecclesiastical authority of the fraternity, an authority suddenly cloaked in the sanctity of the Cambridge Platform. The Windsor brethren smugly, even arrogantly, rejected the council's decision out of hand because it contradicted their understanding of the nature of a congregational polity as well as their portrayal of the traditional source of ecclesiastical decision-making in Windsor. It must have seemed a strange juxtaposition of ideas and events to the clergy, but it was indicative of the growing self-consciousness of Connecticut's reforming brethren and their desire to heal breaches in the church and community on their own terms.

Several more councils convened in the next few years in an attempt to get the church to accept the original council's formula for reunification, but all ended in failure. In the interim the town endorsed First Church's stand by firing both ministers, then started a search for a single replacement.[23] Two men emerged as likely candidates, Samuel Mather of Milford and Isaac Foster of Charlestown, Massachusetts. Mather, especially, wanted to leave Milford quickly, for he detested the congregation. In a 1678 letter to his relative, Increase of Boston, he wrote of his low salary, lack of authority, and his objections to the obstinancy of the brethren, "they being of that perswasion we call anti-synodalianer."[24]

Mather found the same attitudes in Windsor. Both he and Foster were brought for "trials." The criteria for assessment were simple. Would the prospective minister respect local autonomy and eschew synods? Would the prospective minister abide by the power of the fraternity? Neither man fared too well. Mather's reception was cool because he was synodically inclined and that, remarked John Whiting of Hartford, "diverts their thoughts from him."[25] Isaac Foster proved the better preacher, and his reception was enthusiastic, though there were also doubts about his loyalty to "Congregational" principles.[26]

In April 1679 a church committee recommended Foster with reservations. The members continued to have a "doubtfullness . . . concerning his persuasion in point of church order" and suggested the church send two men to Cambridge to interview him "in case they can obtain so much from him as shall capacitate them to assert that he is congregationally persuaded according to the Synods of 48 and 62." Could he be happy in a situation where the brethren determined standards of behavior and the polity of the church? Foster indicated that he could, since the committee subsequently withdrew its reservations.[27]

The town assembled in early 1679 and cast their votes for the two men. Mather was defeated soundly, 71 to 47; Foster carried, 83 to 44. The town then asked the latest council of ministers to help them obtain Foster's services, and the council replied that it had already written several letters to Bay ministers for help. The replies indicated uncertainty of Foster's position "in point of church order." The council then informed the town that it had written a second time to the same Bay ministers asking them to quiz Foster again on his agreement with the synods of 48 and 62. Soon, however, Foster informed the town that he was not coming.[28]

Foster refused Windsor's offer because the "Bay ministers" in question were really only one, Increase Mather, and Increase promoted the interests of his relative, Samuel, by doing everything in his power to keep Foster from going to Windsor. While Windsor worried about Foster's orthodoxy, Increase warned Foster not to go to Windsor because of the "strict congregationalism" of the church. Later, Foster went to Hartford's First Church to replace John Haynes.[29]

Samuel Mather was left as the only candidate for the Windsor position. In March 1680/81, the town voted "unanimously" to ask Mather to come for another trial. He quickly accepted, but his ordination was put off until 1684, again because the brethren were suspicious of his views. John Whiting of Hartford, in another letter to Increase Mather in October 1682, noted that "Mr. Samuel Mather sticks somewhat about Synod Principles, and by that meanes his settlement at Windsor seemes yet uncertaine. This day some of the Elders meete to discourse him."[30]

Old wounds were healing as reforming brethren began to find allies in the town meeting. In the discussions over Mather and Foster, church and town acted virtually in concert, demanding and receiving assurances from each candidate that nothing would be done to upset the emerging pattern of peace centering on the power and unity of the fraternity and cooperation between church members and townsmen. That probably explained why First Church suddenly reversed its stand on the readmission of members of Second Church and accepted the formula of the 1676 council. The breakthrough came in 1682 when the General Assembly "ordered" reunification and First Church agreed without argument. Former members were reinstated automatically while persons never associated with First were required to "address themselves to Mr. Mather, and haveing sattisfyed him about their experimentall knowledg and the ground of that sattisfaction by him declared to the church unto their acceptance, with encouraging testimonie given in reference to their conversion, they be thereupon admitted."[31]

Had First Church lost the struggle? Hardly, for negotiations with Samuel Mather continued until he capitulated in 1684, agreeing to abide by the power of the fraternity and the principles of behavior and ecclesiastical order it would construct. He was ordained quickly, and the members used the occasion to come together for a recitation of covenant obligations. Windsor's "reformation" took place in 1684 or early 1685, and although a copy of the covenant has not survived, it may be surmised that it resembled other reforming covenants in scope and purpose. Most important, it was endorsed by the former members of Second Church, thus satisfying the demands of First Church in regard to reunification. Within the year 155 persons—mostly children—subscribed to a special covenant binding them to the discipline, standards of behavior, and renewed sense of purpose endorsed by their elders earlier. Windsor's reformation was First Church's vindication.

The significance of the reformation may be seen in Mather's records, beginning in 1685 and lasting into the eighteenth century. The church grew steadily in both full and half-way members. By 1690 ten persons per year were entering full communion.[32] Moreover, peace returned to the church and the community, and its maintenance was supervised by the brethren—as the cases of disciplinary action suggested—and by a sympathetic town meeting. Church order remained unaltered, and Mather quietly submitted to the terms extracted from him in his settlement. He may not have liked them—he does not say—but he acceded to the superior force he encountered. Consensus replaced factionalism in Windsor. The power of the fraternity became a viable, operating force underlying the new moral community.

As consensus based on mutual agreement became the principle supporting order in older churches like Northampton and Windsor—churches ravaged by controversy and factionalism—it also emerged in congregations organized after the chaos of the mid-1660's. Likely bastions of the ancient principle of ministerial dominance, the new churches revealed the true extent of the effects of the social and ecclesiastical crises of earlier years. Westfield, Massachusetts, provided an excellent example. Settled in the 1660's, the town led a perilous existence for a number of years. Able to secure a minister, Edward Taylor, in 1671, it could not establish a church because of its small and relatively impoverished population. Finally, in the spring of 1679, Westfield sent invitations to churches up and down the Connecticut River to attend organizational ceremonies in June. But as the date approached, the town faced a rather serious problem. With so many churches and communities represented among the town's inhabitants, numerous proposals came forth for the "correct" manner of church organization. The proposals differed markedly, and each faction seemed convinced that its version was the way of the churches of the land. The dispute grew so heated that Taylor, describing the bizarre situation in his journal, feared that no organization would take place.[33]

The town leaders expressed a single feeling: the plan adopted had to be the traditional approach of other churches, else the community would be disgraced in the eyes of its neighbors. In desperation the leaders commissioned Taylor to contact neighboring churches for advice. Taylor did as he was told and soon received a number of replies full of complicated and often contradictory information. The town was no closer to a decision than before.

The people then held several emergency meetings and haggled over all the proposals. Finally a compromise emerged that seemed to contain the spirit of the advice of neighboring churches as well as much of what seemed proper to local citizens. The plan was put to a vote and adopted. Seven "pillars" were either elected or appointed from among leading male residents to serve as founding members, and a covenant was drafted by the inhabitants to be the mortar binding the members in the ways of Christ. The pillars polished their narratives of conversion experience and, on a warm June day, "took hold" of the covenant and created the church.[34]

To that point the minister played only a minor role in the proceedings, stark testimony to the gap separating 1679 from the 1630's. The entire procedure conformed to popular will as best as it could be determined, and to tradition, if not of Westfield then of the area. Unfortunately, the organizational ceremonies did not proceed as planned. First Solomon Stoddard of Northampton, spokesman for the elders of the vicinity, horrified everyone by speaking disparagingly of church covenants. He then used the Presbyterian tactic of offering the right hand of fellowship to the new church in the name of the elders, not the churches. Second, John Russell of Hadley, oldest of the clergymen present, unleashed a tirade of criticism after watching the seven pillars reenact their moments of conversion, complete with references to blinding light and strange voices. He told Taylor and others that it was the most ludicrous display he had ever witnessed and ample evidence that narratives of experience were worthless. More grumbling followed as the ceremony continued, and several representatives expressed a desire to return to the sanity of their own congregations.

After the service Westfield's inhabitants gathered to take stock of what had happened. Shocked by the reactions of lay and clerical representatives to their painstakingly prepared organization ceremony, they quietly discussed what to do. No attempt was made to secure Taylor's views, nor did anyone look to him for direction or guidance. No lay figure or figures dominated the meeting; at least none is mentioned in Taylor's account. The discussion was open and unstructured and ended in a decision to make no alterations in polity, a decision adopted unanimously.[35] The pattern of order endorsed by church and town—and the principles of peace and consensus upon which it was founded—was reaffirmed despite the objections and hostile attitudes of persons from other towns and other churches.

From the late 1660's to the beginning of the eighteenth century, the lay-inspired "reformation" of behavior and attitude swept Connecticut and the Connecticut Valley from remote and agricultural Northampton in the north and west to noisy, bustling New London on the coast. Nowhere, however, was the transformation more pronounced than in the ravaged communities of Hartford and Wethersfield. Both towns continued with Presbyterian or Presbyterian-like clergymen: Timothy Woodbridge at Hartford First (1684–1724) and Stephen Mix at Wethersfield (1694–1738). Both towns, however, rejected rule by elder for the covenanted policies of consensus set down by a united brethren.

Hartford First continued the church system that emerged from its years of turmoil, a system that focused on the half-way covenant and Samuel Stone's method of admitting new members. The latter, especially, was labeled the "broad" or "Presbyterian" method in the vernacular of the time and placed most of the responsibility for judgment in the hands of the minister, Woodbridge. Woodbridge met privately with prospective members, quizzing them concerning their reasons for seeking admission. If he found genuine interest, he placed their names before the membership and recommended affirmative action. No public relation of experience was required, only a profession of faith and repentence. The church, however, conducted a lengthy examination of the applicant's conduct, both past and present.

That method apparently satisfied the reform-minded brethren, but it represented the only area wherein Presbyterian Woodbridge possessed any real authority. His position was fixed firmly at his ordination, where, in familiar fashion, the once-divided brethren ratified their covenant and its principles of peace and proper behavior, and affirmed their united control of church discipline.[36] Woodbridge's records testified to the new power of the fraternity. In matters of discipline and censure, for example, he had no voice. On May 10, 1703, David Ensigne, convicted of adultery and excommunicated by the brethren, appeared before the church to confess his error. Exercising the compassion of the covenant as well as the practice of consensus, the brethren quickly returned him to full communion. In the same year a woman identified only as "Lydia" appeared to respond to a charge of public intoxication. She, too, confessed and was returned to the fold by the membership.[37] Woodbridge opposed both the fraternity's rule and the polity it endorsed. A loyal supporter of the ministry's reformation, he worked constantly to enhance the ministerial prerogative and promote spiritual awakening, but to no avail.

Wethersfield followed a different course. Sometime between Presbyterian Bulkeley's exodus around 1677 and Stephen Mix's ordination reforming brethren achieved superiority, drafted a new covenant, and affirmed the unity of the laity in morals and polity. The victorious laymen forsook the parish system, however, returning to the exclusive posture of earlier days. The half-way covenant, never a significant issue in the community, was opposed by the church until 1709.[38]

The reforming brethren's flight from Presbyterian rule and parish order was symbolized by a rigid test of membership adopted during or immediately prior to Mix's tenure. The test, consisting of a public profession of religious experience as well as a church trial of the applicant's character, was as stern as any in New England and was meant to divide the church from the world. It also formed the basis for the fraternity's rigid and constant monitoring of the behavior of members.

An example of the brethren's control over behavior emerged from Mix's records. In 1703 Benjamin Church, Jr., a member of Hartford First, returned to Wethersfield, his home, and asked for admission to the church. The church refused until he provided a "public profession." His father, Benjamin, Sr., counseled him to reject the church's demand with the argument that a profession was not required in Hartford and membership in one church entitled a man to membership in another. The brethren disagreed and ordered the father to appear before them for censure. Howver, before any action could be taken, Benjamin, Sr., admitted his error and subsequently received only a mild reprimand.[39] Presbyterian Stephen Mix had little to do with the proceedings. He opposed them, just as he opposed the church's general posture, but there was little he could do. Like Woodbridge, he followed the suggestion of the synods of 1675 that disciplinary differences be downplayed in favor of the promotion of piety. In that regard he had no more success than his Hartford colleague.

The reforming brethren's victory in Wethersfield created a shaky peace in the community, but the subsequent alterations in church order emphasizing exclusiveness did not typify the movement's successes elsewhere. For the most part the brethren of Connecticut and the Connecticut Valley viewed the moral reformation of the congregation as a necessary first step in the pursuit of a greater goal, the reformation of the community. To that end they saw themselves providing a constant and self-generating source of moral energy, reaching out to the community through a number of carefully constructed mechanisms designed to bring men, women, and children under the watch of the fraternity and possibly into its fold.

The key to moral evangelism lay in the formula for admission to the church. While procedures varied widely, as they always had, new patterns began to emerge reflecting the reforming instincts of the brethren. The lay reformation produced three significant changes in admission procedures. First, the decision-making process was taken from the clergy, and in some cases, ministers were kept from any voice in the proceedings. Second, a public examination before the members tended to replace private interviews by elders. Third, and most important, moral behavior gradually replaced conversion experience as the most important criterion for membership —and moral behavior was determined by the applicant's ability to abide by the standards of the group. This is not to say that the relation of conversion experience ceased to exist. On the contrary, as late as 1700 a majority of the churches continued to recognize publicly the test of spirituality. Privately, however, many were allowing it to fall into disuse and were placing their faith in demonstrations of good behavior or "good conversation" in the vernacular of the time. Consequently, it was not until the first three decades of the eighteenth century that many of Connecticut's more reticent reforming congregations publicly disavowed the ancient public narrative of experience.[40]

In Westfield, Massachusetts, for example, the church initially required a lengthy public recitation of the "time and manner" of conversion. Edward Taylor's narration lasted several hours while he laboriously assembled and related the events leading to his conversion, beginning with the earliest recollections of his childhood.[41] Yet in 1727, shortly after Taylor's death, the church voted to discontinue the test of conversion experience and to rely only on the record of past behavior.

Initially in agreement with their minister, many laymen of Westfield gradually became disenchanted with evidence of religious experience. Possibly events in Westfield paralleled those in Farmington, Connecticut, where, despite the minister's objections, the public narration of experience fell into disuse but was not stricken from the church record until many years later. In the 1670's Farmington's official posture required a public narration of experience and evidence of Christian knowledge as criteria for admission. But Farmington's records provide a rare opportunity to observe a trial in process, and the reader will note that the official posture bore little relation to the criteria used to judge an applicant's fitness.

Thomas Hooker's son, Samuel, recorded all of the trial of James Bird on June 15, 1673. The members of the church assembled at the home of Deacon Hart. "After an examination of his knowledge," Hooker wrote, "and a brief narrative given by the said James of his experience, the mind of the church was taken. About 8 brethren voted for his admission, 3 against it; the major part by much chose to suspend acting either way."[42] James Bird, "seeing so many of the brethren to hesitate and suspend, refused to close and write with the church. Whereupon the pastor told the said James that the Church did expect of those that joined, and consequently of him: That he should promise to Submit to the government of Christ in his house, were Church his brethren and serve and keep all the commandments of God, as far as Christ should enable."[43]

Aside from the obvious fact that Hooker played no greater role than that of interlocutor, the most striking aspect of the trial lay in the brethren's unwillingness to judge Bird on the official criteria for admission. Apparently, his narrative and evidence of Christian knowledge proved satisfactory; at least nothing was said to the contrary. Yet, without discussion, the majority of the members refused to take action. Obviously, they knew the man well enough to withhold judgment because of something that was not brought out during the brief trial. The reason for their reluctance came to light during Hooker's concluding remarks. By confining his words to the moral demands made by the brethren on all who would join, he suggested that Bird posessed some character defect which made the members doubt his ability to abide by the covenant. Bird himself alluded to that doubt when he responded to the minister's remarks by saying "that as sometime of old, so be in the present case: As the Lord liveth, I will not close with your proposal."[44]

Hooker tried to soften the blow by reminding Bird that the standard of moral behavior demanded by the church was very high indeed and that some very honorable persons failed to meet those standards. Bird replied that he understood and, without malice or bitterness, left Deacon Hart's home with the remark, "I desire you to take care of my wife." Eight years later he was admitted to membership.[45]

Hooker's record of the Bird case attests to the emergence of moral behavior as the primary qualification for membership in a church committed to the time-tested procedure of examining spiritual experience. Because of the continued and bitter opposition of the ministry and some brethren, however, the church could not dispose of the narrative until 1707, thirty-four years later. In two motions the members gave official status to the procedure employed with James Bird. Taken together, those motions decreed that an "explication given of evidence" was to be automatically accepted by the church "unless it evidently appears to contain a falsehood in it."[46]

Moral behavior slowly replaced the conversion experience as the key to admission in most reform-oriented Connecticut churches, producing some unusual practices in the process. One emerged in the youthful but already dissension-ridden village of Middletown. Formally organized in 1668 with Nathaniel Collins as minister, the church held its installation ceremonies at about the same time as Northampton's "reformation." Middletown's covenant, drafted and ratified by the brethren, dwelt on the same theme—peace—found in the reforming covenants of older churches. The formula for admission to the brotherhood, however, contained the peculiar provision that conversion narratives were required from some persons but not from others. For instance, on December 30, 1668, several hopefuls gained admission to communion by "consenting to the profession of faith and plighting the covenant." That was preceded by a report of their Christian knowledge and the "Ground and reason for their hope," given by the minister to the assembled brethren. A vote of the members completed the process. Yet on January 17th of the same year Samuel Cornwell received full membership by simply "consenting to the Profession of Faith and the Covenant." No mention was made of a narrative of experience or a ministerial conference. So far as can be determined that discrimination continued at least until 1700.[47]

Obviously, from the church's inception, some applicants were judged only on their behavior. Evidently persons not well known to the church followed a more elaborate procedure including a relation of conversion experience and a lengthy ministerial inquiry. Quickly, though, even that small residue of ministerial authority was abandoned. In June 1672 Mary Collins reached full communion by "giveing in writing [which was read] an account of the ground of her hope in Christ,"[48] a procedure followed in all subsequent cases where a relation was required.

The Middletown records failed to explain why separate categories of applicants were maintained, but New London's records did. The New London congregation, one of the oldest and most troubled in Connecticut, conducted a reformation in 1670 or 1671, binding the members with the church's first written covenant of obligations and proclaiming the new power of the fraternity. A complete portrait of the church's Congregational polity does not emerge, however, until the consecutive ministries of two noted Connecticut Presbyterians, Gurdon Saltonstall and Eliphalet Adams (1687–1726), both of whom publicly and privately opposed the development of lay Congregationalism. During those years New London maintained a double standard for prospective members, requiring a great deal more from strangers than from children of the church. Strangers were "propounded" to the members for an unspecified time (probably two weeks) and then brought before the brethren for a relation of experience, consideration of any objections to their behavior, and a vote. They repeated the procedure a second time before the entire congregation, a practice reflecting New London's traditional desire to include nonmembers in church activities. If they passed again, they were admitted.

Children of the church, however, did very little to gain admission. If, upon reaching their maturity, they were found to be blameless in conduct and knowledgeable of Christian principles, they were admitted automatically.[49] Obviously the brethren believed that years of scrutiny made a special procedure unnecessary for those children. At the same time, strangers needed the most taxing examination to prove their worth. Moreover, in New London, as elsewhere, the public relation of experience gradually fell into disuse. It was dropped in 1726, since "divers persons of good character and deportment stand off from joining us because a relation of experience is insisted on."[50] That editorial comment, so uncharacteristic of otherwise sterile church records, offered a succinct analysis of the laity's moral reformation and its attitude toward church polity and individual behavior.

While the fraternity's disenchantment with the conversion narrative angered many clergymen—providing added evidence for the charge of "worldliness"—it seemed to aid those ministers favoring the broad or Presbyterian formula for admission. Their formula, emphasizing moral character and Christian knowledge to the detriment of conversion experience, had gained credence among some moderate Congregationalists and Presbyterians in earlier years but had been stymied by hostility from both laymen and clergy. It remained the concern of a few ministers after 1670, especially suspected Presbyterians like Solomon Stoddard of Northampton, Timothy Woodbridge of Hartford, or Gurdon Saltonstall of New London.

The brethren's gradual and ironic shift toward behavior as the standard of judgment suggested that advocates of the "broad way" were finally gaining the victory denied them earlier. But that was not so. While clerical opposition to evidence of conversion increased in the last decades of the seventeenth century, advocates of the broad way never achieved majority status. On the contrary, the ministers' reformation caused many clergymen to place even greater reliance upon evidence of experience before admission to the Supper. Moreover, behavior replaced experience as the criterion for admission in a variety of churches, not just those with sympathetic clergy, suggesting that the stimulus for innovation came from the brethren. New London, with Presbyterian clergy, embraced the broad way no more quickly than Farmington or Westfield with hostile clergy. Wethersfield held on to the narrative of experience despite a clergyman known to favor another formula.

To recognize that reforming brethren were not simply following clerical adherents to the broad way, it is sufficient to note that in one critical area the two groups were poles apart. Broad-way clergy were either Presbyterians, or Congregationalists outspoken in their attempts to enhance ministerial authority and prestige. In no church were they successful in taking control of the apparatus of church government, and in only a few did they control the process of admitting new members. Behavior as the standard for admission accompanied a broadening and solidification of the power of the fraternity, and that was no ministerial innovation.

There were several outstanding exceptions. One was Timothy Woodbridge, who managed the reforming enthusiasm of his brethren so that he retained a voice and a vote in the membership procedure. Consequently, Samuel Stone's old formula became "Mr. Woodbridge's Way."[51] Another exception was Solomon Stoddard, who promoted a similar method in Northampton. Arriving in 1669, he encountered a church fresh from its reformation and sympathetic to widening the church portals. They were not sympathetic, however, to "Mr. Stoddard's Way," of admitting new members. Not only did Stoddard ask the church to substitute behavior for conversion experience but he also asked for control of the procedure.[52] The latter proved a bone of contention for the next two decades. Finally, in 1690, the church capitulated. The members divided along generational lines. Older members, more jealous of the fraternity's rights and able to recall the 1668 reformation, opposed Stoddard. Younger members voted with him.

"Mr. Stoddard's Way" placed most of the responsibility for determining an applicant's fitness in the hands of the minister. The candidate was interviewed by Stoddard, or Stoddard and other elders, and questioned about the condition of his soul and the reason for his "hope." At the same time the candidate stood "propounded" before the church for two weeks, a measure designed to allow members to present complaints against the "life" or "conversation" of the applicant. If no objections appeared and Stoddard found sincerity in the applicant's desire to close with the church, membership was granted after two weeks. There was no narrative of conversion experience and, apparently, no public trial.[53]

Whatever the politics generated by innovation, shifting the emphasis from conversion to behavior and morality did not relax admission standards in Connecticut or Connecticut Valley churches. The evangelism of the reforming brethren remained guarded and careful and the records reveal that most churches, large or small, grew slowly. Northampton, using conduct as its test for much of the time, averaged eight new members per year between 1679 and 1707; while Hartford, using conduct as its test all the time, averaged twice that number. By comparison, Windsor First, still professing to use the public narrative, averaged ten new members per year.[54]

Throughout the last decades of the seventeenth century, however, no Connecticut or Connecticut Valley church admitted enough people to full communion to match the growth of the surrounding town, not even proportionately. It was to this that the ministers alluded in their jeremiads. The reforming brethren, obviously aware of the lagging numbers of members in full communion, refused to show undue concern. Although committed to growth, they were even more committed to discipline, unity, and the maintenance of the moral purity of the membership. Mindful of past dissension, the ever-present specter of continuing social deterioration, and the possibility of chaos, they established high standards of behavior and demanded conformity to those standards by every member of the group. They showed no interest in lowering standards and admitting all or most to the fellowship. Their thinking, extrapolated from their behavior, offered the explanation that it was better to have a few living by a rigid code of conduct than many living by no code at all.

Although the fraternity maintained full communion as a bastion for the demonstrably moral, it did not leave the education of the community to chance. Most of the churches of Connecticut and the Connecticut Valley went into their towns in force, extending the discipline and behavioral norms of the covenant to the nonelect through various devices. Ironically, those devices represented variations of the half-way covenant, an innovation initially forced upon some churches by irate townsmen. After the initial feuding, however, antipathy between church members and townsmen lessened as reforming brethren made the covenant an integral part of their programs. Clergymen had little to do with the covenant's ultimate success. Presbyterians like Stoddard, Saltonstall, and Woodbridge opposed it, while their churches adopted it. Congregational clergy continued to be divided over its merits; yet their churches adopted it as well. By 1690 Connecticut's clergy were no closer to agreement on the covenant than they had been in 1662 or 1667. Yet by the same year nearly all the churches of Connecticut and the Connecticut Valley had endorsed it.[55]

The half-way covenant emerged in many guises, depending upon the inclinations of local churches and communities. Few used it solely as a means of extending baptism, which was the intent of the synods of 1657 and 1662 and the continued preoccupation of the clergy. Many molded it into a probationary status for adults and children likely to become full members. The requirement for admission was essentially the same as that for full communion—a demonstration of good character—though the examination of conduct was much less rigorous. Those who eventually achieved full membership remained half-way members for periods of time ranging from a few months to as much as ten years. Their ability to abide by the rules of the group dictated the length of their probation.

Most of Connecticut's half-way members, however, failed to achieve full status. Analysis of extant covenant lists indicates that fewer than one person in five gained full membership, a remarkably small figure considering the evangelical orientation of most churches.[56] Creating additional confusion is the fact that eligible adults took advantage of half-way membership in large numbers, submitting to the same examination, albeit less stringent, that applied to full members. They provided evidence of good conduct, "professed" Christianity, and agreed to abide by the awesome obligations of the church covenant. Why then did so few move from satellite membership to full membership?

Ministerial writings at the end of the seventeenth and the beginning of the eighteenth century referred often to the overly scrupulous in the congregation, persons who avoided the Lord's Supper and the full membership it entailed because they felt spiritually unworthy and feared damnation.[57] New London's decision to abolish the narrative of experience in 1726 spoke directly to that problem when the church decided that the conversion narrative unnecessarily kept moral men and women from the Table and "full communion."[58] But if scrupulosity was the sole problem, the reforming brethren's decision to abandon the narrative of experience in New London and elsewhere ought to have produced a marked rise in the numbers of full members. It did not.

The existence of the permanent half-way member may have had less to do with scrupulosity than with the fraternity's high standards of conduct. Lay evangelicalism demanded the extension of the church covenant's principles of peace and order into the community, but it never suggested that the community be brought to the Table. Thus it is very likely that members were quite content to see only one in five moving from half-way status to full membership so long as large numbers of inhabitants continued to seek half-way membership.

That explanation conforms with known evidence. Moral standards for full and half-way members, though superficially similar, differed considerably. Full membership demanded much more. As the Bird case in Farmington suggests, not only was the prospective full member forced to live for years under the scrutiny of the brethren, but he often had to pass a rigorous entrance examination lasting anywhere from several weeks to several months. In the end nearly every full member demanded to be satisfied regarding the applicant's moral superiority, on peril of rejection. Consequently, no matter how righteous the community, few persons were likely to survive such a grueling experience.

This suggests a different perspective for the question of scrupulosity. If the brethren consistently rejected people who appeared to be qualified—like James Bird—and did so for reasons of character, not spirituality, it is possible that the issue of scrupulosity was simply another ploy in the ministers' ongoing attack upon the alleged excesses of the fraternity. In all likelihood many of those characterized as overly scrupulous by the ministers were persons spiritually qualified but morally deficient, at least in the eyes of the membership. They applied for admission, probably with the minister's encouragement, then were rejected. And if that was not enough to raise the minister's ire, in all probability they accepted their fate without bitterness—like James Bird—and went on their way.

Moral evangelism explains some of the varied applications of the covenant by the churches of Connecticut and the Connecticut Valley. There were other reasons. Among them the most important proved to be local tradition and the historical posture of the church toward the community. In churches and towns torn by factionalism and forced by strife to undergo a painful reordering of priorities, the covenant became the heart of a parish system involving a nucleus of full members surrounded by a group of neophytes. In churches little affected by strife, and there were not many, the half-way covenant often conformed to the intentions of the 1662 synod—that is, it simply enabled nonmembers with church ties to have their children baptized.[59] In almost every community the covenant became the church's primary means for extending reformation to the unchurched. But the extent of reformation—that is, the extent to which the covenant reached out to embrace the community—occasionally depended upon the degree to which dissension had molded the town's growth.

Northampton was in the forefront in applying the covenant to the community as a probationary status. Adopted in 1668, Northampton's half-way covenant had two principal parts. One conformed to the pattern set down by the 1662 synod: children of baptized nonmembers were placed under church watch and baptized. The second, however, did not conform: all persons—children and adults—admitted to half-way status were marked for eventual full membership. "Owning the covenant" automatically placed the neophyte in a special "state of education" designed to end in full membership.

In 1672 the brethren went a step further by allowing all baptized "children" of the church who were morally above reproach to enter full membership without examination as they reached adulthood. At the same time the "state of education" was dissolved. Those changes seemed to alter the half-way covenant to conform with the proposals of the 1662 synod. They restricted the covenant to those who could not or would not seek full membership and wanted baptism for their children. But since baptized children were granted automatic full membership as adults (if morally qualified), half-way status actually became a convenient way of collecting and disciplining strangers to the Northampton community.

The 1672 reform continued until 1714, when the church agreed to baptize all interested "professing Christians" and their offspring and to place them under church watch.[60] The adoption of the 1672 reform explained partially why a majority of the church eventually agreed to end the relation of experience. Obviously if children of the church gained membership on the basis of past conduct and an expressed willingness to abide by the terms of the covenant, few persons seeking full membership faced the prospect of a narrative of conversion experience. In Northampton, as in many towns, the narrative simply became excess baggage.

A slightly different version of the half-way covenant appeared in Middletown, Connecticut. As in Northampton, the half-way member became a neophyte, designated by the term "State of Initiation." Middletown, however, was more restrictive than Northampton in defining the scope of the covenant, limiting it primarily to the adult or infant children of full members. On February 25, 1671, for example, the children of several members were brought together and provided an explanation of the meaning of the church covenant, the profession of faith and church discipline, as well as what it meant to look inside oneself for a work of God. They were then allowed to "own" the covenant and enter the state of initiation.[61]

Other individuals admitted occasionally to the state of initiation were those who came to Middletown from another community. Having no prior church affiliation, they entered the state of initiation until the church saw fit to grant them full membership. One such case occurred on January 26, 1672, when "Isaak Johnson being recommended to us from the Church of Christ at Roxbury owneing the confession of faith and order wherein this Church stands Ingaged together with their covenant and was accepted as a member of this Church in the State of Initiation."[62]

The special status granted to new arrivals in Middletown also served newcomers with church ties in other communities. Those persons, seeking baptism for their children and possible full membership for themselves, fell under a special provision adopted by the brethren in 1668. That provision stated that "all members of orthodox, being sound in the faith and not scandalous in life, presenting due testimony thereof, these occasionally comeing from one church to another . . . may have their children baptised."[63] In other words, full members from other churches were also pushed into half-way status. Moreover, the telling phrases "not scandalous in life" and "presenting due testimony thereof," found over and over in other church records of the same time, testified to the rigorous standards of behavior applied even to persons with the highest reference possible: church membership elsewhere. The brethren trusted no one's judgment but their own. The emigrant church member followed the same circuitous path as the emigrant nonmember, justifying his character to gain half-way status, then justifying it again to keep it.

In the 1680's the Middletown records began to list persons "owning the covenant" and having their children baptized. Had the church altered half-way status to conform to the 1662 synod? There is no evidence of such a change. Apparently, newcomers with church affiliation elsewhere were rare in Middletown until the 1680's, when they began to fill the covenant lists. Thus their children were granted baptismal privileges even as these privileges continued to be denied to old Middletown residents with "confederate" ties to the church.[64]

Second Church in Stratford, created after a fierce struggle among members of First Church and the town as a whole, fashioned yet another variation on the theme of the parish way in 1670. Adopting the half-way covenant, the brethren opened it to all professing Christians willing to abide by its terms and able to pass a rigorous examination of their character and past behavior. Nothing was mentioned, however, of baptism or a blood tie to the church as a prerequisite for half-way membership. Many people, in fact, were baptized after admission to covenant status. On May 4, 1670, for example, Moses Johnson, "desiring admission into fellowship with this church; after having been a fortnight propounded, there appearing no objection against his admission he was examined concerning his knowledge in the matters of religion, and desiring after the ordinance and discipline of Christ, and having given a satisfactory account, was admitted, and subscribed the covenant." Five days later the same Moses Johnson was baptized.[65] Thus in attempting to reach nonaffiliated adults,

Stratford Second apparently offered baptism to induce them to either seek full membership or at least to accept the discipline of perpetual half-way status.

In 1678 Second's minister, Hezekiah Walker, and many of the members went to Woodbury. Although Walker supported the covenant, his followers refused to endorse it anew. Not until 1708, when Solomon Stoddard's son, Anthony, served the church, did the brethren adopt the covenant. It lasted until 1720, when it was dropped, but ten years later it was reinstituted. Throughout its troubled history the covenant's form followed the formula devised by Stratford Second. It was open to all professing Christians and often led to baptism.[66] Moreover, the story behind the initial adoption revealed another interesting facet of the covenant's history in Connecticut and the Connecticut Valley. Of some three hundred persons admitted to full communion in Woodbury between 1678 and 1730, nearly 70 per cent were women. To remedy that imbalance the brethren turned to the half-way covenant, where, during Stoddard's tenure, men outnumbered women by 60 to 40 per cent. Moreover, a very large number of these men were husbands of women already admitted to full membership. Thus, for Woodbury, the covenant was intended to entice husbands into the discipline of the church when it was clear that they could not, or probably would not, seek full membership.[67]

Much the same can be said of other churches included in this survey. Between 1670 and 1720 women far outnumbered men in gaining full membership. In nearly every church the ratio was about the same: two women joined for every man. Conversely the half-way lists were dominated by men in about the same ratio found in Woodbury: six men to every four women. In addition, though this can be less easily demonstrated, many of the men were husbands of women in full communion. That offers another insight into a question discussed earlier: why so many churches willingly allowed persons of high moral conduct to remain half-way members indefinitely. Those persons were often husbands of full members.

A picture begins to emerge of the priorities of Connecticut and Connecticut Valley churches as they pursued their "reformations" in the late seventeenth century. First, the statements found in church covenants and the subsequent actions of the brethren suggest that the education of youth received the greatest attention. Second, the covenant lists reveal that men, and especially husbands, received special attention to halt the trend toward a predominantly female "fraternity." How early that trend developed is not known, for most membership lists do not predate 1670, but churches considered it potentially dangerous—especially since women were evidently denied voting privileges—and the remedy applied was half-way status. Third, the churches tried to assimilate strangers in the community. True, they treated strangers very carefully, even if they carried impeccable credentials from other churches. But newcomers could not be ignored. As sources of potential discord, they were urged to become half-way members and live by the principles of the church. Only after they proved their reliability, however, were they admitted to the inner sanctum of the fellowship.

Having stated the rule, it is also necessary to admit that there were many exceptions. Dissension-ridden Hartford, for example, appeared to share few of the problems of other churches. No imbalance existed between males and females, nor were full members likely to be wives whose husbands were half-way members. Between 1692 and 1708 the church averaged twenty new members per year, a very healthy figure. Moreover, husbands and wives often joined together, an oddity in the period.

Half-way status in Hartford appeared to conform exactly to the dictates of the 1662 synod. No one was admitted without prior baptism, suggesting that they were the sons, daughters, or grandchildren of full members desiring only baptism for their own children. Yet in comparing half-way lists to the lists of those entering full communion, a secondary—or perhaps primary—function emerges, not decipherable otherwise. The church maintained one of the highest rates of transfer (over 20 percent) from half-way to full status of any church studied. Moreover, many of the husband-wife combinations appearing on the membership lists also appeared on the half-way lists. They, like those not obtaining full status, were mostly young adults with small families, persons likely to want baptism for their children.[68] Apparently, however, the church saw them in a different light. The brethren wanted them to become full members and treated them as neophytes to be counseled, educated, and disciplined in preparation for full communion.

By 1690 the half-way covenant formed an integral part of the church system in nearly every community in Connecticut and the Connecticut Valley, thus completing at least one phase of the lay-inspired reformation. What about the larger goals of the brethren: the desire to rebuild the institutional church around a new ordering principle—the united fraternity—or the need to extend the principles of peace and moral behavior into the community? Part of the answer comes from the church records of Connecticut and the Valley in the later seventeenth-century and the lay-inspired innovations they reveal. Another part may be gleaned from the jeremiads of the clergy, especially the theme of failure enunciated over and over in the last years of the century. The clergy admitted its inability to restore old authority or to stimulate a spiritual reformation and that admission of defeat bore eloquent testimony to the successes of the reforming brethren.

What of the numbers of persons reached by the lay reformation? Even at its broadest the brethren's field of vision remained rather narrow, including mainly children, husbands, and strangers to the community. Yet the total number of full and half-way members reveals steady growth in most churches in the late seventeenth century. What was the significance of that growth? A comparison of the membership figures for the last decades of the century with the available lists of new members from the 1650's, 60's, and 70's—the decades of widespread dissension—suggests a membership revival of spectacular proportions.[69] However, a comparison of the same figures with statistics for overall population growth in the late seventeenth century reveals that few churches stayed abreast of the growth of their towns.[70]

The results achieved by the reforming brethren were deceptive, for the new church system reflected a hastily contrived and often forced consensus among the laymen—one that glossed over the problems of earlier years more than it resolved them. Presbyterianism diminished in towns like Windsor and Wethersfield because lay Congregationalists won stunning victories. Squabbling between churches and towns lessened because reform-minded brethren neutralized the anger of many townsmen by endorsing the halfway covenant, by lowering the barriers separating church and community, and by often seeking accord, not conflict, with the town meeting. The gap between laymen and clergy actually increased, however, and only the timidity of some of the younger ministers and the general hope that sacramental piety would yield its own revolution in church order prevented an open breach.

If the level of discord declined considerably, the potential remained high, especially between ministers and brethren. Clergymen opposed the innovations of the laity as best they could without reviving the factionalism of earlier years. Still, the new order was established at clerical expense, forcing additional humiliation on the ministers as lay Congregationalism triumphed and cries for spiritual awakening produced only a slight response. By 1700 the reformed church system barely concealed the awesome distance separating ministers and laymen or the extent of the clergy's anger and bitterness.

Seven

THE POLITICS OF

ECCLESIASTICAL DISRUPTION

CONNECTICUT'S reforming synods of 1675 inaugurated more than a spiritual awakening. They marked the beginning of a spirit of cooperation between the clergies of Massachusetts and Connecticut which had proven elusive in the past. The impetus for cooperation resulted from a shared vision of New England's awful condition and, especially, the twin specters of spiritual deadness and ministerial impotence. Consequently, though the days of synods of New England's churches had ended, the three decades between the meetings of 1675 and the Saybrook Synod of 1708 saw the respective clergies informally pooling ideas and solutions to an unparalleled degree.

The institutionalization of the "power of the fraternity" and the steady progress of the lay reformation produced a clerical response in both colonies. Zeal for spiritual awakening received new life through greater emphasis upon the efficacy of the Lord's Supper. Later, even as many ministers pronounced the campaign a failure, New England was besieged by communion manuals designed to encourage the "scrupulous" to come to the Table.[1]

But many of the same ministers who called for a spiritual awakening through the sacraments also argued, eventually, that the reformation had failed to improve the minister's lot one iota. Indeed, most evidence suggested that ministerial authority continued to deteriorate despite all of the appeals and the machinations of the clergy. In response some ministers began to seek a new source for clerical authority which could match and counteract the covenant-produced power of the fraternity. Those ministers—a powerful lot including Cotton Mather, Samuel Williard of Boston, Stoddard, Woodbridge of Hartford, and Saltonstall of New London—found their solution in an ancient New England institution, the ministerial meeting. Used often in the early days of the Bay Colony as a means to find accord on common problems, it had fallen into neglect after 1660.[2] In Connecticut, ministerial meetings appeared with increasing frequency in the last decades of the seventeenth century.[3]

Connecticut's synods of 1667 and 1675 provided ample precedent for a different basis for the ministerial prerogative, emphasizing as they did a ministry operating independently of the whims, desires, or control of particular congregations. But to converse independently was one thing, to impose decisions upon the churches was quite another. The clergy had no vehicle for the latter, for the power of the General Assembly had proved equally deficient. The clergy had to rely on the receptivity of the brethren, something few ministers could count on. Thus as the seventeenth century gave way to the eighteenth, the ministerial meeting began to change to something called an "association" of ministers. Supported by Presbyterians and by Congregationalists disenchanted with lay control, formal associations of clergy appeared in eastern Massachusetts around 1690. Virtually powerless, they met regularly to discuss common problems. A little later Stoddard's Hampshire County colleagues began meeting formally, as did ministers in various regions of Connecticut.

Through those meetings the association became accepted as the most likely apparatus for the restoration of clerical authority, though considerable partisanship developed over how the associations would operate and what powers they would have. Congregationalists revived the theories of "consociationalism" approved by the Synod of 1662, arguing that individual churches were not autonomous but were linked in "communion" under the rule of Christ. Clearly, they asserted, superior direction over consociated churches was both necessary and desirable and could be provided under the proposed associations—with the consent of the brethren. The associations would function as appelate bodies in cases of discipline or in matters arising from church disputes. Presbyterians tended to divide their loyalties. Those influenced by the English model and the Heads of Agreement of 1691 endorsed consociationalism. Those influenced by Scottish Presbyterianism wanted to enlarge the association's functions. Some saw them governing local congregations, while others hoped to create church courts.

Eastern Massachusetts reflected Congregationalism, while western Massachusetts tended toward Scottish Presbyterianism. In Connecticut the eastern portions, especially Fairfield County, followed Scottish Presbyterianism. Hartford County in the west leaned in the same direction. Other areas endorsed Congregationalism. Despite the wide areas of disagreement, however, the ministers worked to produce consensus.[4]

Consequently, throughout the 1690s and the first decade of the eighteenth century many ministers followed concurrent paths of action. Publicly they called for a sacramentally inspired spiritual awakening. Privately, or at least semiprivately, they sought a mutually acceptable yet effective form of ministerial association, one that would free the ministers of complete dependence on particular congregations. They also sought a device to make the brethren acquiesce. Both movements reached fruition in the early years of the eighteenth century.

Their fates were influenced heavily by Solomon Stoddard of Northampton. In the last years of the seventeenth century, Stoddard became a leading figure among the clergies of Massachusetts and Connecticut, championing Presbyterianism and promoting ecclesiastical debate even while lending his powerful support to the campaigns for ministerial associations and spiritual awakening. Then, in 1700, he broke with both schemes and with Presbyterianism when he published *The Doctrine of Instituted Churches*. In

that pamphlet he sketched a system of church order unlike anything ever envisioned in New England and asked his colleagues
to either support him or fight. The ensuing furor, revolving around
Stoddard and Increase Mather, siphoned the energies of clergymen
of both colonies and divided their loyalties at the very moment
most ministers believed themselves to be nearing success in their
strategies against the brethren. Moreover, the struggle initiated by
Stoddard awoke many of the laymen to the aims of the ministry.
The resulting dissension caused the ministry's reformation and the
accompanying association movement to collapse like frail trees
before a storm.

Solomon Stoddard went to Northampton in 1669 as a young
man of twenty-six. Having spent most of his adult life at Harvard
as a student, tutor, and librarian, he grew restless and abruptly left
New England in 1667 for a year or two as a chaplain to the Governor of the Barbados, Daniel Searle. He returned sometime in
1668 and, ignoring the advice of friends, refused an opportunity
for study in England in order to assume the vacant post in the
Connecticut Valley.[5] Even at that early point in his career Stoddard revealed two character traits that later became dominant:
unpredictability and a thirst to be different, to do what others
would not consider. Few wanted Northampton, as remote a settlement as there was. It offered nothing but hard work. Moreover,
any minister taking the post could expect to labor unnoticed and
unrecognized. Why would it appeal to Solomon Stoddard? The
son of Anthony Stoddard, a wealthy and politically influential
Boston mechant, Stoddard could have had any post he wanted.
He was bright, considered one of Harvard's finest products, and
had the connections necessary to ensure a prestigious post and a
brilliant career, perhaps in Boston itself. His friends probably reminded him of those facts. Still, he chose Northampton.
Stoddard lacked ambition, at least the kind driving many of his

friends. Intellectual labor proved painful and the contemplative life of some ministers frightened him. He had little interest in the finer things of civilization, especially the hustle and bustle which was beginning to characterize commercial Boston. The thought of presiding over a church of wealthy, cosmopolitan people like his father left him cold. Much later he remarked that inclination and temperament suited him for the most rigorous post available. Possessing a strong constitution, he found happiness doing the Lord's work among farmers ekeing out a living. He gloried in physical toil as much as he dreaded the time spent in his study. He reveled in activity, and from his youth until his death at eighty-six he pursued a life in which he was a father, farmer, parish minister, political adviser, pamphleteer, and personal counselor to a multitude of persons all over New England. He represented a style of life which caused an early demise of many of his colleagues, one that prompted Judge Samuel Sewall, no laggard himself, to remark that he had never known a man like Stoddard.[6]

William Williams of Hatfield noted that Stoddard possessed an indomitable will, that his life seemed to take on meaning only as he faced and surmounted one challenge after another. Williams knew the complexity of his good friend, knew that beneath the tough exterior lay a very private man who rarely made his inner thoughts known to others.[7] When he did, he revealed a mind troubled not by personal problems but by his singular commitment to the God he served. At an early age he became convinced that God's work was not going well anywhere. The Protestant Reformation lost ground. Even in areas where it dominated, spiritual deadness gripped the faithful. Stoddard devoted his thoughts and his life to a search for an explanation and an antidote.

Perhaps that partially explained his decision to go to Northampton. Not only did it represent a physical challenge, but its position gave him access to both Massachusetts and Connecticut. Though politically linked to the Bay, the river towns were both geographically and economically tied to Connecticut by the great river. Moreover, many of the inhabitants of the western Massachusetts towns were former Connecticut people with relatives still living there. A minister would find his life and thought conditioned as much by events in Connecticut as those in the Bay Colony.

Stoddard exploited his position throughout his life, maintaining a perspective covering both colonies. He operated in concert with the clergy of Massachusetts, participating in synods and traveling to Boston often to attend the courts of election in the spring. Simultaneously he acted as unofficial adviser to the churches and clergy of Connecticut. His son went to a Connecticut church, and many of his daughters married clergymen who then took pulpits in the Connecticut Valley. Stoddard's advice was sought eagerly by laymen and ministers from Connecticut, and his stock among the brethren of the Valley remained high, a rarity in a time of anticlericalism.

Stoddard quickly established himself as one of the leading lights of the New England ministry. It was a position he neither sought nor avoided. Part of his reputation developed from his personality; for of all the ministers of the time, he came closest to recreating the lost aura of the first generation. A stern, occasionally arrogant, but usually fair individual, Stoddard maintained staunch adherence to the code of morality he preached. At the same time, no minister showed greater sensitivity or compassion for human failings. He combined those traits into a public portrait of a demanding yet compassionate judge, a mirror-image of the God he followed. That image put Stoddard in constant demand among the churches throughout Connecticut and western Massachusetts, and he was often called upon to use his wisdom and experience to settle difficult problems of discipline, tasks he undertook with humility and love.[8]

Stoddard's physical strength and endurance brought admiration. More like a farmer than a clergyman, he suffered few illnesses and drove himself like a man obsessed throughout his life. He worked his fields, raised a large family, tended to the many needs of his parish, yet never declined a request to travel arduous miles to visit an ailing friend, speak before the Court or clergy of the Bay, or render advice to a clergyman or congregation in distress. In addition, Stoddard forced himself to write, shutting his massive frame into a cubicle in his small home to address himself to the problems of the churches and to offer solutions. As he grew older and less active physically, he pushed his mind in the same manner he had once pushed his body, writing more as he traveled less. Through all, his strength never failed, and his toughness and stamina stood in stark contrast to the timidity of many of his colleagues. Frontier New England admired physical strength and courage, and Stoddard became a model of tough-mindedness and determination.[9]

Stoddard's good reputation also resulted from his activity in promoting the great concerns of the New England ministry in the late seventeenth century: spiritual awakening and ministerial authority. In both of those areas Stoddard's fame grew from his leadership of a small, contentious minority, differing from the majority in means, not intent. In the debate over authority Stoddard gained notoriety as a Scottish Presbyterian favoring a national church and a complicated apparatus of clerical organizations. As for the awakening, Stoddard became associated with the Presbyterian or "broad way" of admitting persons to the Table, one emphasizing character over spirituality. Few persons, however, considered his views either sinister or unique. Presbyterianism had grown fashionable, especially in the Connecticut Valley, and the broad way or "open communion" as it was sometimes called, had already received substantial ministerial and lay support.[10]

The ideas that determined his actions in later life grew from his Harvard years (1658–1667). Certainly his tenure in Cambridge coincided with events that would have stimulated a young student bent on a career in the ministry. The ministers and churches of the Bay were inflamed by the issues swirling around the 1662 synod, and Boston emerged as the center of much of that activity.

In addition, the political future of the colony appeared endangered by the Restoration of Charles II, and most citizens, especially the clergy, divided over the proper course to be followed toward the restoration government.

Stoddard probably submitted to the excitement. His Harvard tutors did. His Commonplace book, covering the years between 1660 and 1664, contained notes on sermons and lectures by many members of the colony's clerical establishment, especially John Norton of Boston's First Church and Jonathan Mitchell of the Cambridge church. Both men were activists and innovators. Both were major figures in the 1662 synod, leading the fight for the half-way covenant and for "consociationalism," a legal sanction for clerical authority. Norton, whose sermons filled many of the early pages of Stoddard's book, was politically active as well. He made a dangerous voyage in 1662 to plead the colony's case before Charles II and led a group of concerned citizens in an attempt to tone down the Bay government's belligerency toward the new king in 1661 and 1662. Stoddard learned well from the fighting Norton and, in 1663, added his own signature to a petition of Boston non-freemen protesting the government's failure to reach accord with a royal commission sent by Charles to conquer New Amsterdam and investigate conditions in the American colonies.[11]

In that heady atmosphere of dissension, with the loud rumbling of Connecticut's civil and ecclesiastical turmoil echoing in the distance, it was not surprising that a quick young mind considered the country's ecclesiastical problems and toyed with new ideas. Stoddard did just that. Norton and Mitchell remained the objects of his admiration, but he began to question their ecclesiastical allegiances. Samuel Rutherford, the great apologist for Scottish Presbyterianism and antagonist of New England's Congregationalism, became his intellectual mentor. Then he went beyond even Rutherford. He grew interested in a debate that had occupied numerous English divines in the two decades following the Westminister Assembly, a dispute over the sacraments in which Rutherford had been an active participant and polemicist. Stoddard rejected Rutherford's position, turning instead to the minority viewpoint, which argued that the Lord's Supper was a "converting ordinance" open to saints and sinners alike.[12]

It was a radical point of view and a dangerous one for a Protestant to adopt; it would have shocked his Harvard tutors and colleagues had he chosen to share it with them. He did not. His mind worked silently, mulling over the progress of the Reformation, the state of religion in New England, Rutherford's brilliant arguments for Presbyterianism, and the almost ignored paeans of a handful of English writers calling for the restoration of a nearly papist view of the sacraments.

Stoddard arrived at some important conclusions. He decided that the Protestant Reformation lay prostrate, felled by its own preoccupation with the precise nature of the primitive Christian church. That quest—the one Hooker extolled as the reason for New England's existence—had divided Protestants into tiny groups arguing and bickering over meaningless questions of discipline. Meanwhile, the doctrinal truths of the early reformers were forgotten—with predictable results. While Protestant laymen and clergy plotted and intrigued to advance the cause of Presbyterianism or Congregationalism, the Catholic counterreformation recovered most of its lost territory. In areas thoroughly Protestant, like England or New England, conversions diminished in number as the din of partisan debate grew louder. All of that Stoddard attributed to a mistaken quest for a nonexistent pattern of church order buried somewhere in the pages of the New Testament.[13]

Why then his preoccupation with Presbyterianism? Stoddard answered that question and offered the fruits of his youthful speculation in 1700 in his *Doctrine of Instituted Churches*. It was his only printed statement on church order and comprised but a few pages. Yet it was a wide-ranging document that revealed his anguish over the course of the Reformation, his alienation from New England's ecclesiastical heritage, and his reasoning for combining

Samuel Rutherford's Presbyterianism and an obscure doctrine of converting ordinances into something he labeled the "Instituted Church."

In *The Doctrine of Instituted Churches* Solomon Stoddard questioned not only the "New England Way" but some basic tenets of Reformed thought as well. While the Reformation sought the revival of primitive Christianity, Stoddard argued for a church encompassing both Old and New Testaments. He rejected many of the essentials of both Protestant and Catholic traditions because each based notions of polity on the supposed nature of the early Christian church. Catholicism argued that ruling authority passed from Christ to Peter, which justified the existence of an authoritarian church centered around papal power. Congregationalism urged that the authority of Christ passed to the early congregations of Rome, Antioch, and elsewhere as autonomous units. Hence the pure church was a congregation of true believers in which decisions were made by the members. Presbyterians contended that Christ's authority passed to the Apostles, who formed the first consistory of elders. The modern clergyman, they argued, descended from those early "ministers" and possessed ultimate authority in Christ's visible church.

Stoddard also sought purity, but he denied that it was to be found only in the primitive church. God's church, he believed, formed a continuum from Old to New Testaments, and if one wished the restoration of the "pure" church, one looked first at the polity of God's church among the ancient Israelites. According to Stoddard, the church of Israel represented an "instituted church" created, or instituted, by God for the salvation of men. But what form did that salvation assume? According to Stoddard's exegesis, God made a covenant with the Israelites, that if they lived according to His law, they would be saved. Christ's death, however, changed the rules for salvation, for in death Christ atoned for the sins of men; to be saved a man had only to accept Christ as his Savior.

In Stoddard's view, man was, of course, powerless to effect his own salvation, for that was the province of the Almighty. Stoddard emphasized instead the process whereby grace was conveyed from God to man through the ordinances of the Instituted Church. They were Christ's legacy, and as a consequence the real historical significance of primitive Christianity. Christ died to redeem mankind and provided the means for redemption in the ordinances of baptism, prayer, scripture, preaching, censure, and the Lord's Supper.

This, then, represented the heart of Stoddard's complaint against the churches of New England and much of the Reformed tradition as well. Too much time was wasted in speculation about the precise form of the primitive Christian church. The significance of early Christianity was doctrinal, not disciplinary. New England's failure was obvious. Prevailing theories concerning "pure" churches and the sacraments as only "seals" of the Covenant of Grace caused God's anger and the country's decline, and New Englanders starved for lack of spiritual nourishment.

Stoddard's conception of the Instituted Church represented an amalgamation of Old Testament form and New Testament function. The church of Israel was a national church comprising only the Jewish nation. In Christ, God extended his rule and benefits to all men. However, He retained the form of the church of Israel, changing only the rules for salvation. While adherence to the moral law provided sufficient justification for the Jews, a nation of believers, God now confronted a multitude of unbelievers who knew nothing of His power or His law. Obviously, different means were required for their salvation. The Jewish church had existed primarily as a vehicle for divine worship. The new church was that and much more. Its purpose was evangelistic, the saving of sinners. God sacrificed His son, then "instituted" His church—through the ordinances—to convey His message and His gift to the world.[14]

Unfortunately, Stoddard sounded occasionally as though he favored universal redemption, that his Instituted Church was, in truth, meant for all, and that no man could or would be barred from admission. In reality, though he often implied it, he did not mean it. His argument would have made more sense had he stated that Christ died for all visible saints, for that was his intent. In discussing the fit matter for church membership, he always made it clear that membership and the sacraments were intended only for visible saints.

By the standards of most New England Congregationalists, however, Stoddard's definition of a visible saint was so broad and loose that by comparison his communion did appear to be open to almost anyone. His definition proceeded directly from his analysis of the function of the Instituted Church. There were three churches, he argued. The invisible church encompassed the elect. The visible or "catholic" church included all professing "the true faith in Christ." These made their sainthood visible through a blameless life, a sound knowledge of Christian principles, and a sincere desire to close with Christ, not through church membership or proof of regeneration. Thus, it was possible that a man could be a visible saint and not a member of any particular congregation.

The third church was the Instituted Church, or the institutional means for the dissemination of grace. The basic purpose of that church was obvious: to bring all professing Christians to the ordinances so that they might be saved. For Stoddard, no obstacles should be placed in the path of professing Christians, or visible saints, desiring union with the institutional church.[15] He rejected New England's efforts to insure church purity through tests of regeneration. The ordinances lay open to all who wanted and could qualify for their benefits, and a man who thought himself a reprobate had as much right to them as the man who believed himself a saint. The reasons for this were twofold. First, Stoddard found no scriptural warrant in either Testament for any practice limiting membership to proven regenerates. Second, he believed that although a minister could aid in the search for "signs" of redemption, no external test could be devised to determine the condition of something so intangible as the human soul. Moreover, an overzealous attempt to separate wheat from chaff violated the nature and function of the Instituted Church. Men desired membership because they sought the church's saving ordinances. Any attempt to keep them out for reasons other than immorality or ignorance of Christian doctrine denied the meaning of Christ's death.[16]

Thus Stoddard could not accept the Congregational doctrine of the autonomous congregation as a community of saints drawn together out of society to worship God and celebrate the sacraments, bound together and to God by a covenant. The particular church, he argued, was a manifestation of the visible catholic church, and membership in one church constituted membership in all churches. For Stoddard, as for Presbyterians, a particular church was an institution whose "members were bound" by the appointment of God to assemble in one place in a constant way for the celebration of "Publick Worship." The church's importance lay in the dispensation of the sacraments. Particular churches were appointed by God as places where members of the universal catholic church came together to celebrate the sacraments.

In the absence of a binding covenant, the authority of the particular church came from its membership in the national church. Stoddard believed that the church of ancient Israel had been a national unit. God had made a covenant with the Jews, and that relationship applied to the Christian church as well. Each Christian nation was in covenant with God, promising obedience to Him in return for His blessing. Consequently, as in the Jewish church, spiritual authority and power flowed from God through the national covenant to the ruling body of the national church, and from there to particular churches.

The Congregational doctrine of independent churches seemed to Stoddard "too lordly a principle." The experience of New England proved to him that the implementation of such a principle led to ecclesiastical anarchy, with congregations working constantly at cross purposes. The Instituted Church, as he portrayed it, had but a single purpose—the salvation of sinners. To accomplish its mission, it needed effective coordination of the activities of local churches through a centralized governing body. The "light of nature" suggested to Stoddard that the Church of Scotland most resembled the Old Testament model and God's will.[17]

Here Stoddard showed his indebtedness to Samuel Rutherford, the Scottish Presbyterian whose books he had read and admired while a student and tutor at Harvard. Stoddard asserted that ultimate authority in the national church should be vested in a synod composed of all elders of the churches, or if the country were too large, of a few elders representing all the churches. The power of that national synod was both specific and pervasive. It would have full authority in the determination and dissemination of sound doctrine and in the repression of error and heresy. It would judge complaints and impose ecclesiastical censures when necessary. It would also oversee the training and placement of ministers, appointing groups of elders to examine each prospective minister to determine proper qualifications.

To facilitate the government of particular churches, Stoddard urged the division of the national church into provinces, each controlled by a body of elders immediately subordinate to the national synod. In turn, each province was to be divided into a number of classes, bodies composed of elders whose duties were to implement, on the local level, the decisions of the national synod.[18]

Turning to the polity of the local church, Stoddard wrote that the minister and ruling elders had complete authority in matters of doctrine and discipline. These officers formed a "presbytery" with total control over church affairs, total because the minister's power came from God through the national covenant and the hierarchical structure of church government. But Stoddard, like New England's Presbyterians, could not totally escape Congregational theory. The brethren, he concluded, were not without rights. They had the authority to choose their ruling elders, and thus had considerable power in deciding church affairs.

The pastor administered the sacraments of the church and decided who would be admitted to them and who would not. Baptism lay open to any person who was a visible saint. It was not necessary for the applicant to be the child or grandchild of a member. The prerequisites for communion were much the same. A prospective member need only be a visible saint, that is, to "walk blamelessly" and "profess faith in Christ." Yet Stoddard did have another condition: prospective communicants were to have knowledge of the principles of religion. This latter qualification barred infants from the Table.[19]

Solomon Stoddard's decision to champion doctrine above discipline, to question the evolution of the Protestant Reformation, to reject New England Congregationalism and offer an Instituted Church instead, made him a solitary figure in New England's ecclesiastical history. For much of his career, however, he said nothing about his Instituted Church, carefully shielding the exact parameters of his private vision from public view. He built his reputation as a leader of the Presbyterian opposition among New England's clergy, sympathetic to many of the goals sought but often critical of the means applied. He allowed himself to be labeled a disciple of Samuel Rutherford, champion of the "broad way" in church membership and synodical rule in church government. At the same time, however, he sought to mold his Northampton congregation into a small outpost of the Instituted Church.

Stoddard quickly learned about the "power of the fraternity" and the zeal of Northampton's reform-minded brethren. The narrative of conversion experience survived two decades of ministerial education. The rationale for open communion, the converting ordinances, fared worse. At the same 1690 meeting where the brethren abolished the narrative, Stoddard preached a sermon from Galations 3:1, "that the Lords Supper was a converting ordinance."[20] He then asked for a vote and lost by the narrowest of margins. Younger members, reflecting the persuasiveness of Stoddard's personality, voted with him but the older members, including the ruling elder, voted against him. He continued his crusade for ratification for some years after but never again came as close to victory.[21]

Stoddard's efforts to presbyterialize his church by drawing

ruling authority into his own hands and by extending the boundaries of the parish over most of the community also met strong resistance. Even limited success eluded him until 1714, when the church consented to bring all baptized persons in the community under the discipline of the church regardless of whether they had owned the covenant. At the same time, the brethren endorsed the formal organization of the Hampshire Association of ministers, noting that in unspecified areas "church councils" were superior to individual congregations.[22] It was a significant victory but considerably less than the Instituted Church. Solomon Stoddard never successfully curbed or abrogated the power or unity of the fraternity in Northampton.

Northampton's recalcitrance suggests one reason for Stoddard's refusal to reveal publicly his converting ordinances, his hostility to reformed discipline, or his Instituted Church. Consequently, while opponents attacked his Presbyterianism and his advocacy of open communion, only a few ever hinted that they knew of more sinister designs. Boston's powerful Increase Mather was one of the latter. Mather believed Stoddard to be the leader of a sizable number of Connecticut and Connecticut Valley clergymen sympathetic to Scottish Presbyterianism, and he felt their existence imperiled New England Congregationalism. At the same time, Increase suspected that Stoddard was no ordinary Presbyterian and that behind his theory of open communion lay the dangerous notion of converting ordinances. Thus, Mather spent several decades trying to discredit Stoddard and defuse the Presbyterian movement by forcing the Northampton cleric to admit that he did, indeed, believe in converting ordinances.

Mather first accused Stoddard of chicanery in 1679 when the two ministers debated church membership practices at a great "reforming" synod in Boston. Stoddard contended that, despite advocating an "open" communion, he adhered to the doctrine of the "seals"[23] and viewed the sacraments as but part of an individual's "preparation" for grace. Increase suggested that Stoddard was being less than candid. "Inasmuch as my brother amongst all his qualifications fitting to partake at the Lords Supper, saith not a word about regeneration," Mather countered, "one would think that he looketh upon the *sacrament* as a *converting ordinance*. An opinion which hath been maintained by papists, Erastians, and some prelatical men, but is abundantly refuted, not only by those of the Congregational persuasion but by godly learned presbyterians; especially Mr. Gelaspy in his Aarons Rod, and by Dr Drake against Mr Humphrey, and by Mr Vines in his Treatise of the Lords Supper. So that I shall not need to vindicate the truth in that controversy, others having done it so fully . . ."[24]

In the years following the synod Increase continued his attack. When Stoddard published his first book, *The Safety of Appearing at the Day of Judgment in the Righteousness of Christ, Opened and Applied* (1687), Mather refused to write a preface because Stoddard again publicly disclaimed any unusual designs or strange notions. Instead, *Safety of Appearing* supported and defended those seeking to promote a spiritual awakening through the sacraments and church discipline. The book, while no communion manual, directed itself to the concerns of the overly scrupulous and the uncertain; and Stoddard assured those persons that their fears were groundless, for the doctrine of Atonement promised that faith in Christ sufficed for salvation. Once more he denied believing in converting ordinances. On the contrary, he pledged allegiance to the traditional doctrine of the "seals" again by arguing that the sacraments possessed no saving power but existed, primarily, to facilitate preparation for grace. For that reason, and no other, he wrote, he broke with many of his colleagues and endorsed open communion. The logic of sacramentally induced piety demanded, he believed, that only openly immoral or "scandalous" persons be kept from the Lord's Table.[25] Mather, however, refused to accept Stoddard's protestations of innocence, and he later sniped at Stoddard and Connecticut Valley Presbyterians with references to Stoddard's "Design against our Churches," his "plot of undermining the Churches," and his "antichristian Depravation Apostasy."[26]

Another opponent who grew suspicious of Stoddard's intentions was Edward Taylor of neighboring Westfield. A feud between the two began in 1673 when Taylor, attempting to organize a church, asked for Stoddard's help. Westfield needed persons of the "better sort," of known godliness and social distinction. Northampton responded by sending several of its leading citizens to live in Westfield. Taylor wanted more. In July 1673 he wrote Stoddard asking for David Wilton, a Northampton man of considerable stature and a founding member of the church. Taylor informed Stoddard that the addition of Wilton would enable Westfield to organize a church.[27] A few weeks later Stoddard replied that because of poor health, Wilton could not leave. Moreover, he went on, Northampton had already contributed several leading citizens and could ill afford the loss of a man of Wilton's stature. He suggested that Westfield contact another church.[28]

Stoddard's letter drew an angry reply from Taylor. He argued that without Wilton his people would be forced to continue with no formal church. He told Stoddard bluntly that he and his people knew of no reason why Wilton could not be spared, and implied that Northampton's recalcitrance offended him. Despite Taylor's plea, Wilton remained in Northampton and Westfield continued without a church.[29]

A second encounter took place during the formation of the church in 1679. Stoddard extended the hand of fellowship in the name of the elders. Taylor responded with a sermon attacking Stoddard and Presbyterianism while defending the traditional way of the churches. Entitled "A Particular Church is Gods House," the sermon emphasized the congregational view of the peculiar nature of the individual church brought about by its covenant relationship with God. Each congregation formed a distinct unit, Taylor argued, whose legitimacy and authority stemmed directly from God. Taylor denounced the Presbyterian view that a particular church was but an extension of the national church whose authority stemmed from Christ through the eldership.

Taylor also attacked Stoddard directly by emphasizing the need for purity in God's house. The members of a church, in covenant with God and with one another, needed "visible" holiness "manifested first in a Holy and Regular Life Conversion or saintly behavior, and secondly by an Holy and Regular Confession of the same . . . None are to be received and baptized into the church but by a Previous Confession of Faith and Repentence, according to the Custom of the Primitive Church and ours at Present."[30] It was an obvious jibe at Stoddard's notion that unregenerates of "good conversation" had a right to church membership and to the Lord's Supper.

By 1687, however, Taylor assumed that Stoddard was more than a Presbyterian. He wrote a sharp note to his colleague demanding to know why he proposed to open the Lord's Supper to "all above fourteen years of age, that live morally, and having Catechisticall knowledge of the Principalls of Religion."[31] Then answering his own question, he reminded Stoddard that his beliefs were unique in New England and a dangerous apostasy likely to pollute the churches. He also appealed to the course of the Reformation, seeking to denigrate Stoddard by telling him that he represented a minority position historically, "you having so few of the Non-Conformists for you, and therefor it is a thing well to be suspected."[32]

Stoddard's *Safety of Appearing* had just been published in Boston. Nonetheless, with some candor Stoddard explained his action in Northampton in a subsequent reply. He did not admit his belief in converting ordinances but he did not deny that he engaged in an "Endeavor to make Some Alterations as to the way of admitting persons to Full-Communion" nor that he had other innovations in mind. "I shall give you this briefe account of the Reason of what I did," he announced, for "I have been abundantly Satisfied these many years, that we did not attend the Will of God in this matter: and that our neglect therein is the occasion of the great Prophaneness, and Corruption that hath overspread the land . . ."[33]

Stoddard began to reveal his private thoughts. "Prophaneness and Corruption" were neither the products of a deep conspiracy among the brethren, as his Connecticut colleagues believed, nor the result of the absence of eclesiastical unity among the clergy, as his Massachusetts brothers sometimes argued. They represented the fruits of the restrictive Congregational theories of church order which held the land in a viselike grip. He blamed the clergy for the situation, not the brethren, and urged as the only solution the destruction of Congregationalism. He hinted at a plan to undermine the prevailing system of church order. Explaining his role, past and present, Stoddard conceded that he worked actively to promote ecclesiastical debate among the clergy. He pressed ecclesiastical issues and demanded innovations even though friends and enemies alike suggested silence. They feared he might revive the frenzy of earlier years. But that, he revealed, was what he sought. "I judge that it is the Cause of God," he concluded, "and am therefore under Pressures of the Spirit in all Regular Wayes to promote it."[34]

Taylor probably paled. Stoddard confessed a design against the churches. He admitted hatred for New England's most hallowed ecclesiastical principles, admitted a desire to foment contention and disorder at exactly the time many ministers stressed unity of purpose. More astounding, Stoddard conceded that, to a certain extent, his public utterances and private thoughts differed, and, for the first time explained why. His public posture as leader of the Presbyterian opposition represented a façade, a device that masked some of his true intentions. He did not elaborate further. Instead, he conveyed to Taylor the feeling that he viewed himself as a lonely figure pursuing a course which only he understood, a course whose radical nature demanded stealth and, occasionally, subterfuge.

Even as *Safety of Appearing* circulated through New England, Stoddard stepped up his campaign to have his church endorse converting ordinances. The ruse typified a portion of his early career. Publicly, he fostered contention by espousing Presbyterianism even while he supported both ministerial campaigns of the later seventeenth century: the sacramentally induced awakening and the association movement. Privately, he harbored opinions which questioned the legitimacy of many of the central assumptions of Reformed ecclesiology. But why did he consider such bizarre deception so necessary? Apparently his behavior reflected both a quirky nature and a determination to first win the support of his own church. Perhaps he wanted evidence of the success of converting ordinances and the Instituted Church before revealing his scheme to the generality of New England. Whatever his thinking, he chose to go about his business in Northampton as quietly as possible while he taunted Congregationalists and countered the dreams of ministerial unity of some of his clerical brethren with demands for synodical government and red herrings like open communion. A Presbyterian in public, a maverick in private: that was Solomon Stoddard. Some of his tactics were revealed in the soothing assurances of *Safety of Appearing*. Others, however, were reflected in his sparring with Increase Mather and Edward Taylor. To understand the latter it would be helpful to consider further Stoddard's role in the reforming Synod of 1679.

Following Connecticut's meetings by four years, a select group of Bay clergy led by Increase Mather petitioned the General Court for authority to hold a reforming synod. The reasons given for a synod were legion: storms, disease, Indian wars, drought, the decline of personal piety and enthusiasm for religion among laymen, heterodox opinions such as those offered by the Baptists, Massachusetts' precarious position vis-à-vis England, and a host of other problems. All were interpreted as signs of God's displeasure with his people and of impending disaster for the country. The synod's duty would be to determine the reasons for "God's controversy" and to suggest a path to "reformation." Underlying the clergy's petition, however, was the haunting fear of rising anticlericalism in the colony, and a very real belief that its authority was slipping from its grasp.

The ministers believed—or feared—that "God's controversy" might be with them and that anticlericalism, the decay of religion, and their own decaying authority represented divine retaliation for ministerial contentiousness. The synod would find the sources of God's anger and offer solutions. Above all, it would end bickering among the ministers. Points of disagreement over church polity would be aired and compromises found. To that end the petitioning ministers added that "It may now seem very necessary for us so to do, at least by owning and asserting the same faith and order of the Gospel in which these churches were at first established, and of which our Fathers witnessed a good Confession in such an Assembly at Cambridge, in the year 1648."[35]

The General Court misinterpreted the wording and assumed that the clergy intended to revise the Cambridge Platform to account for dissenting views, lest Boston become another Hartford or Cambridge another Windsor. "In answer to a motion made by some of the reverend elders that there might be a conveneing of the elders and messengers of the churches in forme of a synod, for the revisall of the platforme of discipline agreed upon by the churches, 1647, and what else may appear necessary for the preventing schismes, haeresies, prophaneness, and the establishment of the churches in one faith and order," the Court consented.[36]

Despite the confusion over the synod's intent, elders and laymen convened in September 1679 with an agenda resembling those of the Connecticut synods of both 1667 and 1675. Although the basic question remained the "decay" of religion, most of the debate revolved around three related issues of church discipline: the responsibility of churches to their children; the respective spheres of authority of elders and brethren and the associated issues of consociations and synods; and the requirements for church membership. Of those the last generated the most excitement. A few ministers submitted a proposal "that persons should make a Relation of the work of Gods Spirit upon their hearts, in order to coming into full Communion."[37] Others objected and a formal debate was suggested and accepted. Solomon Stoddard was chosen to argue the affirmative of the question "Whether those Professors of Religion as are of good Conversation, are not to be admitted to full Communion, provided they are able to examine themselves, and discern the Lords body."[38] Increase Mather took the negative, and Urian Oakes was appointed to act as moderator.

The debate grew spirited, particularly on Mather's part. "After some time," wrote Peter Thacher in his *Journal* of the synod, "the rest of his arguements were deferred and at present it was Eased."[39] The synod then searched for a statement on church membership which would satisfy both parties. The resulting proposal was full of ambiguous wording yet acceptable to Stoddard. He wrote at a later time that "the result was that they blotted out that clause of Making a Relation of the work of Gods Spirit, and put in the room of it, The Making a Profession of their Faith and Repentence; and so I Voted with the Rest and am of the same judgment still."[40]

Stoddard disrupted the meetings with his advocacy of open communion, but he desisted just short of an open breach. The climate of contentiousness he fostered, however, was typified by an incident involving himself and Ralph Wheelocke. Wheelocke was a member of the General Court, founder of the town of Medway and, at seventy-nine, one of the oldest lay brethren present. During one of the early discussions of the "sins" of the people, Wheelocke, obviously rankled by the ministers' debate, rose and "declared that there was a cry of injustice in that magistrates and ministers were not rated." That outburst against high authority, recorded Peter Thacher, "occasioned a very warme discourse. Mr. Stodder charged the deputy [Wheelocke] with saying what was not true and the Deputy Governor told him [Wheelocke] he deserved to be Laid by the heals . . . after we broke up the deputy and several others went home with Mr. Stodder and the deputy asked forgiveness of him and told him he freely forgave, but Mr. Stodder was high."[41]

Despite his opposition, Solomon Stoddard eventually gave his approval to the synod's findings and to a program for reformation which would guide the clergy for several decades. The synod endorsed the compromise plank on church membership, called for the churches to uphold discipline and to elect a full complement of officers, and carefully skirted the issue of the Cambridge Platform by noting that "It would tend much to promote the Interest of Reformation . . . for us to declare our adherence . . . in the Platform of Discipline."[42] In addition, the synod adopted most of the reforming tools outlined by Connecticut colleagues earlier, including a sacramentally oriented spiritual awakening.

By the 1690's the ministerial counterattack against the brethren was in high gear. Sacramental manuals began to appear and to become popular, and the association movement—with Stoddard, Cotton Mather, Samuel Willard, and Timothy Woodbridge lending their support—gained momentum. Ministerial unity had never seemed more important, though Solomon Stoddard continued to be the primary source of contention. While working to organize the ministers of Hampshire County into an association, he hinted that he was writing an elaborate treatise on church polity for publication and that he was prepared to engage in a debate over discipline and the sacraments. Moreover, he finally acknowledged that his real views were not what they had seemed and that he was willing to do battle with the entire clerical establishment if necessary.[43] He was changing his tactics. Possibly the rebuff from his church in 1690 had ended his hopes of an Instituted Church in Northampton. More likely, he knew that his deception was crumbling because of his activities in Northampton and the wariness of adversaries like Edward Taylor and Increase Mather.

He was right. Taylor sounded the alarm while both Increase and Cotton Mather let it be known that if Stoddard wanted a battle he would have it. In the process the Mathers broke with the conclusions of the Synod of 1679 by blaming the religious decline of the country on Presbyterians, of whom Stoddard was cited as the leader. It seemed a desperate move, a blunder perhaps, for they appeared to drive a wedge between Presbyterians and Congregationalists at exactly the moment when consensus was needed to bring the clerical reformation to a successful conclusion.

Stoddard accepted the challenge. He continued to talk of the forthcoming manuscript, and the Mathers' frenzy increased accordingly. Increase issued a stern warning that if Stoddard published, he, Increase, would use all his strength to oppose him, and he hurriedly began a lengthy treatise on church government to answer the Brattle Street Church's manifesto as well as Stoddard, if necessary.[44] Cotton, his son, worked hard on his lengthy ecclesiastical history of New England, giving it a strong anti-Presbyterian bias and publishing selected portions of it before issuing the whole work in 1702.[45]

The *Magnalia Christi Americana* indicated how quickly and completely the Mathers, erstwhile spokesmen for the clerical reformation and leaders of the awakening, had swallowed Stoddard's bait. Clearly a polemic against Presbyterian deviators, especially Stoddard, *Magnalia* sought to assess the thoughts of the great lights of the past—the ecclesiastical founders—for evidence that all had intended rigid adherence to a Congregational posture and that life in the old days was, to paraphrase John Whiting's earlier assessment, better in every way. If the quality of life had indeed deteriorated, and everyone believed it had, then the reason stemmed from the incursion of an alien ideology like Presbyterianism.[46]

Moreover, to rid Congregationalism of any taint of guilt, Cotton Mather portrayed the lives of eminent divines from 1630 to 1690 as that of continuing adherence to an exact set of doctrines and practices so that New England's decline could not be attributed to any dissension or backsliding among the faithful. Even the great Connecticut disputes of mid-century were explained away. He characterized them as minor, isolated disagreements revolving around petty local problems. Commenting on Hartford's interminable turmoil, he wryly observed that from his vantage point the matters at issue seemed totally obscured.[47]

He used the same approach in reciting the facts of the lives of certain divines whose "orthodoxy" appeared questionable. Men like Thomas Parker and John Woodbridge of Newbury, Massachusetts, Samuel Stone of Hartford, John Russell of Wethersfield, John Warham of Windsor, even John Davenport of New Haven, emerged as essentially mindless. Mather emphasized their piety or their effectiveness as preachers, or their stature among their people. But in the galaxy of New England's greats, their careers, though glorious, were lackluster when compared to Cotton, Hooker, Norton, Mitchell, Shepard, and Wilson.[48]

Consequently, in Mather's view, the ecclesiastical history of New England through much of the seventeenth century emerged as a time of tranquility produced by unswerving adherence to Congregational discipline. But, he lamented, in the last decade of the century, certain foolish "younger" divines (Stoddard was nearly sixty by that time) flirted with dangerous notions. Presbyterianism, heretofore foreign to New England's rarified atmosphere, made inroads among the young. A "great design" arouse—with Stoddard presumably at the helm—to destroy the purity and, of course, the tranquility of the New England churches. Already it had achieved some success. Presbyterianism led to an increase in worldliness, disrespect for authority, and a host of similar problems, all contributing to the general decay of religious interest of the populace. Consequently, God showed His wrath toward His people for breaking with His, and New England's, "way." The inescapable conclusion was that unless Presbyterianism was uprooted immediately, New England's demise appeared certain.[49]

Written on the eve of the publication of *The Doctrine of Instituted Churches*, the *Magnalia* was a call to arms designed to provoke Presbyterians into a bellicose response. Reflecting the thinking, presumably, of both Increase and Cotton, it reversed the conclusions of the 1679 synod, laying the blame for all social and religious evil at the feet of Presbyterian innovators. It announced to all that New England's health demanded a bitter fight to the finish, a clerical bloodletting in which either the innovators or the guardians of orthodoxy were banished from the scene. For most ministers the Mathers' manifesto presented a chilling prospect. Seeking victory in their decades-old struggle with the fraternity, they were asked to dispense with that concern and enter the lists. Only one minister, Solomon Stoddard, complied happily.

Eight

THE STODDARD-MATHER DEBATE

SOLOMON STODDARD's proclamation of war against Congregationalism and Reformed discipline, *The Doctrine of Instituted Churches*, heralded a decade of bitter, occasionally venomous, debate among New England's clergy.[1] The debate proceeded in two stages. The initial stage, covering the first two or three years of the new century, dwelt on the merits of Congregationalism, Presbyterianism, and the Instituted Church. The second, concluding about 1710, concerned the efficacy of the sacraments and especially Stoddard's converting ordinances. The major arguments, however, appeared in 1700 and 1701 in four important publications. The first was Increase Mather's *Order of the Gospel* (1700), followed quickly by Stoddard's *Instituted Churches*. Mather then countered by publishing an English sacramental manual by a Presbyterian, John Quick, appending a lengthy introduction denouncing Stoddard. Finally, in 1701, three Presbyterians—Benjamin Colman, Simon Bradstreet, and Timothy Woodbridge—published an anonymous attack on both Stoddard and Mather entitled *The Gospel Order Revived*.[2]

New England had never witnessed such a display by its ministers. Public disputes occurred occasionally; some even appeared in print; but nothing equaled the Stoddard-Mather clash.[3] In both Connecticut and Massachusetts ministers reported intense interest among the brethren. Clergymen not involved in the fracus expressed dismay over the pamphleteering and its possible effects on laymen. Their dismay was well-founded. The debates promoted factionalism. Worse, they publicized the ministers' campaigns to restore clerical authority, for beneath the rhetoric lay some common assumptions about the good society which the brethren could read with interest. The debaters agreed that the good society prized order and harmony above all things, that it cherished the public weal—determined by magistrates and ministers—above private interest, and that it demanded obedience to properly constituted authority, whether civil or ecclesiastical. The debaters agreed also that order and stability depended upon a strong religious basis—determined by the number of conversions—and that religiosity dissipated without ministerial guidance and leadership.

The Stoddard-Mather clash forced the ministry's private thoughts into the open. The good society, the orderly society, the religious society, the debaters announced, depended upon the enlightened rule of the few, especially the ministers, and the obedience of the many. New England had fallen because of the subversion of that principle. The many ruled the churches and presumably the commonwealth as well, and the debaters concurred that until that situation was corrected, New England would continue its descent. Only blindness or deafness could have prevented the brethren from understanding the significance of what they read and heard. Decades of ministerial rhetoric concerning the sins of the people and New England's decline; the ministerially inspired, sacramentally oriented spiritual awakening; the new and burgeoning association movement—all were intended to produce a social and ecclesiastical revolution whose first phase involved the replacement of the power of the fraternity by a clerical oligarchy. No wonder ministers not involved in the debate felt anxiety about lay interest.

Increase Mather's *Order of the Gospel* appeared in early 1700. It had a dual purpose. Primarily, it attacked the members of the unorthodox Brattle Street Church of Boston and refuted the contentions of its *Manifesto*, written by the minister, Benjamin Colman, in 1698.[4] Secondarily, it tried to discredit Stoddard before his pamphlet appeared. Still unaware of the revolutionary implications of Stoddard's position, Mather perpetuated the theory of Presbyterian conspiracy he had held for at least twenty years by assuming that Colman and his followers had fallen under Stoddard's domination and that all could be refuted with the same bold sweeps of the quill. Foremost, he adopted the argument that they were false Presbyterians, charlatans hiding their designs against the churches of New England behind the façade of a respectable polity. True Presbyterians, he noted, had no quarrel with Congregationalists, thanks to the declaration of the United Brethren of London of 1690—an amalgamation of English Presbyterians and Congregationalists—which revealed basic agreement in many fundamentals of discipline. Mather, of course, participated in those meetings, but he meant to do more than praise his own efforts. He knew of Stoddard's allegiance to the Scottish model just as he probably knew that Benjamin Colman was an English Presbyterian. He was aware also of the traditional split between English and Scottish Presbyterians in Connecticut and of the rapid rise of the latter. Employing a neat rhetorical trick, he tried to anger men like Colman, in order to feed their natural antipathy toward the Stoddards and to break the conspiracy through internal dissension.[5]

Increase then shifted his argument to an analysis of the historical development of the Protestant Reformation and New England's peculiar position in that development. He defined the thrust of the Reformation as the quest for the reestablishment of the polity and purity of the primitive Christian church. The early churches of the Reformation, he explained, rediscovered the meaning of primitive Christianity in their adoption of rigorous admission policies and in the maintenance of strict discipline by the laity. "Now that wherein these Churches did Chiefly Excel," he announced, "was their *Order*, Especially in their great strictness as to Admission to the Lords Supper."[6]

However, he went on, in time those "pure" churches declined, because they relaxed entrance standards and congregational discipline. This was especially true of Reformed churches in Switzerland, France, and England. To counteract that trend a new Reformation began in England and on the Continent, directed not against Papists but against existing Reformed churches. A second attempt began to recapture the meaning of primitive Christianity, and it was out of that attempt that "our fathers" came to the American wilderness. They went into "voluntary exile" to create a congregational polity—the correct "Order" of the Gospel—away from the corrupting influences of the Old World.[7]

Next, Mather focused on the ecclesiastical history of New England, previewing the argument to be used so effectively by his son Cotton in the *Magnalia*. New England, Increase wrote, began as a great experiment. God gave His people a second chance, offering them a world untouched by European man or his institutions. God told His chosen to go to the new world and create a holy commonwealth to serve as a beacon for the reformation of mankind. Consequently, Increase went on, the founders of New England established churches imitating the congregational order and purity of the early church. In that manner they fulfilled their divine mission.[8]

However, he continued, New England declined and her people became corrupt and ungodly. They strayed from the wisdom and guidance of the founders and lost God's favor. Thoughtful New Englanders sought the reason for declension. Increase knew the reason: Presbyterianism. Once before, Increase warned, Reformed churches had stumbled by rejecting congregational order and purity, relaxing discipline, and polluting the membership with questionable saints. Now some persons suggested that New England's churches should make the same mistakes. Orthodox Congregationalism was endangered by the Presbyterian doctrines of Stoddard and the Brattle Street group. Each time a church or minister succumbed to those doctrines, Mather warned, the people deteriorated further and God showed His wrath through storms, pestilence, drought, and Indian wars.[9] Thus Mather concluded that religion would thrive again only when the country's ecclesiastical constitution was upheld and unsound doctrine dispelled.

Increase did not list Stoddard's converting ordinances as a dangerous innovation, though he admitted knowing something of Stoddard's heretofore unpublicized beliefs.[10] Apparently, though, he still did not know enough about Stoddard's private position to sense the relationship between the ordinances and his Presbyterianism, or to see his hostility to Reformed discipline. Consequently, Mather treated the converting ordinances in exactly the same offhand manner as he had done at the Synod of 1679, noting simply that "as for that objection that the Sacrament is a Converting Ordinance, and therefore that there is no need of Examining members about their Conversion in order to their being admitted to partake thereof, it is a Popish Assertion."[11]

Throughout the *Order of the Gospel* Mather tried not to anger the laity, whom he viewed as a powerful ally in his struggle with the great conspiracy. He concluded by assuring his lay readers that their views and his were too alike for quibbling, especially when confronted by the ominous menace of Presbyterianism or pseudo-Presbyterianism. "It is not my own cause, but Yours, which I have here undertaken and plead for," he told the fraternity. "Did I say Yours? Nay, it is Christs Cause. The defense of these Truths is now become the Cause of Christ and of his Churches in New England. I am also very sensible the young Divines, who have not Studied these Controversies, are apt to think, that what has been Ordinarily professed and practised in the Churches of New England, is Novelty and Singularity. It may in that respect be a Service to the Churches that something be written which may be for the Information and Illumination of such, in Questions of this nature."[12]

If Mather wrote his *Order of the Gospel* for the "Information and Illumination" of young divines in the traditional "controversies," his attitude of nonchalance quickly dissipated when he read

Stoddard's *Instituted Churches*. He rushed into print a treatise written some years earlier by an English Presbyterian, John Quick, offering a different view of the nature of the sacraments.[13] In his introduction, which was longer than Quick's text, Mather warned the reader of the menace lurking in the hinterland of Massachusetts. Stoddard endangered the "Happy Union" of the New England churches, he announced, and represented a force more pernicious than all the Presbyterians combined. Compared to the Northampton cleric, the Brattle Street group was harmless. Obviously something Mather read in the *Instituted Churches* had taken him by surprise.[14]

What surprised him was Stoddard's rejection of so many of the principles of the Proestant Reformation and his obvious interest in seeing the "Enclosures about the Churches demolished, and whatever distinguishes them from the wide and wild World Extinguished."[15] Stoddard rejected what Mather considered the basis of the Reformation: the attempt to distinguish saints from reprobates so as to create churches composed solely or largely of God's elect. For centuries, Mather argued, "Papists" had polluted Christian doctrine with unsound notions while filling their churches with known unregenerates. The Reformation had sought to undo that tangle by studying the New Testament for sound doctrine and practice and by imitating the practices of the early Christian churches. Mather supported this effort, and he believed that Congregational doctrine and discipline flowed from it. Stoddard appeared alien to that tradition, for he sought no primitive church in the pages of the New Testament. Instead, he argued that the discipline most reflecting God's wishes was the church of the Israelites, a comprehensive, corporate, national church which made only a token attempt to distinguish saints from reprobates. In Mather's eye, it differed little from the corrupt Roman Catholic Church that Protestants had repudiated.

Thus, for Increase Mather, representing New England's Congregationalists, Stoddard posed a significantly greater threat to New England than the Brattle Street group or Presbyterians in general. The latter challenged New England's ecclesiastical system as Mather saw it, but did so within the framework of Reformed ecclesiology. Stoddard questioned one of the major theses of the Reformation, the search for the primitive New Testament Church. "We shall not concern ourselves," Increase announced, "with his Doctrine, That Elders have not only power over their particular Churches, but also over others; and his Essay to Erect Provincial and National Churches (and these must Consist only of the clergy) as of Divine Right." Instead, he concentrated on Stoddard's scriptural model for the "Instituted Church," the Old Testament Church of the Israelites. "We see now the fault of our Platform of Church discipline," he concluded, "tis too much compiled out of the books of the New Testament."[16]

While asserting that the Instituted Church contradicted Reformed doctrine, he also declared that the Jewish church was not the national church Stoddard portrayed it to be. In one concise paragraph Mather touched on both his ecclesiological and historical objections to Stoddard's position. "To tell us," he wrote, "that the Constitution of the Church of Israel and of the Synagogues as particular Churches under it, in the land of Canaan, is an Institution for the Churches of the New Testament, will rather Astonish than satisfy Considerate Christians . . . But almost all the Traditions that we have about the Church Governments of the Synagogues, are either the Fabulous, or at best, uncertain Reports of the Talmuds, which were not in being, til several Hundreds of years after our Saviour."[17]

The use of the Jewish church as a model for Reformed Christian churches was only half of Stoddard's argument. Stoddard claimed that the requirements for man's salvation had changed since the days of the Israelites from conformity to the Law to faith in Christ's atonement, and from that he drew the inference that Christ had instituted the ordinances for the transmission of saving grace. Once Mather understood the context from which Stoddard argued for the notion of converting ordinances, he hammered at the theme that Stoddard's position was "Papist" and, although upheld by a few early Lutherans, was rejected by other Protestants because of its similarity to Catholicism.[18]

Mather buttressed his attack with evidence that no major Protestant group accepted Stoddard's position. He cited the Heads of Agreement as proof that neither Congregationalists nor Presbyterians deviated from the doctrine of the "seals."[19] He used Samuel Rutherford as further proof of Presbyterian rejection.[20] Even the Church of England, which in many respects conformed to Stoddard's notion of a national church, kept unregenerates from the Lord's Table. The opposition of New England's Congregationalists was well known, and he doubted that New England Presbyterians would be any more sympathetic. For Mather, Reformation polity represented an attempt to recreate primitive Christianity. Reformed theology sought the same end, rejecting the institutionalized salvation of Catholicism for the more personalized view of the confrontation of God and man without earthly mediators. Stoddard's polity and divinity came close to the institutionalized salvation of the "Papists." Thus Mather rejected Stoddard because Stoddard questioned the Reformation.[21]

Reading the *Instituted Churches* may have convinced Mather that Stoddard's ecclesiology was unlike that of other New England Presbyterians, but it did not convince him that Stoddard was a maverick. Nor did he take solace in the knowledge that apparently his old tactic had worked and Stoddard had finally admitted his heresy and shown himself to be a dangerous innovator and a charlatan. Quite the contrary, the close temporal proximity between the formation of the Brattle Street Church and the appearance of Stoddard's treatise seemed more than coincidence. Mather linked the two and assumed the worst. An unholy alliance had formed between Stoddard and the Presbyterians, an elaborate plot hatched in the Connecticut Valley and directed toward New England Congregationalism. Had not Stoddard said as much in his treatise? Had he not blamed New England's woes on her congregational polity and warned that he would not be silent until the polity he espoused was enshrined as New England's discipline? Consequently, Mather treated Stoddard's work as the war cry of New England's Presbyterians, most of whom were located in the Connecticut Valley. He assumed, as he always did, that Stoddard spoke from a broad and solid base of power. How could he attack the Bay establishment unless he could count on the support of the clergy and laity of the Valley? Mather therefore filled his preface to Quick's treatise with dire warnings of the "Presbyterianism that runs down the Connecticut River." He attacked Rutherford, whom he saw as fashionable among younger Valley clergy, and reminded them that one of their forebears had thoroughly refuted Rutherford. "You our Brethren in the Colony of Connecticut," he warned, "that Exceed all the rest of New England for proclaiming your Indisposition to the Order wherein your Churches have so long flourished, wilt above others attend; Because t'was Rutherford that was against your Thomas Hooker, whom though he were (with your leave) the greatest man that ever your Colony saw, yet now the most Raw Youths amongst you can . . . Confute him!"[22]

If Mather hoped to provoke a Presbyterian rejoinder, he did not have to wait long, for soon after the publication of Quick's *Young Mans Claim* a lengthy treatise entitled *The Gospel Order Revived* appeared in Boston. The pamphlet, published anonymously in New York, represented the thoughts of three clergymen: Benjamin Colman of Boston's Brattle Street Church, Simon Bradstreet of Charlestown, and Timothy Woodbridge of Hartford's First Church.[23]

The purpose of *Gospel Order Revived* was to defend a tradition—New England Presbyterianism—against Increase Mather on one side and Stoddard on the other.[24] Its authors disagreed completely with Mather's ecclesiastical position and could accept neither his view of New England orthodoxy nor his characterization of Presbyterian innovators. Moreover, they sought to dissociate Presbyterianism from Stoddard. They rejected his Instituted Church, and they wanted New England and the world to know that they, not Stoddard, spoke for New England's Presbyterians.

They agreed with Stoddard on many questions of polity—membership requirements, synodical authority, and particular church covenants—but the discipline they espoused was New Testament, not Old. They sought, like Mather the revival of primitive Christianity, and they abhorred Stoddard's emphasis on the Old Testament Jewish church and his argument for institutionalized salvation through converting ordinances.

Mather's mistake, the authors argued, was in assuming their views were identical to Stoddard's. Nothing was further from the truth. They accepted Quick's denunciation of Stoddard's conception of the Lord's Supper. Stoddard did not speak for all Presbyterians—Connecticut or otherwise—but only for himself. "Had the attestation," they concluded, "been only to recommend the following Treatise of the excellent Mr. Quick's to our perusal and Practice, no Minister in New England, that calls himself a Presbyterian, but would cheerfully subscribe it; but we believe few would considerate in its Reflections on the Reverend Mr. Stoddard, or favour that worse Report, That under the Umbrage of the Name of Presbyterians some would bring in Innovations, ruinous to our Churches, and contrary to the Doctrine and Spirit of Mr. Quick's Book."[25]

Colman, Bradstreet, and Woodbridge did not dwell as much on their differences with Stoddard as on those with Mather, but they did not have to. They had made their point, and lengthy refutation of the Northampton divine would only have weakened their position. Instead, they lashed out at Mather's conception of New England's ecclesiastical history and the Congregational orthodoxy that supposedly dominated its development. "It is a groundless Calumny which is suggested," they wrote, "that a latitude beyond what our Author [Mather] contends for, is but a betraying the liberties and priviledge; which our Lord Jesus Christ has given to his Church, or the Brethren of the Church."[26] Mather argued that deviators from New England's orthodoxy blasphemed the memory of the founders and endangered the success of their errand. The authors replied that the true intent of the founders "has been somewhat differently conveyed unto us."[27] Their desire "was to be freed from the imposition of Man in the Worship of God," or, as Samuel Willard once phrased it, "to sequester themselves into a quiet corner of the World, where they might enjoy Christ's unmixt Institutions, and leave them uncorrupted to Posterity."[28] The authors knew of no intention to establish and enshrine a particular discipline. "Some indeed," they went on, "would make the design of our first Planters to consist in some little Rites, Modes, or Circumstances of Church Discipline and those such, as the Word of God no where requires. These are the men who dishonour their country, and their Fathers Memory, by making their great design to lie in so small matters."[29]

But did the founders' disinterest in any particular discipline mean that New England should have no ecclesiastical constitution? Yes, replied the trio, if having one meant ruthless extermination of opposing views. That much conformity, they believed, was never intended by the founders nor was it ever the situation in New England. After the initial settlement the founders divided over questions of church government "and it is notorious there has been no agreement in these points from the beginning," the authors noted ruefully. Yet Increase Mather argued as though his beliefs were God's own truths and dissenters were "not on the Lords side, [but were] enemies to the cause of Christ, and the Churches of New England."[30]

In a sense Woodbridge, Colman, and Bradstreet reflected the thoughts expressed by John Woodbridge in his letters to Richard Baxter thirty years before. How, they asked, could New Englanders profess loyalty to one discipline when, in fact, the country seethed with factionalism? Hypocrisy represented the real source of strife to the Presbyterian trio. Instead of searching for agreement on fundamentals, Presbyterians and Congregationalists—spurred mainly by Congregationalist intolerance—sought a death struggle, little realizing the inherent danger to the country. Messrs. Woodbridge, Bradstreet, and Colman called for harmony rather than warfare. They pleaded for the establishment of an ecclesiastical constitution encompassing both polities, one based on tolerance and compromise, not intolerance and suppression.[31]

Despite the authors' disavowal of partisanship, however, *Gospel Order Revived* was a polemic. Woodbridge, Colman, and Bradstreet spent little time discussing the fundamentals linking Congregationalists and Presbyterians. Instead, they wrote a point-by-point refutation of Mather's objections to the Brattle Street Church. Commenting on the old New England practice of a public "tryall" before admission to communion, for example, they quoted Samuel Willard's observation that "God had appointed the preaching of the Gospel, the Sacraments . . . for edification, and the promoting of Christian love among his people; but we read nothing of these imposed relations . . . nor is there any appearance of such a Custom in the primitive Church."[32]

Turning to church covenants, they rejected any covenant "entered into by some Persons of a Christian Society, exclusive of the rest, whereby they being in Covenant one with another, should thereby call themselves a Church of Christ, making the Ordinances of Christ, or any of them to depend on this Covenant, so that those who scruple it, or refuse to joyn in it, shall on that account, not enjoy them. And that those who are thus covenanted, or the major part of them have power to make or unmake Officers, to admit or reject Church Members, to manage Discipline, to order the affairs of Christs House in his Name, as if they had warrant and communion from him so to do."[33]

By discarding church covenants the Presbyterians denied the autonomy of the congregation. Like Stoddard, however, they went further by attacking the essential element of a congregational polity, the "power of the fraternity." They recited the Congregational argument that Christ delegated a portion of His spiritual authority to the church through the covenant, thus allocating to members the power to manage their own affairs and, more important, to convey spiritual powers to officers, especially the minister, through election. The argument suggested that church officers had no authority outside their own congregations. It also implied that church officers meeting in synods or councils lacked authority unless blessed by the churches.

The Presbyterians argued that Christ bestowed spiritual and ruling powers on the Apostles, the original elders, and not upon the laity. Thus assemblies of elders, not covenanted congregations, held the "keys" in matters of doctrine and discipline, and they needed no authorization from churches. Conversely, ruling power lay with the elders in particular churches as well. "We can never believe," the trio wrote, "that our Lord Jesus Christ has left every private Brother an equal Vote with any of his Officers, in ruling or managing his Church."[34]

The intent of *Gospel Order Revived* was explicit. Countering Increase Mather's assertion that Congregationalism represented the New England way, it argued that New England labored under a legacy of continuing struggle between Congregationalists and Presbyterians. Still, the authors contended that their purpose was not to enlarge that struggle. Mather had to be answered, but it was just as important to dissociate legitimate Presbyterianism from its offspring in Northampton. They recognized that their own views and Stoddard's were much alike, but they could ill afford to let Mather succeed in his attempt to place all Presbyterians in Stoddard's camp. So, in refuting Mather's *Order of the Gospel* and his use of *Young Mans Claim*, they also rejected any affiliation with Stoddard. They might endorse parish organization, open communion and rule by elder in the local church but Stoddard was neither their spokesman nor one of them. So far as they were concerned, his sacramental church placed him outside the pale of Reformed ecclesiology.[35]

At the same time, *Gospel Order Revived* deftly glossed over the Scottish-English split among Presbyterians. Instead, the authors tried to counter both Stoddard and Mather with a call for reason, conciliation, and an ecclesiastical constitution, one essentially Presbyterian but encompassing the arguments of both sides. They urged readers to reject all appeals for ecclesiastical strife, to reject the predictions of Mather and Stoddard that New England would founder if dissenting notions survived. Above all else, they tried to restore ministerial unity and save the clergy's "reformation."

The Stoddard-Mather debate continued for the rest of the decade, but it could not maintain the luster or intensity of its first two years. Mather successfully separated Stoddard from the Presbyterians, while the Presbyterians isolated both Stoddard and Mather by refusing to participate in a war of attrition. Stoddard provoked factionalism among his colleagues and incited the brethren by revealing the clergy's quest for power; but lacking Presbyterian aid, the Instituted Church garnered only brickbats. The debate quickly degenerated into a minute discussion of the converting ordinances. Stoddard knew he could not win that argument. He had hoped for a general conflagration, not a seminar on the sacraments, and he had failed.

Solomon Stoddard roasted slowly on an open fire. Not a single clergyman or layman came to his defense, while his opponents merrily sniped from pulpit and press. His assumed strength in the Valley and Connecticut never materialized, and no church publicly endorsed the Instituted Church and its converting ordinances.[36] Stoddard discovered that his personality and reputation could not force endorsements for his ecclesiology. Presbyterian friends like William Williams of Hatfield quietly disassociated themselves from his views. Congregationalist friends like Samuel Mather of Windsor repaid old debts by remaining silent (though Mather wrote a lengthy anti-Stoddard tract which he placed among his private papers). Even his few disciples deserted him. Stephen Mix of Wethersfield, Gurdon Salstonstall of New London—both maintained a discreet public silence, though Saltonstall, in a sermon to his church in 1703, did endorse converting ordinances.[37]

Most clergymen, especially in Connecticut, viewed the Stoddard-Mather clash as a disaster. It jeopardized hopes for a spiritual awakening and doomed the association movement. Stoddard became a liability. Revealing his personal idiosyncrasies cost him the prestige and awe he had carefully nurtured for decades. Everywhere but in his own Hampshire County he became known as a troublesome maverick. Increase suffered as well. The leadership of the association movement in Massachusetts, centered in the Cambridge Association and its potent spokesmen, Benjamin Colman and Samuel Willard, severely criticized his overzealousness. Its counterpart in Connecticut, guided by Timothy Woodbridge and Gurdon Saltonstall, did the same.[38]

The excitement of the Stoddard-Mather debate forced association supporters into quick action. At the yearly convention of the Bay ministry in Boston in 1704 the members circulated a letter calling for stronger associations. A year later representatives of five Massachusetts associations drafted proposals for the legal establishment of area associations as well as an annual general council of representatives of the churches. The purpose of the general council was vague, but the powers of the association were explicit. They would deliberate any issue causing dissension in the churches and would function as licensing bureaus for young ministers seeking employment. They would resolve cases of discipline by creating councils of ministers *and* laymen to hear evidence and render decisions. Supporters of the association movement received a stunning blow, however, when their proposals failed to receive support from either the General Assembly or the churches.[39] After that, the association movement in Massachusetts foundered, though informal gatherings continued.

Stoddard played no direct role in the debacle surrounding the Proposals of 1705 or the ministers' subsequent humiliation, though his tactics had obviously aided enemies of the associations. He continued to work for a legal association in Hampshire County supported by neighboring Presbyterians like William Williams of Hatfield. Cut off from the Massachusetts Assembly, the Hampshire ministers chose the only route remaining, the churches. Most of the ministers wanted a presbytery but were forced ultimately to settle for an association reflecting thecontent of he Proposals of 1705. Finally ratified in 1714, the Hampshire Association's charter did reveal a Presbyterian flavor. It included no laymen, only clergy, and its architects, notably Stoddard and Williams, won endorsement of a sentence revealing the intentions of Valley Presbyterians. "We judge it our duty," the charter noted, "to be subject to a Council of the County, until there be some Superior Council set up in the Province unto which we may appeal."[40]

In Connecticut the association movement surfaced in 1703 when some of the ministers, Presbyterians and Congregationalists, active in the creation of Yale College suggested a new synod. Led by Timothy Woodbridge, they sent a letter to the churches asking them to "peruse the assemblies [Westminster] Confession of Faith, as also that made by the Synod held at Boston, May 12, 1680, and manifest in convenient season the concurrence with us in addressing our Religious government . . . that they would please to recommend to our people and their posterity the following Confession of Faith, viz., that agreed upon by Reverend Assembly at Westminster, as it is comprised in and Represented by the Confession made by the Synod in Boston, May 12, 1680."[41]

The reaction indicated guarded enthusiasm. The failure of the Bay Proposals of 1705 did not dampen that enthusiasm. On the contrary, the Connecticut Assembly's sanction was assured in 1707 when New London's Gurdon Saltonstall became the colony's governor. In May the Connecticut Assembly issued a call to the churches for the ministers to meet in each "countie town." "This Assembly," the proclamation stated, "from their own observation and from the complaint of many others, being made sensible of the defects of the discipline of the churches of this government, arising from the want of a more explicite asserting the rules given for that end in the holy scriptures, from which would arise a firm establishment amongst ourselves, a good and regular issue in cases subject to ecclesiastical discipline, glory to Christ our head, and edification to the members, hath seen fit to ordain and require . . . that the ministers of the churches . . . meet together at their respective countie towns."[42] They would meet with selected laymen to draw up a platform of church discipline "conformable to the word of God." They would then select two representatives to convene with all of the other county representatives at Saybrook in order to compare plans and draft a single proposal for presentation at the General Assembly's October meeting.[43]

The representatives of the churches met in the summer of 1708 and searched for the agreement on fundamentals suggested by the authors of *Gospel Order Revived*. From the beginning, however, the composition of the group determined that the platform would be more Congregational than Presbyterian. Presbyterians dominated the Hartford County delegation (led by Timothy Woodbridge) and the Fairfield County group. The other delegations supported Congregationalism and submitted proposals reflecting the intent of the Massachusetts Proposals of 1705—that is, they asked that any governing body above the individual church have the consent of the brethren.[44]

The work of the representatives proceeded smoothly. First, they turned to consideration of a united confession of faith. Presbyterians suggested endorsement of the Westminster Confession, but the majority voted for the Congregationalist Savoy Confession of 1658.[45] Second, they endorsed the theological assumptions of the Heads of Agreement of 1691, the joint declaration of the London Congregationalists and Presbyterians. True to the spirit of the Saybrook meeting, the doctrine found in the Heads forged common ground between the competing disciplines without really resolving any of the traditional points of argument. For example, in the ancient dispute over the nature of Christ's visible church, the Heads merely noted the distinction between Protestant and Roman Catholic doctrine:

> We acknowledge our Lord Jesus Christ to have one Catholick
> Church, or Kingdom, comprehending all that are united to
> Him, whether in Heaven or Earth. And do conceive the
> whole multitude of visible Believers, and their Infant-Seed
> . . . to belong to *Christ's Spiritual Kingdom* in this world; But
> for the notion of a *Catholick Visible Church* here, as it
> signifies its having been collected into any formed Society,
> under a Visible common Head on Earth, whether *one* Person

singly, or Many Collectively, We, with the rest of Protestants, unanimously disclaim it.[46]

Saybrook's statement on admission requirements reflected the same desire for unity. For generations Connecticut's churches had argued over the correct method for admitting new members. The definition of the visible saint contained in the Heads provided sufficient latitude for the narrowest or broadest admission policy:

> That none shall be admitted as Members, in order to Communion in all the special Ordinances of the Gospel, but such persons as are knowing and sound in the fundamental Doctrine of the Christian Religion, without Scandal in their Lives; and to a Judgment regulated by the Word of God, are persons of visible Holiness and Honesty; credibly professing cordial subjection to Jesus Christ.[47]

The only real partisanship occurred over the issue of church government. Presbyterians tended to favor Timothy Woodbridge's plan while Congregationalists drifted toward the plan presented by Nicholas Noyes for New Haven County. The majority preferred the New Haven plan, "but some Clauses were put into it, in Conformity to Mr. Woodbridge of Hartford and some others, who were inclined to the Presbyterian Side."[48]

The resulting plan of church government, differing little from the Proposals of 1705, became part of the Saybrook Platform. A general council or synod of all the churches was to meet yearly to discuss common problems and to make recommendations, although no substantive powers were assigned to that body. The plan envisioned the creation of county councils to determine cases of discipline and render decisions in church disputes, as well as associations of ministers to license and regulate the clergy and "consider and resolve questions and cases of Importance which shall be offered by any among themselves or others."[49]

The completed platform went to the Connecticut Assembly in October. Acting quickly, the Assembly declared its "great approbation of such a happy agreement," and announced "that all the churches within this government that are or shall be thus united in doctrine, worship, and discipline, be, and for the future shall be . . . established by law."[50]

Nothing remained except the arduous task of securing the approval of the churches. That, however, appeared to be a manageable problem, since lay representatives had already concurred. Furthermore, the Assembly had decided that the associations could function even without complete support from the brethren. Dissenting churches would be allowed to exercise "worship and discipline in their own way."[51] Connecticut's ministers were ecstatic. Despite Stoddard's onslaught and the humiliating failure of their Massachusetts colleagues, their perseverence was about to produce yet another revolution in Connecticut—and without either bitterness or rancor. The resurrection of ministerial authority seemed assured. Unity had triumphed.

FROM THE SAYBROOK PLATFORM
TO THE GREAT AWAKENING

CONSIDERING Connecticut's turbulent history, the ministers' hope for quick acceptance by the fraternity seemed unrealistic. But the ministers remained optimistic, for their Platform was constructed to hide much of its significance. On the surface it seemed to confirm the status quo. Its doctrinal and disciplinary pronouncements were vague enough to condone almost any existing practice. More important, it did not appear to challenge the ultimate power of the fraternity or any lay-inspired innovations in polity.

While much of the Platform's vagueness stemmed from ecclesiastical debate among the ministers, a portion resulted from the clergy's desire to placate the brethren, if not to deceive them. The clergy asked for endorsement of the associations and agreed to legitimize the existing structure of the local church in return. Moreover, as a bonus Assembly and clergy held out the right of dissent, showing their apparent willingness to go to any length to patch up the decades-old rift between ministers, magistrates, and brethren.

The Platform tried to avoid direct confrontation with the fraternity's prerogatives. For example, it failed to define the respective spheres of authority of minister and brethren in the local church. In addition it characterized the association as a supplement to the power of the fraternity, not as an antagonist. The Platform argued that the association would provide either an independent forum to solve potentially disruptive church disputes or an appellate body for cases of discipline. In either role the Platform directed the association to protect the consensus established and nurtured by the covenant. Finally, the ministry agreed to clean its own house by using the association to examine and license prospective ministers in order to protect the churches from incompetent or otherwise ill-qualified persons.[1]

But behind the façade of rhetoric and reassurance lay the apparatus for an ecclesiastical revolution. Anyone able to remember the church disputes of the seventeenth century knew that they often developed from schisms between ministers and brethren. They knew as well that ministerial authority had carried no legal or ecclesiastical sanction to counter the sheer number of opponents, especially when councils and Assembly edicts proved ineffective. The Platform remedied that traditional defect in Connecticut's ecclesiastical order through the association, a source of ministerial authority based on statute, not congregational election.[2] A beleaguered minister could now expect aid from his association whose decisions, in some cases, would have the force of law. Consequently, though the Platform did not abrogate the fraternity's power, it created the machinery that could. A minister buttressed by a powerful and sympathetic association was likely to be much tougher than one forced to rely on the old powerless council of neighboring elders.

In the same vein, though the Platform did not create a new ecclesiastical system, its machinery could be used for that purpose. Assuming the eventual demise of the power of the fraternity, the new mechanisms for clerical dominance—the annual all-colony meeting, the associations, and the dominant local minister—could draft a new institutional definition of the local church. Its nature would depend on the wishes of the majority of ministers. Should they desire Scottish Presbyterianism, the General Association and area associations could be quickly converted into a national church complete with all the hierarchical apparatus of the Scottish system.[3] Should English Presbyterianism emerge triumphant, the emphasis could immediately shift to the local clergyman and his dominance over the parish. The area associations and the yearly meeting would perform advisory functions, aiding and supporting the local minister in his actions and decisions. Finally, if the clergy opted for Congregationalism, the Platform could recreate an ecclesiastical system similar to Connecticut's first days. Individual clergy would preside over covenanted bodies of saints, sharing authority with the brethren while retaining the ultimate responsibility for determining the nature and direction of the church's development. The associations would act as advisory bodies, asserting their authority and denying the autonomy of the congregation only when the church was threatened with schism, a power not unlike that given to the General Court in the ancient Fundamental Orders.[4]

The Platform emerged as an ingenious device solving the immediate problem of clerical impotence while providing an apparatus to heal ecclesiastical division. But despite the optimism of the clergy and the skill of its architects, the Platform fooled few churches. Many brethren passed over the sections on doctrine and focused on the proposed associations, labeling them "Presbyterian" and destructive of congregational autonomy. The brethren transformed the debate over the Platform into a test of lay Congregationalism. The issue was never in doubt. The associations were emasculated, stripped of their power to render binding decisions in either disputes or cases of discipline, and the clergy's carefully prepared counteroffensive collapsed like a sand castle. Only Fairfield County emerged unscathed as Presbyterian clergy violated the intent of the Platform by attempting to transform the county association into a church court.[5]

The Saybrook Platform did not die quickly, for it remained in the book of statutes until 1784. But it never functioned as intended. A few churches ratified all of its provisions, but it needed majority support—something it never received. Some churches, like East

Windsor, rejected it out of hand; others merely deleted the sections on church government. Some gave it conditional approval, ratifying its provisions while reaffirming lay authority and congregational autonomy and instructing ministers to do nothing as association members without specific instructions from the churches. Still other churches accepted the associations but added amendments carefully diluting its authority. The churches of New Haven County, for example, created an association with barely enough power to convene or adjourn its meetings.[6]

Even worse, the Platform opened old wounds and produced dissension in nearly every church, thus subjecting ministers to new humiliations. The reaction in Norwich typified the Platform's reception in many locales. John Woodward, the Congregationalist minister, asked for approval. When his church learned of the nature of the Platform, especially its proposals for the formation of ministerial associations, a bitter contest ensued. Some members supported Woodward but most did not, calling the Platform "Presbyterian" and urging quick defeat. Woodward fought for ratification, but his side eventually lost, forcing him to resign.

His resignation, however, did not end the dispute. His successor, Benjamin Lord, began preaching in 1716. The church, fearing that Lord would make a new attempt at ratification, decided to continue "to practice that Form of Church Government, called Congregational, as formerly practiced by the Generality of the Churches of New England, and according to the Agreement of the Synod, at Cambridge, 1648." As a condition of settlement, Lord agreed to respect the church's opposition to the Platform.

Eventually he changed his mind. In 1724 he asked the church for permission to attend the meetings of the New London County Association. He assured the laity that he would inform the Association that his attendance implied neither his own consent to the Platform nor that of his church. He would explain that he attended because he "often thought that it was a damage . . . to live as one Alone upon the Earth." The church agreed and the matter ended.[7]

Woodward and Lord suffered embarrassment by supporting the Platform. Some of its architects experienced the same fate. Timothy Edwards of East Windsor was such a minister. Father of Jonathan, Timothy worked diligently before, during, and after the synod for the Platform's creation and ratification. His church, formed in 1699 from former members of First Church, rewarded his labors by rejecting the entire document.[8] The dean of Connecticut Presbyterians, Timothy Woodbridge in neighboring Hartford, achieved only slightly greater success. First Church endorsed the Platform, then undercut the authority of the Hartford City Association. Created to handle difficult cases of discipline, the Association grew frustrated by the church's refusal to let it hear those cases. In July 1719, for example, the church charged Major Joseph Talcott with an offense against the brethren. When no decision was reached, the church ignored the Association and demanded a hearing before Solomon Stoddard, John Williams of Deerfield, and William Williams of Hatfield. Woodbridge consented, and on January 13, 1720, the three upriver clergymen notified the Hartford Church that "if you do freely over looke and Passe by all things that have passed between Major Talcott and yourselves as matters of offence and do upon his desire withdraw your charge you have Laid against him to prosecute it no farther and do receive him to your charity and communion, manifest your consent hereunto by your Silence. Which was done by the Church."[9]

Solomon Stoddard's Hampshire Association experienced similar difficulties. Despite the boastful phrases of the Association's charter, it proved a disaster from its inception. Nearly half of the county's churches rejected it immediately, in spite of the years of careful preparation and the toned-down Presbyterianism it reflected.[10] The remaining clergy—Stoddard, William Williams, John Williams of Deerfield, Isaac Chauncey of Hadley, Daniel Brewer of Springfield First, and Nathaniel Collins of Enfield—continued to meet despite opposition from many of their own laymen. Apparently no church, not even Stoddard's, accepted the association quietly. In tiny Enfield opposition grew unchecked and Collins suffered constant criticism for his preaching and general deportment. Eventually the church decided to deny his right to serve communion.

Enfield became the first test of strength for Stoddard's "ecclesiastical council." In 1714 a group of representatives from churches near Enfield met but failed to find a solution. The next year the matter went to the Association, whose decision absolved Collins of blame. In a letter to the Enfield church the Association wrote that "we do not understand that Mr. Collins has given any occasion of grievance. Several persons belonging to other places, who have occasionally heard him abroad and at home have given an Account that his preaching hath been profitable and worthy to be accepted and some of your [selves] that remain unfaithful have given testimony that his preaching has mended."[11] The letter concluded by pointing out that though the church had requested the intercession of a council the year before, it had chosen to ignore the Association's advice. Now, apparently, it wanted a different tribunal to endorse its position. The Association, the letter declared emphatically, would not provide that support.[12]

Three years later the dispute still raged. The Association, a failure in its attempt to restore peace, sent a bitter letter to the church in which Stoddard, John Williams, and William Williams indicated that the only alternative for Collins was to seek employment elsewhere. "Brethren," they wrote:

In answer to your letter of July 29th, we judge that the church of Enfield have had no cause of such dissatisfaction these many years, but have cause to reflect upon themselves, having manifested an unpeacable and disorderly Spirit and layed God much temptation before Mr. Collins . . . the discord is grown to so great a height, and rejects all remedies, so that it proves an overbearing discouragement and impediment to Mr. Collins in his work, and a great hindrance to the peoples edification and edification of their children, we judge it not unwarrantable to Mr. Collins to lay down his work in that place, hoping that God will make provision for him that he may be more servicable in another place.[13]

> Sol: Stoddard
> John Williams
> Wm. Williams

Collins left Enfield soon after and the Association, its power successfully challenged, never recovered.

The morale of the clergy of Connecticut and the Connecticut Valley sank to its lowest ebb in half a century. The misfortunes of Nathaniel Collins of Enfield and Benjamin Lord of Norwich added new names to an already lengthy list of ministerial casualties. The failure of the Hampshire Association, the Massachusetts Proposals of 1705, the futility of the Stoddard-Mather clash and Solomon Stoddard's reforms, and the light from the still-glowing embers of the Saybrook Platform—all contributed to an increasing sense of gloom and frustration among the once proud and powerful heirs of the Protestant Reformation.

Only Solomon Stoddard avoided the general malaise. Even as his own struggle with the Mathers continued, and optimism in Connecticut over the Platform reached its height, the Northampton warrior, now seventy years old, abruptly and radically changed tactics. He knew he had lost his battle. So, attacked from nearly every quarter, he quietly began to turn against his own Instituted Church. In 1708 he published a treatise entitled *The Inexcusableness of Neglecting the Worship of God Under a Pretense of Being in an Unconverted Condition*. In it he returned to the position that any ordinance, least of all communion, existed primarily for conversion. Rather, he went on, the sacraments existed mainly for preparation, though it was conceivable that an unregenerate might be converted at the Table. Concerning the Supper, around which much of his debate with Mather had centered, he now argued that it was no more than a "memorial to Christ's death."[14]

As he had in 1687, he again urged the necessity of open communion, because of the importance of the ordinances in preparatory work. Rather than admit a change of heart, however, he simply stated that he had been misconstrued by critics who punished anyone daring to "depart from the ways of our Fathers" though "it may be a vertue . . . to depart from them in some things."[15] He continued the same refrain the next year in another pamphlet, *An Appeal to the Learned*.[16] After that he wrote no more on the Instituted Church.

Though he continued to press his own church for reforms for a time, Stoddard seemed eager to withdraw from public debate. Not only had he lost, but, more important, his fertile mind was already rethinking the enormous problems of the age and weighing possible solutions. He retained his intense desire to reach New England's unconverted as well as his hostility to Reformed discipline, especially Congregationalism. He saw continued signs of religion's decay, and he still blamed New England Congregationalism and the Reformed mentality that had fostered it. Moreover, he continued to view the restoration of clerical authority as the cornerstone of any revival of religion. Consequently, too long a frontier minister to be foiled by adversity, Stoddard worked quietly, creating a new plan for New England's redemption.[17] Even as his church voted on the authority of "ecclesiastical councils" and the Saybrook Platform crumbled, Solomon Stoddard's plan began to unfold before New England's reading public.

In 1718 Stoddard explained his decision to drop the Instituted Church in a blistering little pamphlet entitled *An Examination of the Power of the Fraternity*.[18] *An Examination*, a savage attack on Congregationalism and the Cambridge Platform sounded typically Stoddard, but it was not. He wrote it to confess publicly a serious error in judgment. For decades he had assumed that New England Congregationalism represented the collective thoughts and actions of only the clergy; so, in seeking reform, he had attempted to alter the thinking of his colleagues. Few accepted his program, but many had come to agree that change was necessary and had worked actively to bring it about. Their efforts, and his, had reached fruition in devices like the Saybrook Platform and the Hampshire Association.

In retrospect, Stoddard lamented, they achieved nothing, for the real power in the churches lay with the brethren, and they resisted every attempt at reform, no matter how innocuous. The brethren, Stoddard argued, were the true paladins of Congregationalism, although it was not the Congregationalism of the clergy, synods, or the Reformed tradition. Rather, it masked the very godlessness he and others had labored so long to destroy. The brethren were hypocrites, claiming to protect their rights and privileges in God's name while seeking only self-interest. They labeled all existing practices and beliefs traditional, and therefore sacrosanct, and resisted reform even when shown how, in the name of the "power of the fraternity," their recalcitrance contributed to the collapse of true religion.[19] For the first time Stoddard drew a sharp distinction between lay and clerical conceptions of a congregational polity. The former, not the latter, constituted the real enemy. The Instituted Church foundered not as a result of Increase Mather's logic but because of the ignorance and hostility of the laiety. Smug and secure in their churches, fearful of change in any form, the brethren cloaked worldliness in the guise of Congregationalism while arguing that no alteration in either doctrine or discipline was possible without the approval of the fraternity—approval the fraternity never granted.

The brethren rationalized the "power of the fraternity" with constant appeals to the Cambridge Platform, and Stoddard turned his fury on that document and its creators. "The mistakes of one Generation," he announced, "many times become the calamity of succeeding generations. The present generation are not only unhappy by reason of the darkness of their own minds, but the errors of those who have gone before them have been a foundation of a great deal of Misery." The Platform was contrary to the "experience" of the churches in that it was written "before they had much time to weigh those things . . . and some of their posterity are mightily devoted to it, as if the Platform were the Pattern in the Mount." And what was the "experience" of the churches? A century of life in New England demonstrated that the "community" was unfit to judge and rule in the church. The brethren lacked both understanding or wisdom, for few had "read or studied." "If the Multitude were to be judges in Civil causes," Stoddard warned, "things would quickly be turned upside down."[20]

Stoddard offered "practical" objections to the Platform as well, evidently assuming that laymen would respond to that approach. He devoted his energies to refuting specific arguments against clerical rule, repeating a litany he had uttered for half a century. He chided those willing to let elders act only as "moderators" of meetings. To those who feared "corrupt" elders, he replied that lay power was a poor defense against corruption, since corrupt rulers always indicated a corrupt people. He spoke also of those who feared rule by elder because it tended to "exalt the minister or debase the Brethren." In that, he added sarcastically, there was no more danger than "the confining of Preaching to the Minister."[21]

More than ever Stoddard blamed New England's preoccupation with church discipline for the sad state of religion. By 1718 he believed he possessed a clearer understanding of the problem, and it was far worse than even he had imagined. Buttressed by the Cambridge Platform, clerical Congregationalism had wrought a social revolution. The brethren, blindly following the dictates of deluded minds, used the Platform to justify godless ways and protect them from all clerical attempts at reform. Trapped by ancient rhetoric, the clergy continued to seek a solution in discipline, little realizing that synodical decisions paled before the "power of the fraternity." Stoddard was just as critical of his own thinking. His Instituted Church, an alternative to Congregationalism and Presbyterianism, had been aimed at clerical ears. That it had generated no enthusiasm meant little, for he realized now that, even had he won hosts of ministerial supporters, the fraternity would have stopped him, just as it had in Northampton. Thus, perhaps sadly, Stoddard wrote the epitaph for his sacramental church.

To destroy the grip of the brethren on the structure of the churches, to resurrect clerical authority, and to reach New England's ever-growing multitudes of unconverted, Stoddard adopted a new tactic and gave it theological justification. By his own claim one of New England's most successful soul-winners, Stoddard measured his ministerial experience to find the secret to his success. His own personality, he decided, was the key. Not that he attributed any special power to his own efforts—for whatever he possessed was God's—but he had been the agent in the conversion of many souls and, he concluded, whatever he had done must have been right in the sight of God.

The position Stoddard now adopted was not so much new as an elaboration of skeptical ideas presented in *The Safety of Appearing*. The Gospel was the sole means to conversion. Before conversion, however, every sinner underwent preparatory work, though that work had no saving power in itself. Preparatory work proceeded in two stages: humiliation and contrition; and its progress was aided by the ordinances of the church: baptism, preaching, the Word, communion, and the like.[22]

His new evangelicalism was patterned on this outline, though in a considerably modified form. Searching his own experience in Northampton, he decided that God most often used the ordinance of preaching as the vehicle for the dispensation of Grace.[23] Thus he concluded that if religion in New England languished, it did so primarily because of the low quality of ministers and their lack of training in the workings of the Spirit, often due to their own unconverted state. Also, it languished because of the pathetic state of preaching and the shortage of many "powerful preachers."[24]

Simply stated, Stoddard's plan involved little more than an attempt to upgrade the quality of ministers by conveying to them what he, in his success, had learned of the true nature of the ministerial function. What he passed on by book and pamphlet between 1713 and 1729 were his secrets. In *A Guide to Christ* he explained the workings of the Spirit and the "varieties of religious experience," and offered to young clergymen his wisdom and expertise in guiding sinners through preparatory work. In the same work he emphasized the absolute necessity of a converted ministry, arguing that no one could understand another's travail until he had followed the same path. Only six years earlier he had written that a converted ministry was not really necessary to God's work.[25]

In the writings of his last years, Stoddard developed his conception of "powerful preaching," including the proper use of emotionalism and the fear of damnation. He stressed constantly the correct manner of preaching—his manner—as well as the successful combination of preaching and Word which had wrought so many conversions in Northampton. The Gospel, while the only means of conversion, seemed most efficacious in the hands of the experienced and converted minister of the Lord who developed its truths in the manner used by Stoddard. Such a message was not novel in New England, for it invoked images of Shepard and Hooker, as well as an earlier Stoddard.[26] Yet for the aged warrior it represented a breakthrough, for it suggested a tactic that would simultaneously reach the unconverted, raise the level of ministerial importance by making clergy so vital in conversion, and provide a lever to unhinge the "power of the fraternity" and diminish the importance of church discipline in the minds of both clergy and laity.

Meanwhile, other Connecticut and Connecticut Valley clergymen began to share Stoddard's contempt for ecclesiastical discipline and synodical decisions. As their writings suggest, they flocked to his new plan. The Word was the only source of salvation, and it was most efficacious when applied by the "powerful preacher." The ministry must be upgraded, not by formal education but through experience of the workings of the Spirit and practice on guiding souls through preparation. Suddenly, as never before, ministerial writings discovered St. Paul as the archetype of the powerful preacher and agent of conversion. He was described as an itinerant evangelist, dispensing the Word and bringing souls to Christ. Paul had argued, the evangelicals believed, that there were two principal ingredients in conversion, minister and Word. Properly handled, they were devastating.[27]

As Stoddard hoped, the Connecticut evangelicals' emphasis upon gospel preaching led them to open hostility toward Congregational discipline. Their intent was to create a Great Awakening, and to facilitate its coming, they advocated an itinerant, evangelical ministry. The realization of that ideal began haltingly in efforts like Stoddard's Hampshire Association's establishment of weekly public lectures around 1712 in which members exchanged pulpits and gave reforming sermons designed to stimulate religious revivals.[28] In the 1720's the practice became more informal and subject to abuse by laymen who traveled about posing as trained clergy. Ultimately, of course, the trend toward an itinerant ministry would find fruition in the career of George Whitefield.

Evangelicalism also scuttled the clergy's campaign for sacramentally induced piety, thus satisfying another of Stoddard's intentions. Zeal for gospel preaching minimized the importance or efficacy of the sacraments and the decades-old campaign to buttress the institutional church while elevating ministerial importance suffered irreparable harm. Stoddard argued that, like his Instituted Church, it had only nurtured the power of the fraternity. Evengelicals agreed, and by 1718 controversy over the sacraments ceased. Soon, interest in communion manuals began to lag as well.[29]

Evangelicals continually looked for signs of an "Awakening." In the 1720's revivals and mass conversions or, in the ministerial rhetoric, great "outpourings of the Spirit" appeared frequently. In 1721, for example, Eliphalet Adams of New London traveled to Windham, Connecticut, to mark a revival in that community and praise the minister whose preaching had brought it about. He told a throng that revivals, although still widely scattered, were no longer uncommon and a "great Awakening" appeared imminent.[30]

Adams was correct, of course, though it is doubtful that the results were those intended or expected by the clergy. In Norwich, for example, evangelicalism only added fuel to the deep seated personal and institutional antagonisms already present in church and community, especially those between church and minister, church and town, and brethren and brethren. Instead of reviving religion and restoring ministerial authority, revivalism in Norwich resulted in the destruction of the church.[31] In Northampton where Stoddard's grandson and successor, Jonathan Edwards, gave revivalism an intellectual justification far superior even to Stoddard's, Edwards' reward was exile to missionary work among the Indians.

The pattern in Norwich and Northampton was the pattern of the Great Awakening in Connecticut and the Connecticut Valley.[32] Lay Congregationalism, the institutional cement of many churches, cracked, though the result was not so much heightened religiosity as social and ecclesiastical chaos. A plethora of new sects emerged, and anticlericalism remained, as did the trend toward secularism or "worldliness." Moreover, the fragmenting effects of the Awakening appeared in secular institutions, disrupting traditional patterns of authority, weakening institutional relationships and, some have argued, creating fertile ground for a revolutionary mentality.

For churchmen, both lay and clerical, it meant another ecclesiastical revolution. The unity of the clergy disappeared in the battles of old lights and new lights. The lay reformation ended in a nightmare of intramural squabbles, schisms, and separations. The power of the fraternity and its covenant crumbled, as did its ability to dictate either the goals of the church or the behavior of the community. The search for the moral community collapsed in renewed frenzy for spiritual rebirth. Dissenters demanded an immediate wedge between the church and the world, regenerate and unregenerate. Revivalism spawned a renewal of the sectarian/antisectarian arguments of the founders. Connecticut's Puritans continued to mouth the values of the past—order, harmony, consensus, communal perfection—but the Awakening left the gap between rhetoric and reality wider than ever before.

CONCLUSION

AN examination of the character of eighteenth-century society in Connecticut and the Connecticut Valley is beyond the scope of this essay. Many historians agree, however, with Richard Bushman's thoughtful analysis of Connecticut life on the eve of the American Revolution. While noting the continuing influence of Puritanism upon Connecticut society, he writes that "perceptive leaders" were searching for new ideals and institutions to fit a society becoming more "open and heterogeneous." "By the eve of the Revolution," he continues, "Connecticut was moving toward a new social order, toward the republican pluralism of the nineteenth century."[1] The "new social order" released the ambitions and desires of the individual in politics, religion, and economic activity. It produced a "flowering of individualism" in the nineteenth century, "a magnificent display of economic and artistic virtuosity."[2] How did it all come about? Repeating some cherished assumptions about society in seventeenth-century New England, Bushman suggests that the desires of individuals were held in check by a "close-knit, tightly controlled, homogeneous" Puritan social order rooted in the founders' piety. That social order eventually collapsed before the onslaught of the combined forces of economic ambition and religious dissension in the eighteenth century.[3]

The portrait of a monolithic, "close-knit, tightly controlled," communally-oriented Puritan social order in Connecticut and the Connecticut Valley in the seventeenth century reflects myth more than fact. Its terminology describes some Puritan values but not Puritan behavior. The institutional order in the Valley grew out of the conflict of ideas, not consensus. Ideological conflict, in turn, bred social and ecclesiastical disorder, not communal harmony. As a consequence, the economic ambition and religious dissension that Bushman discovers in eighteenth-century Connecticut did not undermine Puritan social order so much as it indicated its continuing weakness. Dissension was a bitter fact of life in the seventeenth century, and the more Valley Puritans sought to control it, the more they fostered ideological conflict and widened the gap between ideals and behavior.

The evolution of the Valley's church system reflected a continuing search for mastery as well as a series of failures. The Puritans who settled Connecticut and the Connecticut Valley hoped that their "congregational" churches would provide the moral basis for an ordered, harmonious, tightly structured, communally oriented society. But the churchmen possessed no single vision as to how that would be done. Their problems were immense. They rejected a church encompassing all—though most of the first churches included nearly everyone—just as they questioned a church encompassing only a few. Most sought a middle way, a church system composed of the visibly elect which would stay abreast of the growth of the community. But they could not agree on the configuration of such a system. They had similar difficulties determining the proper locus of ecclesiastical authority. Their theories intimated that ultimate sovereignty lay with the brethren, but tradition combined with reverence for particular clergymen to give the ministry control over the church apparatus.

The ministers searched for a common definition of the function and order of the church, but they failed to find one, ultimately dividing into factions supporting one solution or another. They urged new and often conflicting innovations upon the brethren. The brethren resisted, and the churches lapsed into decades of bitterness and rancor. Dissension spread, engulfing the colony. When it subsided, ruling authority in the churches had passed to the brethren, and an awesome gulf separated ministers from the new "power of the fraternity." The search for a single definition of church order produced a surprising result.

After 1670 laymen and clergy linked their heritage of ecclesiastical dissension to new perceptions of a deteriorating moral order and a society near collapse. Their shared analysis of society's ills produced a common obsession for reformation and social salvation. At the same time, historical antipathy toward each other led them to adopt conflicting means and ends and to work at cross-purposes. The clergy sought spiritual awakening, while the brethren demanded conformity to universal and clearly-defined standards of behavior. Both sought to make the church system the mechanism for a new moral order. As a consequence, zeal for reformation led them into a new struggle for control of the church system. The result was another round of dissension, one that led directly to the theological assumptions and the social and ecclesiastical chaos of the Great Awakening.

Throughout a century of discord the churches of the Connecticut Valley showed the effects of dissension. Internally unstable, the church system changed often as it bent before the onslaught of forces from within and without. Overall, the influence of the churches in the towns gradually deteriorated as decades passed, despite the apparent success of lay Congregationalism. From a church system serving all or most of the inhabitants it evolved into one serving only a fraction of the populace in the early eighteenth century. An explanation for that deterioration lay embedded in the confused thinking of the churchmen and the behavior it spawned. Unable to find a common definition of church order and plagued by a continuing struggle for control of church government, the Puritans made dissension a way of life.

The cycle of internal disharmony and social change that engulfed Puritan English colonists in the first century of settlement in the Connecticut Valley indicates the fallacy of our long-cherished assumption that society in eighteenth-century New England grew, Phoenix-like, from the ashes of a Puritan social order. Cut off from the institutional sanctions of England, the legacy of those early Puritans was one of drift, dissension, and institutional instability. A frenetic, confused search for ideological consensus and conformity between values and behavior left an institutional order weakened by dispute and torn by a growing argument over the locus of authority in church and society. A century of discord suggests that the Puritan's search for one kind of social order created the values and institutional apparatus for quite another.

BIBLIOGRAPHICAL ESSAY

A search of secondary material is likely to be a frustrating experience for anyone interested in the history of Connecticut and the Connecticut Valley in the seventeenth century. Despite sizable manuscript collections in the Connecticut Historical Society, the Connecticut State Library, and the Massachusetts Historical Society, modern scholarship has virtually ignored Connecticut in favor of meticulous analysis of intellectual and institutional developments in neighboring Massachusetts. Many of these studies provide valuable insights into the history of the Connecticut Valley. I have been influenced by the research and the conclusions of the "town" studies, especially Sumner Powell's *Puritan Village: The Formation of a New England Town* (Middletown, Conn., 1963); Darrett B. Rutman, *Winthrop's Boston: Portrait of a Puritan Town* (Chapel Hill, N.C., 1965); Kenneth A. Lockridge, *A New England Town: The First Hundred Years* (New York, 1970); and Michael Zuckerman, *Peaceable Kingdoms: New England Towns in the Eighteenth Century* (New York: 1970).

Massachusetts-oriented studies of New England Puritanism and the New England "mind" have been helpful as well. The list of these books has grown very long, but I would be remiss if I did not mention a few that influenced my thinking. Among the most important are Perry Miller's *The New England Mind: The Seven-*

teenth Century (Cambridge, Mass., 1939), and *The New England Mind: From Colony to Province* (Cambridge, Mass., 1953); Edmund S. Morgan, *Visible Saints: The History of a Puritan Idea* (New York, 1963); Perry Miller, *Orthodoxy in Massachusetts, 1630–1650* (Boston, 1933); Darrett B. Rutman, *American Puritanism: Faith and Practice* (New York, 1970); Robert Middlekauff, *The Mathers: Three Generations of Puritan Intellectuals, 1596–1728* (New York, 1971); Larzer Ziff, *Puritanism in America: New Culture in a New World* (New York, 1973); and, especially, David D. Hall, *The Faithful Shepherd: A History of the New England Ministry in the Seventeenth Century* (Chapel Hill, N.C., 1972). Institutional histories similar to the author's are surprisingly few, but one, Robert G. Pope's *The Half-Way Covenant: Church Membership in Puritan New England* (Princeton, N.J., 1969), has been important because of its lengthy discussion of Connecticut and Connecticut Valley churches in the seventeenth century.

No student of early New England religion and culture can proceed without considerable familiarity with the historiography of Tudor and Stuart England. Again the bibliography is large, but some books have been especially helpful for this study, chief among them Patrick Collinson, *The Elizabethan Puritan Movement* (Berkeley and Los Angeles, 1967). Others are William Haller, *The Rise of Puritanism* (New York, 1938); Alan Simpson, *Puritanism in Old and New England* (Chicago, 1955); Charles H. and Katherine George, *The Protestant Mind of the English Reformation, 1570–1640* (Princeton, N.J., 1961); Geoffrey Nuttall, *Visible Saints: The Congregational Way, 1640–1660* (London, 1957); C. G. Bolam, *et al.*, *The English Presbyterians from Elizabethan Puritanism to Modern Unitarianism* (London, 1968); John F. H. New, *Anglican and Puritan: The Basis of their Opposition, 1558–1640* (Stanford, Cal., 1964); David Little, *Religion, Order, and Law: A Study in Pre-Revolutionary England* (New York, 1969); Michael Walzer, *The Revolution of the Saints: A Study in the Origins of Radical Politics* (Cambridge, Mass., 1965), and the early chapters of Hall's *Faithful Shepherd*.

For Connecticut and the Connecticut Valley in the seventeenth century I have used Mary Jeanne Anderson Jones, *Congregational Commonwealth: Connecticut, 1636–1662* (Middletown, Conn., 1968); Albert Van Dusen, *Connecticut* (New York, 1961); Richard S. Dunn, *Puritans and Yankees: The Winthrop Dynasty of New England, 1630–1717* (Princeton, N.J., 1962); Robert C. Black III, *The Younger John Winthrop* (New York, 1966); and Richard Bushman, *From Puritan to Yankee: Character and the Social Order in Connecticut, 1690–1765* (New York, 1967). Bushman's study includes an excellent bibliography of printed and manuscript sources, as well as secondary accounts, which should be used to supplement my own highly selective survey.

Much of the best writing on early Connecticut is still to be found in the scattered products of another age. Of these, I have relied upon M. Louise Greene, *The Development of Religious Liberty in Connecticut* (Boston, 1905); Joseph B. Felt, *The Ecclesiastical History of New England* (2 vols., Boston, 1855, 1862); Benjamin Trumbull, *A Complete History of Connecticut Civil and Ecclesiastical . . .* (2nd ed., 2 vols., New London, Conn., 1898); and Williston Walker, *Creeds and Platforms of Congregationalism* (2nd ed., Boston, 1960). The latter three works are as much primary as secondary sources. Felt and Trumbull, especially, contain evidence no longer available to the scholar in manuscript form. Finally, any student of early Connecticut should consult the pamphlets published in the 1930s by the Tercentenary Commission of the State of Connecticut.

Despite the paucity of modern literature on early Connecticut, a rich vein of material awaits the student sufficiently motivated to invest considerable time and energy perusing the products of nineteenth-century antiquarianism, the New England local history. Though varying markedly in quality of analysis and in scholarly apparatus, the local histories of Valley towns and churches, written primarily between 1850 and 1900, provide much of the raw data for the Valley's history in the seventeenth century. Even the best of them, however, must be used carefully, for interpretation was influenced often by filial piety and partisan local issues, many of which originated in the colonial period. Despite these problems, local histories are essential to modern research, for two reasons. First, historians like James Trumbull or Henry Stiles often had access to documents no longer available; hence their accounts of many events and their descriptions of some ancient documents are akin to primary evidence. Second, most of the local historians printed fragments or whole sections from old church and town records, letters, diaries, journals, commonplace books, and legal records, as well as statistics regarding births, deaths, population, land acquisition, emigration and immigration, church membership, and social and economic class structure based on church records, tax records, wills, deeds, and other types of public and private documents. Many of those documents are now missing. In one town history, for example, *The History of Northampton* (2 vols., Northampton, Mass., 1898), James Trumbull inserted without comment fragments of town records into his narrative. Many of the early records of the town (1654–1700) have since vanished but much can be learned simply by studying Trumbull's fragments.

Among the town and church histories, several deserve particular mention. Trumbull's *History of Northampton* is excellent. Henry R. Stiles, *The History of Ancient Windsor* (New York, 1859), and Frances M. Caulkins, *History of New London* (New London, 1895), are the most scholarly of all the local histories, excelling in the lucidity and perceptiveness of their analyses and also containing long excerpts from local records. Bernard Steiner's *A History of the Plantation of Menunkatuck and the Original Town of Guilford, Connecticut* (Baltimore, 1897) and Ralph Smith's *History of Guilford, Connecticut, from its First Settlement in 1639* (Albany, 1877) are uneven in quality but contain extensive accounts of the early years of that important community. Sherman W. Adams and Henry R. Stiles, *The History of Ancient Wethersfield* (2 vols., Wethersfield, 1904) is inferior to Stiles's portrayal of Windsor but contains much ecclesiastical material. The opposite is true of J. Hammond Trumbull's monumental *Memorial History of Hartford County, 1633–1884* (2 vols., Boston, 1886), which is short on ecclesiastical material but rich in needed supplementary data on early Hartford. Finally, among histories of particular churches, none reaches the plateau of excellence and utility occupied by George L. Walker's *History of the First Church in Hartford, 1633–1883* (Hartford, 1884), which skillfully blends the facts of Hartford First's development with a more than adequate narrative of Connecticut's ecclesiastical history in the seventeenth century. Of all the local historians Walker, Stiles, and Caulkins stand out by virtue of their grasp not only of the significance of local events but also in their general understanding of the history of New England. As a result, their analyses are of infinitely more value than those of any other students of Valley history except Benjamin Trumbull and Sylvester Judd of Hadley, Massachusetts. Judd deserves special mention, not only for his *History of Hadley* (Springfield, 1905), but also for his magnificent collection of copied records (54 volumes), which are now the property of the Forbes Library, Northampton. The Judd manuscript, though weak on ecclesiastical material, is a vast collection of miscellaneous records relating to the history of the upper Valley in the colonial period. Judd spent the last twenty years of his life meticulously copying documents, and his Manuscript is the point of departure for any study of early western Massachusetts.

Much of Connecticut Valley's ecclesiastical history remains buried in the colonial records. Chief among these are the Connecticut colonial church records maintained in manuscript and on microfilm in the Connecticut State Library, Hartford. The complete or partial records of several hundred churches may be found there, with about half pertaining to the colonial period. As might be expected, however, records for the seventeenth century are scant. The Library possesses full or partial records for approximately nineteen churches in that century. These may be augmented by fragments of now nonexistent Connecticut church records to be found in such publications as *The New England Historical and Geneological Register*. The student interested in the church records will note quicky that their compilation tends to follow a pattern. Generally, separate volumes were maintained for baptism and membership lists, cases of discipline, and records of meetings of the membership. Also, some ministers kept their records as personal journals (Stephen Mix, for example).

Understanding the ministerial "mind" of Connecticut and the Connecticut Valley in the seventeenth century is not an easy task. The reasons are several. First, Connecticut had no printing press until the early years of the eighteenth century, and ministers bent on publication had to utilize distant presses in Boston, New York, or, occasionally, London. Second, there are no large manuscript collections relating to particular Valley ministers. To find the requisite letters, diaries, etc. needed for an intellectual and institutional portrait of the collective ministry requires a great deal of time spent perusing unlikely collections. I did, however, discover several valuable documents buried in the Miscellaneous Bound Manuscripts of the Massachusetts Historical Society and made similar findings in the miscellaneous collections of the Connecticut State Library and the Connecticut Historical Society. Another significant collection of documents pertaining, in part, to Valley clergy is in the Gratz Collection, Historical Society of Pennsylvania, Philadelphia, under the heading "American Colonial Clergy." Also helpful, especially for the eighteenth century, are the Curwin Papers in the American Antiquarian Society, Worcester, Massachusetts. This collection includes many letters to and from various ministers in the Connecticut Valley of western Massachusetts.

Much can be ascertained about the thoughts and actions of the Valley clergy through local histories and printed documents. Of the latter several deserve special mention. The Massachusetts Historical Society's *Collections* are standard for any study of New England. Particularly helpful for the Valley ministry are the Winthrop Papers (especially series 4, Vols. 6 and 7) and the Mather Papers (series 4, Vol. 8). The *Collections* of the Connecticut Historical Society are equally useful, and the interested student is directed especially to the Wyllys Papers (Vol. 21) and the Hoadly

Memorial (Vol. 24). Much documentary material may be found in Trumbull's *History of Connecticut* and Felt's *Ecclesiastical History of New England*. Finally, the reader is directed to the published writings of the ministers themselves. I have used James Hammond Trumbull's *List of Books Printed in Connecticut, 1709–1800* (n.p., 1904) supplemented by Charles Evans' *American Bibliography* (14 vols., Chicago, 1903–59) and a lengthy search through the excellent pamphlet collection of the Connecticut Historical Society. The result is a list of approximately one hundred titles by Valley ministers between 1670 and 1730 (almost nothing was published by Valley clergy before 1670). Most of these are to be found among the American Antiquarian Society's microcard reproductions of the titles on Evans' list. Many of the titles not found in Evans may be found in the Connecticut Historical Society.

For the story of the Valley brethren the reader is directed to the town histories and the manuscript church records. However, I relied heavily on the local histories and published records for much of the material on church order to be found in the early chapters of this book. Special mention must be made of the lengthy Records of the Hartford Controversy contained in Vol. 2 of the *Collections* of the Connecticut Historical Society. For the later chapters I relied extensively on the church records supplemented by printed records like the *Historical Catalogue of the First Church in Hartford, 1633–1885* (Hartford, 1885), the Connecticut Historical Society's *Some Early Records and Documents Relating to the Town of Windsor, Connecticut, 1639–1703* (Hartford, 1930), and *The Records of the Congregational Church in Suffield, Connecticut, 1710–1836* (Hartford, 1941).

Finally, much of the story of the ecclesiastical development of the Connecticut Valley is to be found in the public records of both Connecticut and Massachusetts. The Ecclesiastical Manuscripts in the Massachusetts Archives, Boston, are very helpful for western Massachusetts and are available to the distant scholar on microfilm. The Ecclesiastical Manuscripts in the Connecticut Archives are necessary for any study of early Connecticut and are made doubly useful by the detailed index compiled by Hadley's Sylvester Judd. Equally important are *The Public Records of the Colony of Connecticut, 1636–1776*, Vols. 1-3, ed. J. H. Trumbull; and Vols. 4-15, ed. C. J. Hoadly (15 vols., Hartford, 1850–1890).

NOTES

PREFACE

1. Michael Zuckerman, *Peaceable Kingdoms: New England Towns in the Eighteenth Century* (New York, 1970). I have used the 1972 Vintage paperback edition.

2. The literature of consensus is vast, although some of the most provocative arguments are quite new. The reader should begin with Perry Miller's two-volume *New England Mind* (New York, 1939, and Cambridge, Mass., 1953) and go on to Darrett Rutman, *American Puritanism: Faith and Practice* (New York, 1970); Kenneth Lockridge, *A New England Town: The First Hundred Years* (New York, 1970); John Demos, *A Little Commonwealth: Family Life in Plymouth Colony* (New York, 1970; I have used the 1971 Oxford paperback edition); Phillip J. Greven, *Four Generations: Population, Land, and Family in Colonial Andover, Massachusetts* (Ithaca, N. Y., 1970); and Zuckerman's *Peaceable Kingdoms*. Some of these writers may resist my loose categorization of such a diverse and sophisticated literature. This is especially true of those who have attacked Miller's alleged "monolithic" analysis of New England society and the tendency of his disciples to attribute everything in New England to a common source, Puritanism. Some revisionists have gone so far as to describe New England society without reference to Puritanism. Others—myself included—have attempted to question Miller's colossus by rewriting minor themes.

Still, revisionism has tended to replace one monolith with another. The decline of "Puritan" as a descriptive adjective has coincided with an increasing fascination for interdisciplinary analyses. The disciplines chosen, especially anthropology and sociology, offer fascinating insights into well-known evidence, but they do so through a functionalist methodology which stresses continuity over change. Change, the historian's traditional preoccupation, does not lend itself well to such undertakings and is usually tacked on as an afterthought, often in the form of cataclysmic developments similiar to those once held responsible for the decline of the "New England Way." My assumption is that change and continuity were subtly entwined throughout New England's history, and I have tried to cast my book in that mold.

3. The standard work remains Miller's *New England Mind*, although the reader is urged to consult David Hall's *The Faithful Shepherd: A History of the New England Ministry* (Chapel Hill, N.C., 1972).

4. See, for example, Lockridge's *A New England Town*.

5. Until recently the term "yankee New England" conjured up visions of a bustling, commercial society marked by social and economic mobility and rampant individualism. It represented a transitional stage in the process of Americanization, separating the Puritan seventeenth century from the democratic nineteenth. See, for example, Richard Bushman's *From Puritan to Yankee: Character and the Social Order in Connecticut, 1690–1765* (New York, 1967; I have used the 1970 Norton paperback edition). But the whole notion of early America's "uniqueness" is under new and careful scrutiny and, consequently, the Puritan-to-Yankee-to-democracy theme has garnered considerable criticism. Zuckerman, for example, argues that communal instincts were as important in the eighteenth as the seventeenth, although he notes that the Puritan's consensus stemmed from shared convictions while that of their descendants came more from compromise (*Peaceable Kingdoms*, p. 7). From another vantage point Lockridge, among others, argues persuasively for consideration of America as an extension, not a violation, of evolutionary patterns common to England and western Europe. He argues that eighteenth-century America moved closer to the stratification and diversification of English society in the same period. By 1750, England and her American colonies were developing along parallel lines (see Lockridge, *A New England Town*, chap. 9).

6. The literature is familiar to every student of the period. See, for example, Brooks Adams, *The Emancipation of Massachusetts* (Boston and New York, 1887); James Truslow Adams, *The Founding of New England* (Boston, 1921); Vol. I of Vernon Louis Parrington, *Main Currents in American Thought* (New York, 1927); and the more

subtle arguments of Charles M. Andrews, *The Colonial Period of American History* (4 vols., New Haven, 1934-38).

7. It is often argued that some of these writers were guilty of bias, occasional distortion, and shaping evidence to fit presuppositions. It is not my intent to defend their integrity. Rather, I seek to revive a theme that grew from their evidence—conflicting ideals and dissension over the locus of authority in church and society. Contemporary writers have not disproved the older arguments as much as they have made them either inconsequential or irrelevant. The Antinomian controversy, Roger Williams' banishment, the battles between deputies and magistrates in Massachusetts—incidents that allowed Adams and others to make exaggerated claims for nascent democracy or libertarianism—have been labeled minor ripples on an otherwise tranquil sea by modern writers. Perhaps that is so, but early Connecticut was full of similar ripples which, when viewed collectively, made a very large wave.

8. Documented in Michael McGiffert's "American Puritan Studies in the 1960s," *William and Mary Quarterly*, 3rd ser., 27 (1970), 36–67.

INTRODUCTION

1. Albert E. Van Dusen, *Connecticut* (New York, 1961), pp. 19–20.

2. A brief but readable summary of Connecticut's growth may be found in Dorothy Deming, *The Settlement of the Connecticut Towns*, Publications of the Tercentenary Commission of the State of Connecticut, 6 (New Haven, Conn., 1933); see also Rising Lake Morrow, *Connecticut Influences in Western Massachusetts and Vermont*, Publications of the Tercentenary Commission of the State of Connecticut, Vol. 58 (New Haven, Conn., 1936).

3. Van Dusen, *Connecticut*, pp. 42–43, 61. It is almost commonplace to assert that no period of American history has received the attention lavished on early New England. Some scholars view this development with pride. Writing in 1966, Edmund Morgan concluded that "the historiography of early New England has reached in the past forty years a level of sophistication unmatched in the study of any other part of American history." "The Historians of Early New England," in Ray Allen Billington, ed., *The Reinterpretation of Early American History: Essays in Honor of John Edwin Pomfret* (San Marino, Calif., 1966), p. 41. To others it is a burden. Zuckerman feels that current scholarship is counterproductive, going over and over the same mater-

ial, always viewing the colonies as though they existed in a cultural vacuum. He admits a high degree of sophistication in New England studies, but urges us to compare our findings to other cultures; to "become anthropologists, social psychologists, and comparative historians" or "we will never know the significance of what we know." "Michael Zuckerman's Reply," *William and Mary Quarterly*, 3rd ser., 24 (1972), 467–468.

"What we know" about seventeenth century Connecticut—a rather significant part of early New England—is very little. General studies are few, monographs are practically nonexistent. Most of the material for the first half of this introductory chapter came from four works, which comprise much of our knowledge of this important colony. I have used Benjamin Trumbull's, *History of Connecticut* (2 vols., New London, 1898), still the most complete general study; Van Dusen's *Connecticut*, the best modern treatment; Mary Jeanne Anderson Jones, *Congregational Commonwealth: Connecticut, 1636–1662* (Middletown, Conn., 1968), the only recent monograph on the early period; and early chapters of Bushman's *Puritan to Yankee*. There are other works dealing with segments of early Connecticut's history—the Tercentenary pamphlets, Richard Dunn's *Puritans and Yankees: The Winthrop Dynasty of New England* (Princeton, N.J., 1962), and several volumes dealing with Phillip's war or the New England frontier— but the sum total of this scholarship is not great. In addition, students may find considerable Connecticut material in books dealing with Massachusetts' topics and evidence. These usually consider Connecticut data as illustrative of conclusions based on Massachusetts sources, and I have found them to be of dubious value. If one is inclined to view Connecticut only as an extension of the Bay, we probably do know enough already, but if one adopts the view that Connecticut may have possessed a geographic, political, social, intellectual, or economic integrity of its own—certainly the view of its first inhabitants— its history remains obscured.

4. Population estimates are from Evarts B. Greene and Virginia D. Harrington, *American Population before the Federal Census of 1790* (New York, 1932), pp. 12–61. Secondary material on early Connecticut's economic life is scanty, but what there is indicates an economy near the subsistence level (the major exception being an early surplus of corn). See, for example, Bushman, *Puritan to Yankee*, pp. 26–31; Van Dusen, *Connecticut*, pp. 60–62; 83–84; Charles Andrews, *The Beginnings of Connecticut, 1632–1662*, Publications of the Tercentenary

Commission of the State of Connecticut, 32 (New Haven, Conn., 1934), pp. 64–68. Massachusetts' early and spectacular agricultural development is assessed in Darrett Rutman's "Governor Winthrop's Garden Crop: The Significance of Agriculture in the Early Commerce of Massachusetts Bay," *William and Mary Quarterly*, 3rd ser., 2 (1963), 396–415.

5. *The Public Records of the Colony of Connecticut, 1636–1776:* Vols. 1–3, ed. J. H. Trumbull; Vols 4–15, ed. C. J. Hoadly (15 vols., Hartford, 1850–1890), 3: 294–301. Hereafter cited as *Connecticut Court Records.*

6. Bushman, *Puritan to Yankee*, chap. 2. His conclusions are echoed in Jones, *Congregational Commonwealth*, pp. 110–113, 154–156; and Van Dusen, *Connecticut*, pp. 59–62, 111–112.

7. Van Dusen, *Connecticut*, p. 112. Bushman notes that additional land could be attained through periodic divisions of the common land by the town. He also points out, however, that such grants depended upon an individual's willingness to abide by the dictates of the community, a stifling prospect for the would-be entrepreneur (*Puritan to Yankee*, pp. 34–35); Jones, *Congregational Commonwealth*, pp. 138–142. Anyone interested in town planning is invited to consult Anthony N. B. Garvan, *Architecture and Town Planning in Colonial Connecticut* (New Haven, Conn., 1951).

8. Bushman, *Puritan to Yankee*, p. 30; Van Dusen, *Connecticut*, p. 60; Roland Mather Hooker, *The Colonial Trade of Connecticut*, Publications of the Tercentenary Commission of the State of Connecticut, Vol. 50 (New Haven, 1936), 14. See also Henry Bronson, "A Historical Account of Connecticut Currency, Continental Money, and the Finances of the Revolution," *Papers of the New Haven Colony Historical Society*, 1 (1865), 171 ff.

9. Hartford's failure in this regard is implicit in the Report of 1680. New London was the colony's principal port and commercial center, but it was unable to challenge Boston. Connecticut's officials tended to relate New London's inadequacies to imperial regulations (*Connecticut Court Records*, 3: 301).

10. Bushman, *Puritan to Yankee*, p. 83. Dorothy Deming's pamphlet on the settlement of the Connecticut towns (Tercentenary pamphlets, Vol. 6) briefly reviews the settlement of each town in the seventeenth century. Incidences of flooding, and other natural disasters, were usually recorded in the colonial records.

11. The preceding discussion of Connecticut's economic boom in the

late seventeenth and early eighteenth centuries is based on Richard Bushman's excellent analysis in Parts II and III of *Puritan to Yankee* (see esp., chaps 3, 5, 7, and 8, and pp. 83–86).

12. Van Dusen, *Connecticut*, pp. 19–23; a more extensive discussion may be found in Andrews, *Beginnings of Connecticut*, pp. 1–18, 32–37.

13. Van Dusen, *Connecticut*, pp. 41–43. The significance of the Fundamental Orders has been debated for centuries. From Benjamin Trumbull's late eighteenth-century perspective, it looked like a precursor of the Declaration of Independence. "Thus happily did they [the inhabitants of Connecticut] guard against every encroachment on the rights of the subject," he wrote. "This, probably, is one of the most free and happy constitutions of civil government which has ever been formed. The formation of it, at so early a period, when the light of liberty was wholly darkened in most parts of the earth, and the rights of men were so little understood in others, does great honor to their ability, integrity, and love to mankind" (*History of Connecticut*, 1: 77). To the modern scholar it is no longer the fount of democratic liberalism, but its significance continues to be debated. Mary Jones's *Congregational Commonwealth* is oriented, primarily, toward the origins and significance of the Orders. Her argument is that the document was an expression of a Congregationalist/Puritan mentality; hence it was unique. "The fathers of Connecticut," she writes, "combined the traditions they had known in the towns and villages of England with their experience in New England, first in Massachusetts Bay and then on the Connecticut River from 1633 until 1639, with a determination to move away from their past and improve on it by substituting more expedient practices for archaic forms in order that their state might conform more exactly to an ideal Congregational community" (pp. 61–62). She assumes that Puritanism molded their thoughts on politics, society, and religion into a single "mind" which produced congregational churches and a congregational commonwealth. Albert Van Dusen simply notes that Connecticut's infant government bore a striking resemblance to that of neighboring Massachusetts. He argues that the Orders grew from a real need for a "more formal statement of Fundamental Law" (p. 41) and that the colonists looked to Massachusetts for an example. He does not attribute governmental principles to the colonists' Puritanism.

14. The political problems of securing a charter and the events leading to King Phillip's War are covered adequately in Trumbull, *Connecticut*, 1, chaps. 12 and 14; the best account of King Phillip's War is to be found in Douglas Leach, *Flintlock and Tomahawk: New*

England in King Phillip's War (New York, 1958); a short but useful discussion is contained in Wesley Frank Craven, *The Colonies in Transition, 1660–1713* (New York, 1968), chap. 4 (see pp. 118–124).

15. Leach, *Flintlock and Tomahawk*, pp. 59–60; Van Dusen, *Connecticut*, p. 89.

16. The preceding discussion is based on the account provided in Bushman, *Puritan to Yankee*, chap. 6.

17. See chaps. 1 and 3. Few historians have succeeded in conveying the imprecision or changing character of these terms in their seventeenth-century context. Most are eager to provide lengthy and precise definitions to simplify and clarify their arguments. In so doing, however, they create endless confusion by trying to give form to the formless. They often argue over terms which are their own, terms which have little meaning for either the period, the men, or the issues under consideration. I have tried to avoid this problem, in part at least, by using the labels and definitions of the seventeenth century. This may create some confusion for the reader because labels were never precise, and definitions changed considerably over time. Since the actors themselves spent considerable time arguing over who or what was a Congregationalist or a Presbyterian, however, I can only conclude that some confusion is unavoidable in conveying the ambiguities of seventeenth-century ecclesiastical thought.

18. Mainly because of the influence of Perry Miller's *Orthodoxy in Massachusetts, 1630–1650* (Cambridge, Mass., 1933), and his subsequent two-volume study of the New England mind, a generation of students of New England Congregationalism believed it to be a natural and consistent offspring of a unified Puritan mentality. They believed, also, that its intricacies were worked out in careful detail in England and on the Continent, then assembled in America as "The New England Way" of church government. Since Edmund Morgan's brilliant *Visible Saints: The History of a Puritan Idea* (New York, 1963), scholars have reassessed both the origins and the character of the Puritan "mind." For the most part they have dismissed the notion that the term "Puritan" referred to a single cluster of ideas or that all New Englanders shared the same thoughts. Moreover, they have shown that many of the distinguishing ecclesiastical practices and theological arguments of the New England Way were products of the colonial experience.

An early and perceptive critic of the Miller approach to the Puritan mind and New England society was Clifford Shipton. In a series of articles he argued against the notion of "orthodoxy" in thought or practice (see, for example, his "Locus of Authority in Colonial Massachusetts," in George Billias, ed., *Law and Authority in Colonial America* (Barre, Mass., 1965). Other important revisionist arguments are to be found in Darrett Rutman, *Winthrop's Boston: Portrait of a Puritan Town, 1630–1649* (Chapel Hill, N. C., 1965); Norman Pettit, *The Heart Prepared: Grace and Conversion in Puritan Spiritual Life* (New Haven, 1966); Robert Pope, *The Half-Way Covenant: Church Membership in Puritan New England* (Princeton, N. J., 1969); Rutman's *American Puritanism*; Lockridge, *New England Town*; Hall, *Faithful Shepherd*; and Robert Middlekauff, *The Mathers: Three Generations of Puritan Intellectuals, 1596–1728* (New York, 1971). An important article is David Kobrin's "The Expansion of the Visible Church in New England, 1629–1650," *Church History*, 36 (1967), 189–209.

19. Hall, *Faithful Shepherd*, chap. 1; John T. McNeill, *The History and Character of Calvinism* (New York, 1954), chap. 13. The Anabaptists discussed here are primarily Spiritualists, as noted by Hall (p. 8) and defined and discussed at length by George H. Williams, ed., *Spiritual and Anabaptist Writers* (London, 1957), pp. 19–38, and his later, exhaustive study, *The Radical Reformation* (Philadelphia, 1962). See also Franklin Littell, *The Anabaptist View of the Church* (Boston, 1958), chap. 1.

20. My understanding of the Elizabethan Puritan movement owes much to Patrick Collinson's *The Elizabethan Puritan Movement* (Berkeley, Calif., 1967), esp. Parts I–IV and VII, as well as such older accounts as William Haller, *The Rise of Puritanism* (New York, 1938), and Marshall Knappen, *Tudor Puritanism* (Chicago, 1939). Also instructive were John F. H. New's *Anglican and Puritan: The Basis of their Opposition, 1558–1640* (Stanford, Calif., 1964), esp. chap. 2; Rutman, *American Puritanism*, chaps. 1–2; and Hall, *Faithful Shepherd*, chap. 2.

21. See Collinson, *Elizabethan Puritan Movement*, Part VIII.

22. Hall, *Faithful Shepherd*, pp. 37–47.

23. The literature on revolutionary England is staggering in both quantity and quality. I have found David Little's *Religion, Order, and Law: A Study in Pre-Revolutionary England* (New York, 1969) a fascinating introduction to the relationship of religion and society in late sixteenth- and early seventeenth-century England. Much the same may be said for Christopher Hill's *Society and Puritanism in Pre-Revolutionary England*, 2nd ed. (New York, 1967), and Michael Walzer's *The Revolution of the Saints: A Study in the Origins of Radical Politics* (Cambridge, Mass., 1965). Equally important for

novice and specialist alike are William Haller, *Liberty and Reformation in the Puritan Revolution* (New York, 1955), and Lawrence Stone, *The Crisis of the Aristocracy, 1558–1641* (New York, 1965). Books useful in distinguishing the ecclesiastical divisions of the Civil War period are Geoffrey Nuttall, *Visible Saints: The Congregational Way, 1640–1660* (Oxford, 1957), and C. G. Bolam, et al., *The English Presbyterians: From Elizabethan Puritanism to Modern Unitarianism* (London, 1968).

24. See Rutman, *American Puritanism*, pp. 26–47.

25. Hall, *Faithful Shepherd*, p. 66.

26. My use of the term "Presbyterian" is conditioned by evidence offered in Bolam, et al., *The English Presbyterians*, esp. chaps. 1 and 2.

1. "THE DISCIPLYNE OF THE CHURCHES," 1636–1650

1. Van Dusen, *Connecticut*, pp. 20–24.

2. Robert Stansby to John Wilson, April 17, 1637, "The Winthrop Papers," Massachusetts Historical Society, *Collections*, 4th ser., 7 (Boston, 1894), 11; Morgan, *Visible Saints*, pp. 105–108; Hall, *Faithful Shepherd*, p. 98.

3. See Van Dusen, *Connecticut*, chaps. 2–4.

4. *Connecticut Court Records*, 1: 21. An extensive discussion of the Fundamental Orders is to be found in Jones, *Congregational Commonwealth*, chap. 3.

5. Thomas Hooker, *A Survey of the Summe of Church-Discipline* (London, 1648), preface.

6. Ibid.

7. Ibid., Part I, p. 3.

8. Ibid., Part I, chap. 2, pp. 14 ff., where visible sainthood is discussed at length.

9. Ibid., preface.

10. Ibid., Part I, p. 191.

11. Ibid.

12. Ibid., p. 192.

13. Ibid., preface.

14. Ibid., Part I, p. 192. The outward and inward calls and their relationship to ordination and election are described and analyzed in Part II, chap. 2.

15. See Hall, *Faithful Shepherd*, pp. 48–66.

16. There is no modern biography of Hooker. Students of his career

in England, the Netherlands, and New England will find useful information in George L. Walker, *Thomas Hooker, Preacher, Founder, Democrat* (New York, 1891); Warren Archibald, *Thomas Hooker*, Publications of the Tercentenary Commission of the State of Connecticut, 4 (New Haven, 1933); and Perry Miller, "Thomas Hooker and the Democracy of Early Connecticut," *New England Quarterly*, 4 (1931), 663–712.

17. Hooker, *Survey*, Part II, p. 19. See also *The Application of Redemption By the Effectual Work of the Word, and Spirit of Christ, for the bringing home of lost sinners to God* (London, 1659), pp. 195–197.

18. In discussing the distinctions between Pastor and Teacher in the church Hooker made it clear that the former worked, primarily, in the greater community, while the latter nurtured the congregation. The teacher "gathers and perfects" the congregation, Hooker wrote. "The aime and scope of the Doctor is, to informe the judgement, and to help forward the work of illumination, in the minde and understanding, and thereby to make way for the truth, that it may be settled and fastened upon the heart" (Part II, p. 21). For the early history of Hartford First Church see George L. Walker, *History of the First Church in Hartford, 1633–1883* (Hartford, 1884).

19. Preparation for salvation is a continuing and dominant theme in Hooker's writings. Some of the more important treatises are *The Application of Redemption* (London, 1659); *The Soules Exaltation* (London, 1638); *The Unbeleevers Preparing for Christ* (London, 1638); and *The Soules Implantation* (London, 1637). The importance of preparation to the maintenance of the church becomes apparent in the *Survey*, especially Part II, pp. 19–20. The development of preparationist attitudes among early New England evangelicals is discussed in Hall, *Faithful Shepherd*, chap. 7, and Pettit, *The Heart Prepared*, chap. 4.

20. Hooker, *Survey*, Part I, chap 2; Part III, pp. 4–6, 14.

21. Ibid., Part III, p. 4.

22. Ibid., Part I, pp. 14–15; Part III, pp. 4–6.

23. Governor George Wyllys to George Wyllys, October 28, 1644, "Wyllys Papers," Connecticut Historical Society, *Collections* (Hartford, 1924), 21: 58.

24. Significantly, Hall finds most of the first-generation clergy of Massachusetts Bay embracing evangelicalism and generally adopting a posture identical to Hooker's. Hall then argues that second- and third-generation clergymen turned away from the prophetic, conversionist,

evangelical ministry of their forebears in favor of a "higher" definition of the ministerial office, one that reflected an awareness of the primacy of the minister's position as head of the institutional church and, especially, as custodian of the sacraments. Hall refers to this evolution as the "Americanization" of the clergymen, arguing that it reflected their response to changing social conditions. See *Faithful Shepherd*, chaps. 7 and 12.

25. The distinctions among Congregationalists discussed in this chapter are based in part on ministerial factions analyzed and labeled by John Woodbridge, minister at Killingworth, in a letter to the English divine, Richard Baxter, dated March 31, 1671. That letter, an earlier one (dated February 3, 1669), and Baxter's replies have been edited and published by Raymond P. Stearns in the *New England Quarterly*, 10 (1937), 557–583. Taken together, the Woodbridge letters reveal a great deal about Connecticut's early ecclesiastical history.

The letters published by Stearns were found among the Baxter papers in Dr. Williams' Library. A second pair of manuscript letters from Woodbridge to Baxter, with identical dates, may be found in the Connecticut State Library, Hartford. I have used the Connecticut letters because they differ in content from the published versions. They are longer and contain material not found in the letters used by Stearns. I can only assume that the Connecticut letters represent drafts that were edited and toned down before going to Baxter.

26. Bernard Steiner, *A History of the Plantation of Menukatuck and the Original Town of Guilford, Conn.* (Baltimore, 1897), pp. 12–15. See also Isabel M. Calder, *The New Haven Colony* (New Haven, 1934, 1962; I have used the 1970 edition, published by Archon Books), pp. 70–73.

27. Steiner, *Guilford*, p. 22.

28. Ibid., p. 35; Ralph D. Smith, *History of Guilford, Connecticut, from its First Settlement in 1639* (Albany, 1877), pp. 56, 151; Calder, *New Haven*, p. 87.

29. Steiner, *Guilford*, pp. 35-36, 39.

30. Ibid., p. 40; Smith, *Guilford*, p. 89; Calder, *New Haven*, pp. 107–108.

31. Steiner, *Guilford*, pp. 75–76; Higginson was no stranger to the Guilford church or community. He had served as "Teacher" under Whitefield (Calder, *New Haven*, p. 87).

32. See Woodbridge to Baxter, March 31, 1671.

33. Jones, *Congregational Commonwealth*, pp. 55–56.

34. Cotton Mather, *Magnalia Christi Americana; or, The Ecclesias-*

tical History of New England (New York, 1967), 1, 434–438. Mather characterized Stone as "both a Load-Stone and a Flint-Stone" (p. 435).

35. Ibid., p. 437. In 1652 Stone published *A Congregational Church is a Catholike Visible Church. Or An Examination of M. Hudson his Vindication concerning the Integrity of the Catholike Visible Church. Wherein also satisfaction is given to what M. Cawdrey writes touching that subject, in his Review of M. Hooker's Survey of Church Discipline* (London, 1652). The book was not a systematic treatise on polity but concerned an argument with Presbyterian Samuel Hudson over whether individual churches, taken together, gave sustenance to the whole. It was not meant to be a blanket endorsement or defense of Hooker's *Survey*.

36. Joseph B. Felt, *The Ecclesiastical History of New England* (2 vols., Boston, 1855–1862), 2:38.

37. Samuel Stone, "Against A Relation of Experience" (n.d.), Notebook of Joseph Gerrish, 1697, Massachusetts Historical Society.

38. Frances M. Caulkins, *History of New London* (New London, Conn., 1895), pp. 111–117, 130–145. Utilizing records no longer available, Caulkins found no evidence of formal church organization before 1670. The earliest ministers, Blynman and Gershom Bulkeley, were not ordained by the church, and the third minister, Simon Bradstreet, was ordained in 1670. Apparently in that same year the church adopted its first "covenant."

39. Ibid., pp. 130–145.

40. Jones, *Congregational Commonwealth*, pp. 13, 28.

41. William B. Sprague, *Annals of the American Pulpit* (9 vols., New York, 1857–1869), 1:11.

42. Walker, *Hartford*, p. 431.

43. Windsor, Connecticut, First Congregational Church Records, Connecticut State Library, Vol. 3, "Creed and Covenant," October 23, 1647; Henry A. Stiles, *The History of Ancient Windsor, Connecticut* (New York, 1859), p. 75. Apparently, Hooker spent more than a decade trying to convert Warham to evangelical Congregationalism. For example, in a notebook kept by one Windsor inhabitant, Henry Walcott, are notes on several of Warham's sermons between 1638 and 1641. They seem to show the Windsor minister moving toward a more restrictive definition of church membership. See Douglas H. Shepard, "The Wolcott Shorthand Notebook Transcribed" (unpublished Ph.D. dissertation, University of Iowa, 1957).

44. Stiles, *Windsor*, pp. 172–175. See also "Matthew Grant's Old Church Record," appended to Stiles, *Windsor*, p. 846.

45. Stiles, *Windsor*, pp. 76, 846; Mather, *Magnalia*, 1: 441-442.

46. "Petition of William Pitkin and others to the General Court, 1664," in Walker, *Hartford*, pp. 195-196. See also John Warham, "On the Form and Matter of a Church" (n.d.), Taylor MS, Prince Collection, Boston Public Library.

47. Felt, *Ecclesiastical History*, 1: 490, 600 ff. Most writers have been aware of the lack of participation by Connecticut's ministry, but they have interpreted collective silence as an indication of consent to the synod's conclusions. Generally, it is argued that Hooker's *Survey* reflected the thinking of the synod and that it spoke for Connecticut's clergy. Recent appraisals of the Cambridge Synod have characterized it as a forum meant to forge a compromise on disputed questions of discipline. Hall argues that the resulting Platform indicated that the clergy was moving away from the evangelicalism of the 1630's toward what he labels "sacerdotalism" (*Faithful Shepherd*, pp. 115–120). The ministers were developing a higher definition of the ministry, one similar to that of Connecticut's moderate Congregationalists. A different interpretation of the synod's origins and significance emerges from Robert E. Wall's *Massachusetts Bay: The Crucial Decade, 1640–1650* (New Haven, Conn., 1972), pp. 225–228.

48. Sherman W. Adams and Henry R. Stiles, *The History of Ancient Wethersfield, Connecticut* (2 vols., New York, 1904), 1: 135–138, 142, 144–145, 148; *Connecticut Court Records*, 1: 87.

49. To be discussed in Chap. 2.

2. CONTENTION AND SEPARATION

1. This chapter and the two following will attempt to analyze the ecclesiastical and nonecclesiastical issues that prompted dissension and strife in early Connecticut between 1650 and 1675. Much of my research centers on the problems of the ten towns included in the General Court's annual "list of persons and estates" before the acquisition of a charter in 1662. The towns were Hartford, Stratford, Windsor, Wethersfield, Farmington, Middletown, Saybrook, Norwalk, Fairfield, and New London (see *Connecticut Court Records*, 1: 373). Nine of the ten experienced serious division between 1650 and 1675. The length of the controversies varied between one to two years and the epic twenty-year struggles of Hartford and Windsor.

Twelve towns were added to the yearly rate between 1662 and 1675. Most were either the towns of old New Haven Colony or those located on Long Island, far from the original river settlements. I have been able to document dissension in several of the newer towns even though the histories of many are obscured by the absence of records. Contemporary accounts, however, make frequent references to disturbances all over Connecticut without citing locations or issues involved. I have included three of the early Massachusetts river towns (Northampton, Hadley, and Springfield). Northampton experienced a long period of dissension. Although the latter two were only brief skirmishes, their growth fits the patterns discerned among the Connecticut towns.

2. Samuel Stone, "Against a Relation of Experience"; Benjamin Trumbull, *A Compleat History of Connecticut; Civil and Ecclesiastical, from the Emigration of its First Planters, from England, in the year 1630, to the year 1674; and to the close of the Indian Wars* (2 vols., New London, 1898), 1: 248-257; Walker, *Hartford*, pp. 150–180.

3. Samuel Stone's "Remonstrance," June 1657, reprinted in Walker, *Hartford*, p. 164; "Records of the Hartford Controversy," Connecticut Historical Society, *Collections* (Hartford, 1870), 2: 70–71; hereafter cited as "Records of the Hartford Controversy."

4. "Records of the Hartford Controversy," pp. 70–71; *Connecticut Court Records*, 1: 3.

5. Testimony of Rev. John Higginson of Guilford before a Council from Massachusetts (n.d., probably 1657), MS, Connecticut Historical Society. "Records of the Hartford Controversy," pp. 94–97.

6. Bay Ministers to the Hartford Church, 1656, "Records of the Hartford Controversy," pp. 59–63; Massachusetts Churches to the Hartford Church, September, 1656, ibid., pp. 64-68.

7. Hartford Dissenters to Massachusetts Churches, March 1657, "Records of the Hartford Controversy," pp. 68–69.

8. "Records of the Hartford Controversy," pp. 83, 94–95; Trumbull, *History of Connecticut*, 1: 248.

9. Samuel Stone to the Hartford Church, May 1657, "Records of the Hartford Controversy," pp. 70–71.

10. "Records of the Hartford Controversy," pp. 73-75; Walker, *Hartford*, p. 164.

11. "Records of the Hartford Controversy," pp. 75–76.

12. *Connecticut Court Records*, 1: 311.

13. Ibid., p. 319.

14. Hartford Dissenters to Governor Eaton and John Davenport, December 1657, "Records of the Hartford Controversy," pp. 82–86.

15. Trumbull, *History of Connecticut*, 1: 251.

16. Samuel Stone to the General Court, March 11, 1658, Wyllys Papers, Connecticut Historical Society, *Collections*, 21: 128; *Connecticut Court Records*, 1: 333.

17. Trumbull, *History of Connecticut*, 1: 254.

18. Connecticut General Court to Churches of Boston, Cambridge, and Roxbury, August 26, 1658, "Records of the Hartford Controversy," p. 102; Petition of Samuel Stone to the General Court, May 2, 1658, *Connecticut Court Records*, 1: 317.

19. Trumbull, *History of Connecticut*, 1: 256–257.

20. Decision of the Council, October 7, 1659, "Records of the Hartford Controversy," pp. 112–125.

21. Adams and Stiles, *Wethersfield*, 1: 159–163.

22. Felt, *Ecclesiastical History*, 2: 189. See also Walker, *Hartford*, p. 192.

23. Felt, *Ecclesiastical History*, 2: 190. Felt claimed to have seen and compared both sets of proposals. He also suggested that Massachusetts refused Connecticut's request for a complete discussion of the merits of a Presbyterian settlement.

24. Trumbull, *History of Connecticut*, 1: 253–254. The proposals have not survived.

25. Jonathan Brewster to John Winthrop, Jr., 1657, Winthrop Papers, Massachusetts Historical Society, *Collections*, 4th ser., 7 (Boston, 1865), 85–86.

26. Many, of course, were members of English parishes, which meant that English membership no longer sufficed in New London.

27. Brewster to Winthrop, Jr., Winthrop Papers, pp. 84-87.

28. *Connecticut Court Records*, 1: 311.

29. Ibid., p. 333.

30. Walker, *Hartford*, pp. 195–196.

31. *Connecticut Court Records*, 1: 438.

32. Ibid.

33. Connecticut Historical Society, *Some Early Records and Documents Relating to the Town of Windsor, Connecticut, 1679–1703* (Hartford, 1930), p. 13. This collection also includes Matthew Grant's "Old Church Record," from which this selection is taken.

3. A WIDENING CHASM

1. According to Sibley's *Harvard Graduates*, Woodbridge graduated in 1664, Bulkeley in 1655, and Haynes in 1656. Haynes spent five years

at Cambridge, England, before returning to New England in 1661 or
1662. (Samuel E. Morison, *Harvard College in the Seventeenth Century*, 2 vols., Cambridge, Mass., 1936, 1: 330). Portions of this chapter
have been printed in Paul R. Lucas, "Presbyterianism Comes to Connecticut: The Toleration Act of 1669," *Journal of Presbyterian History*, 50 (1972), 129–147.

2. "Solomon Stoddard's Commonplace Book" (microfilm copy),
Widener Library, Harvard University. The original belongs to the
Library of the Union Theological Seminary, New York.

3. For Russell see Adams and Stiles, *Wethersfield*, 1: 159–163, as well
as the "Complaint of members of the Wethersfield Church against
John Russell," August 17, 1658, Connecticut Archives, Ecclesiastical
Affairs, Vol. 1, Connecticut State Library. Samuel Stone's position
emerged from his controversy with his church. See the "Records of
the Hartford Controversy," especially 70–79, and Samuel Stone,
"Against a Relation of Experience." See John Davenport's letter to the
Connecticut General Court, 1657, reprinted in Felt, *Ecclesiastical History*, 2: 189.

4. The evolution of English Presbyterianism is ably discussed in
Bolam, et al., *The English Presbyterians*, and I am indebted to it for
aiding my attempts to categorize Connecticut's Presbyterians. Lacking
ministerial literature, it is exceedingly difficult to define precisely
shades of Presbyterianism, but the English influence may be seen in the
letter from John Woodbridge to Richard Baxter of March 1671.

The Scottish influence is more difficult to detect. Gershom Bulkeley,
generally cited as the leader of the Presbyterian faction, was the most
visible Presbyterian in the events surrounding and pertaining to the
synod of 1667 and was the Presbyterian representative on the committee favoring toleration a year later. Thus it may be assumed that he
exercised considerable influence on the questions submitted for discussion at the 1667 synod and contributed Proposition Sixteen,
"Whether a Synod have a decisive power" (*Connecticut Court Records*, 2: 55). The clearest evidence of Scottish influence on Connecticut or Connecticut Valley is to be found in the thought of Solomon
Stoddard. Stoddard was about the same age as Woodbridge and a few
years younger than both Haynes and Bulkeley. See Solomon Stoddard,
The Doctrine of Instituted Churches (London, 1700).

5. Caulkins, *New London*, pp. 131–139.

6. Adams and Stiles, *Wethersfield*, 1: 322–324.

7. Connecticut Historical Society, *Some Early Records of Windsor*,

p. 13; "Henry Rowlandson's History of the Windsor Church, 1801," Windsor Church Records, Connecticut State Library, Vol. 3; *Connecticut Court Records*, 2: 73 ff.

8. Trumbull, *History of Connecticut*, 1: 390.

9. Windsor Dissenters to the General Court, 1668, Wyllys Papers, CHS, *Collections*, 2: 183; Stiles, *Windsor*, p. 176.

10. Windsor Dissenters to the General Court, October 1668, Wyllys Papers, p. 183; Stiles, *Windsor*, p. 176.

11. Stiles, *Windsor*, p. 179; Davenport to Winthrop, Jr., June 14, 1666, Isabel M. Calder, ed., *The Letters of John Davenport* (New Haven, 1937), p. 263.

12. Walker, *Hartford*, pp. 183–185.

13. Davenport to Winthrop, Jr., June 14, 1666, *Davenport Letters*, p. 263.

14. It was their second attempt to join First Church. See the Petition of William Pitkin and others to the General Court, 1664, Walker, *Hartford*, pp. 195–196.

15. The Notebook of the Rev. Samuel Whiting of Windham, Connecticut, 1666, MS, Connecticut State Library; Walker, *Hartford*, p. 200.

16. John Woodbridge to Richard Baxter, March 31, 1671.

17. *Connecticut Court Records*, 2: 53–54.

18. Trumbull, *History of Connecticut*, 1: 390; Felt, *Ecclesiastical History*, 2: 53–54.

19. *Connecticut Court Records*, 2: 53–54.

20. Ibid., p. 55.

21. Felt, *Ecclesiastical History*, 2: 466–468.

22. *Connecticut Court Records*, 2: 55; Felt, *Ecclesiastical History*, 2: 467; Walker, *Hartford*, pp. 200–202.

23. Felt, *Ecclesiastical History*, 2: 468; *Connecticut Court Records*, 2: 84, 107, 109; Walker, *Hartford*, pp. 202–203; Trumbull, *History of Connecticut*, 1: 390. The law, as passed by the Court, referred to no specific group, but John Woodbridge's 1671 letter to Richard Baxter called it the law granting toleration to Presbyterians.

24. Walker, *Hartford*, pp. 205–208; Trumbull, *History of Connecticut*, 1: 392; Hartford First Church, *Historical Catalogue of the First Church in Hartford, 1633–1885* (Hartford, 1885), p. 17, hereafter cited as *Hartford Catalogue*.

25. See Hartford, Connecticut, Records of First Congregational Church, Connecticut State Library, Vol. 10.

26. Stiles, *Windsor*, pp. 163–164.

27. Council's Decision, January 31, 1677, Connecticut Archives, Ecclesiastical, Vol. 1.

28. Petition of Windsor Church to the General Court (n.d. probably 1678), Connecticut Archives, Ecclesiastical, Vol. 1, documents 66a-c.

29. Ibid.; *Connecticut Court Records*, 3: 82.

30. Woodbridge to Baxter, February 3, 1669.

4. CHURCH, TOWN, AND THE HALF-WAY COVENANT

1. Windsor, Connecticut, First Congregational Church Records, Connecticut State Library, Vol. 3, "Creed and Covenant," October 23, 1647; Stiles, *Windsor*, pp. 172-173.

2. Robert G. Pope, *Half-Way Covenant*, p. 124.

3. There is a continuing debate over the degree of exclusiveness of New England's churches. In *Congregational Commonwealth*, Mary Jones writes that "the membership in the churches [of Connecticut] during the period of the Fundamental Orders included only a minority of the town's population" (p. 48). This is a common view reflecting the churches' stated emphasis upon regenerate members but making no attempt to measure statistically members and nonmembers. Kenneth Lockridge, in his study of Dedham, shows the danger of the approach when he notes that despite exclusiveness "admissions during this period [the first twenty years] were frequent enough to make the membership of the congregation and the town substantially the same" (*A New England Town*, p. 31). It was many years, he concludes, before there were a significant number of nonmembers in Dedham.

Early Connecticut's problem is that there are so few church or town records extant that statistical analysis is nearly impossible. Nonetheless, I think Lockridge's conclusion is substantially correct, though I feel the process was accelerated considerably. My conclusion is based on three related arguments: (1) membership practices differed markedly from church to church and few were as severe as Jones believes or as Lockridge found in Dedham (see my "Presbyterianism Comes to Connecticut," pp. 131–135); (2) many of Connecticut's first towns were founded by wandering congregations, suggesting a close initial approximation between church members and town inhabitants. Of those which were not, several followed Dedham's pattern as subsequent discussions of Wethersfield and New London will show; (3)

of?

the church-town divisions of the 1650's and 1660's document the emergence of sizable numbers and nonmembers. The only explanation for that split would envision church members adopting one stance in the church, another in the town meeting—a rather implausible theory.

4. The townsman's responsibilities relating to the church are discussed by Jones in *Congregational Commonwealth*, chap. 2.

5. Adams and Stiles, *Wethersfield*, 1: 159–160.

6. Complaint of Wethersfield Church against John Russell, August 17, 1658, Connecticut Archives, Ecclesiastical Affairs, Vol. 1; Adams and Stiles, *Wethersfield*, 1: 160–161; Sylvester Judd, *History of Hadley, Massachusetts* (Springfield, Mass., 1905), p. 9.

7. *Connecticut Court Records*, 1: 319.

8. Adams and Stiles, *Wethersfield*, 1: 163–164; Judd, *Hadley*, p. 9.

9. In discussing Wethersfield's turmoil, Adams and Stiles remarked that a majority of the town "in those days really controlled the church" (*Wethersfield*, 1: 160).

10. *Connecticut Court Records*, 1: 311.

11. Ibid., pp. 330–331.

12. Ibid., p. 342.

13. Ibid., p. 363.

14. Caulkins, *New London*, pp. 111–117, 130–145. See also Jonathan Brewster to John Winthrop, Jr., 1657, Winthrop Papers, pp. 84–87.

15. Brewster to Winthrop, Jr., Winthrop Papers, pp. 84–87.

16. *Connecticut Court Records*, 1: 356, 361–362; Trumbull, *History of Connecticut*, 1: 259.

17. *Connecticut Court Records*, 2: 240.

18. Pope, in *The Half-Way Covenant*, writes that "Enlarged baptism dominated the churches of Connecticut by 1690" (p. 125). However, he continues, "of the churches whose adoption of the half-way covenant we can date, 70 per cent made the change by the end of 1671" (p. 124). Pope, whose analysis of the churches adopting the covenant in Massachusetts and Connecticut represents the most ambitious and comprehensive survey to date, discusses the covenant's emergence in Connecticut in chap. 4.

19. "Henry Rowlandson's History of Windsor Church, 1801," Windsor Church Records, Connecticut State Library, Vol. 3; *Connecticut Court Records*, 2: 73–74; Stiles, *Windsor*, pp. 173–176.

20. "Records of the Hartford Controversy," pp. 70–76; Walker, *Hartford*, pp. 183–185.

21. Walker, *Hartford*, p. 183; Lucas, "Presbyterianism Comes to Connecticut," pp. 143–144.

22. Walker, *Hartford*, pp. 184–185. See also Davenport to Winthrop, Jr., June 14, 1666, in Calder, *Letters of John Davenport*, p. 263.

23. The Haynes-Whiting turmoil is recounted in Walker, *Hartford*, pp. 184–208. Second Church issued an elaborate statement describing its ecclesiastical order. Included among its practices was the half-way covenant, though in a form consistent with the plan of the Synod of 1662 (p. 208). See also Trumbull, *History of Connecticut*, 1: 391–393.

24. Trumbull, *History of Connecticut*, 1: 393.

25. Petition of Dissenters to the church in Stratford, February 9, 1665, and the church's reply, April 16, 1666, Connecticut Archives, Ecclesiastical, Vol. 1.

26. Stratford Town Vote, December 18, 1666, Connecticut Archives, Ecclesiastical, Vol. 1. For reasons that are unclear the dissenters did not formally organize a separate church until May 1, 1670 (Woodbury, Connecticut, Records of the First Congregational Church, Connecticut State Library, Vol. 1, May 1, 1670). The early records of Stratford's Second Church are contained in the first volume of the Woodbury records.

27. Documents 25 to 34, November 11, 1668, to September 10, 1669, Connecticut Archives, Ecclesiastical, Vol. 1; Trumbull, *History of Connecticut*, 1: 393.

28. First Church Stratford did not adopt the covenant until 1689, and it had "no significant effect on Stratford's membership" until 1698 (Pope, *Half-Way Covenant*, pp. 101–102). Though it cannot be documented, it may be that church-town bickering continued until the church capitulated in 1689. Then, as a kind of protest, the church may have simply ignored the new status.

29. James R. Trumbull, *History of Northampton, Massachusetts, from Its Settlement in 1654* (2 vols., Northampton, 1898), 1: 25–41, 56–57, 82–83.

30. Ibid, pp. 66–69, 82.

31. Ibid., pp. 74–80.

32. Records of the First Church of Christ of Northampton, Massachusetts, Forbes Library, Northampton, Vol. 1, June 18, 1661. The estimate regarding church membership is based on population figures provided by Trumbull and membership lists contained in Volume 1 of the church records.

33. Trumbull, *Northampton*, 1: 201–202. Evidently, Mather was ill during much of his stay in Northampton, for in 1662 the town hired Joseph Eliot to assist him. To provide for such an occasion the town had set aside a parcel of land earlier for use by the minister. The

decision was made to give part of that land to Eliot and that sparked another controversy. The result was a petition from nine persons to the town meeting in late 1662 asking that the land be taken back. It is likely that opposition to Eliot was sparked by Mather's stand on the covenant.

34. Eleazer Mather published nothing during his life, but after his death his brother Increase edited and published some of his sermons. The resulting pamphlet, a jeremiad, contained several comments suggesting that the author's stay in Northampton was less than happy. The tone of the piece reveals a writer despondent either from the effects of controversy or prolonged illness or both. Eleazer Mather, *A Serious Exhortation to the Present and Succeeding Generation in New England* (Cambridge, 1671), esp. pp. 1, 10–11, 27–28.

35. Northampton Church Records, Vol. 1, entries dated January 29, February 16, and February 22, 1668. The "state of education" is commonly and erroneously attributed to Solomon Stoddard.

36. Trumbull, *Northampton*, 1: 211.

37. Whether town meetings were gaining similar authority in Massachusetts at this time is not known. However, Paul Boyer and Stephen Nissenbaum in *Salem Possessed: The Social Origins of Witchcraft* (Cambridge, 1974), have found that a church-town division over the retention of a minister was part of the pattern of social and economic cleavage which led, eventually, to the witchcraft hysteria in Salem. The incident occurred in the 1670's and revolved around the ministry of James Baily in Salem Village. The issue was whether the Village, a "parish" of Salem Town with no church of its own, or the members of the church of Salem Town controlled the hiring and firing of the Village's minister. Colony law specified that only church members had that right, but the General Court, recognizing the peculiar legal status of Salem Village, decided for the Village. When in 1689 the Village did organize a church, the "inhabitants" refused to surrender their authority to the church members. The authors do not see this development as part of a colony-wide movement. Rather, they view the persistence of dissension as the product of "structural defects" peculiar to Salem Village (see pp. 45–53).

38. The victories of the towns in the midseventeenth century led directly to some important ecclesiastical practices in the eighteenth. In 1697 and 1699 the General Assembly formalized participation of nonmembers in church affairs with two laws guaranteeing all householders the rights to join in the selection of a minister and the determination of his salary (*Connecticut Court Records*, 4: 200–201, 316).

Moreover, as towns grew larger in the late seventeenth and early eighteenth centuries, more than one church per town became common. To provide for this, towns were divided into parishes. Not surprisingly, the practice of dual government emerged intact in the parish system. Spiritual questions (the nature of baptism, church membership, etc.) continued to be the province of the church members. All other matters (and those once decided by the town meeting) were referred to the "society," an arm of the parish including both members and nonmembers. The society handled financial matters, cared for the church building, levied ecclesiastical taxes, and retained a voice in the selection or retention of the minister. See J. M. Bumsted, "Revivalism and Separatism in New England: The First Society of Norwich, Connecticut, as a Case Study," *William and Mary Quarterly*, 3rd ser., 24 (1967), 589.

5. "THE RIGHT WAY TO ESCAPE DESERVED RUINE," 1670–1700

1. This analysis of ministerial attitudes is a composite of published writings of the 1670's and 1680's and, especially, the conclusions of the synods of 1675.

2. The situation in Connecticut and the Connecticut Valley in the 1670's is masterfully recounted in Leach's *Flintlock and Tomahawk*. His analysis of the war and its effects, both physical and psychological, on the frontier settlements is unmatched. Earlier disasters in the Valley, such as drought, disease, and famine, are chronicled in Vol. 2 of *Connecticut Court Records*.

3. Much has been written by scholars about the jeremiads of late seventeenth-century New England, but the standard account remains Perry Miller's *New England Mind from Colony to Province*, esp. chap. 2. Miller, however, largely confines his analysis to Massachusetts, as have most subsequent students of the phenomenon. One recent study worthy of attention is Middlekauff's *The Mathers*. Middlekauff argues that the jeremiad and the declension theme resulted from Puritan typology. Whereas first-generation clergy saw New England as an extension of old England, second-generation ministers sought to give it a sense of mission and an identity of its own. They turned to ancient Israel and subsequently applied the theme of a declining people to New England. Consequently, Middlekauff discounts the significance of

societal changes as an explanation for the clergy's altered stance (see esp. chaps. 6 and 7).

4. James Fitch, *An Holy Connexion, Or a True Agreement between Jehovahs Being a Wall of Fire to his People, and the Glory in the Midst Thereof* (Cambridge, 1674). Apparently the first jeremiad by a Connecticut or Connecticut Valley minister was Eleazer Mather's *A Serious Exhortation*, previously cited, but the jeremiad appeared in Massachusetts a decade earlier. See Robert F. Scholz, "The Reverend Elders: Faith, Fellowship and Politics in the Ministerial Community of Massachusetts Bay 1630–1710" (unpublished Ph.D. dissertation, University of Minnesota, 1966), chap. 5.

5. Fitch, *An Holy Connexion*, pp. 7, 16.

6. James Fitch, *An Explanation of the Solemn Advice Recommended by the Council in Connecticut Colony, to the Inhabitants in that Jurisdiction resolving the Reformation of those Evils, which have been the Procuring Cause of the late Judgments upon New England* (Boston, 1683), p. 2. See also *Connecticut Court Records*, 2: 389. Massachusetts held its own Reforming Synod in 1679.

7. Fitch, *An Explanation of Solemn Advice*, p. 5.

8. Ibid., p. 13.

9. The clergy's analysis of the ills of the country and its plan for spiritual reformation is to be found ibid., pp. 8–38.

10. Ibid.; *Connecticut Court Records*, 2: 280–283. At its May 1676 session the General Assembly offered a prescription for reformation which was based on the ministers' conclusions. See also Elmer Brooks Holifield, *The Covenant Sealed: The Development of Puritan Sacramental Theology in Old and New England 1520–1720* (New Haven, 1974), esp. chaps. 6–7.

11. Fitch, *An Explanation of Solemn Advice*, p. 23.

12. James Fitch, *The First Principles of the Doctrine of Christ* (Boston, 1679), p. 73.

13. Holifield, chaps. 3–4.

14. Fitch, *First Principles*; Holifield, pp. 182–185, 186 ff. In March 1675/6 the clergy made its report to the General Assembly, which then ordered the report distributed among the churches (March 7). The ministers' report dutifully listed the sins of the people. Of prime importance were the following: "not maintaining a strict discipline in Churches according to the Rule of Christ, Many persons not coming to the Lords Supper or So much as Seeking the Enjoyment of such a Gospel priviledge, and yet there is Reason to fear not so much from

Tenderness of Conscience as making light of the ordinance as a means of honouring and enjoying communion with the Lord Jesus Christ, and therein also greatly Slighting the express Command of Christ. Many Baptized Adult persons neglecting and too many refusing to Own their Baptismal Covenant, and acknowledge themselves Subject to the Discipline and Government of Christ in the Church" (Wyllys Papers, CHS, *Collections*, 21: 237).

15. Fitch, *An Explanation of Solemn Advice*, pp. 69–71; *Connecticut Court Records*, 2: 281–282.

16. *Hartford Catalogue*, p. 22.

17. John Whiting, *The Way of Israels Welfare* (Boston, 1686), p. 27.

18. This occurred in both the Windsor and Hartford disputes.

19. *Connecticut Court Records*, 2: 64–65.

20. Ibid., p. 65. The Assembly repeated some of the recommendations made in 1676.

21. Samuel Wakeman, *Sound Repentence, The Right Way to Escape Deserved Ruine* (Boston, 1685).

22. Ibid., p. 15.

23. Ibid., p. 22.

24. Ibid., p. 23.

25. Ibid.

26. Ibid., p. 32.

27. Ibid., p. 31.

28. Whiting, *Way of Israels Welfare*, p. 22.

29. Ibid., p. 30.

30. Ibid., p. 34.

31. Gurdon Saltonstall, *A Sermon Preached before the General Assembly* (Boston, 1697), p. 53.

32. Ibid., p. 54.

33. Ibid.

34. Ibid., p. 55.

35. Ibid., pp. 74–76. In demanding obedience and reverence for civil rulers, Saltonstall may have made an oblique reference to a resolution passed by the Assembly in 1690. Commenting on repeated attempts by members of the Assembly and "all inferior officers and ministers of justice" to make and enforce laws for moral reformation, the assemblymen angrily concluded "that instead of the reformation sincerely aymed at, vice and corruption of manners, in most places rather abound and increase more than ever" (*Connecticut Court Records*, 4: 29).

36. Richard Bushman's *Puritan to Yankee* ably demonstrates how

land speculation and land hunger affected political and legal affairs in Connecticut in the 1680's and 90's and led to corruption and factionalism in government and in the courts. Saltonstall, Bushman points out, lashed out at this situation in his sermon, singling out Capt. John Fitch of Norwich, who had used his office as a magistrate and judge in New London County to influence decisions on disputed titles (pp. 87–95).

37. *Connecticut Court Records*, 3: 79–82; Trumbull, *History of Connecticut*, 2: 399.

6. THE SEARCH FOR A NEW MORAL ORDER, 1665–1700

1. Windsor, Connecticut, Records of the First Congregational Church, Connecticut State Library, Vol. 3, membership lists.

2. Here I am indebted to Middlekauff's perceptive study of the Mathers. He argues that the second- and third-generation clergy—not the first—defined and delineated New England's mission. It is my argument that second- and third-generation laymen defined the purpose and practice of Connecticut Congregationalism.

3. The "reforming covenant" has caused confusion among scholars studying the records of some churches. Often they have missed the specific purposes of these agreements and have assumed the signers were becoming either half-way or full members of the churches. This has created some confusion concerning the number of persons joining the churches as well as the nature of membership practices. In general, however, those covenants bore no relationship to membership, either full or half-way. As an example the reader is directed to the Hartford covenant of 1695, which has been called a half-way covenant. In fact, it was a reforming covenant directed specifically toward the young people of the church. Signing the document had no effect on membership status.

4. Students of the New England mind have argued for decades over the meaning of New England's declension. Perry Miller attributed it to secularization, capitalism, and federal theology's inability to adjust to a changing world and the dictates of American experience. Since Miller, declension has been treated largely as an ideational phenomenon virtually unrelated to social and institutional change. One recent commentator, surveying the churches in the late seventeenth century, castigates intellectual historians for ignoring social realities and giving "us a distorted view of New England's transformation from the world of John Winthrop into the world of Cotton Mather" (Robert Pope,

"New England versus the New England Mind: The Myth of Declension," *Journal of Social History*, 3, 1969–70, 96). Still, Pope couches his own argument more as a response to the ministers than the historians. He rejects ministerial arguments for declining piety, falling church membership, and spiritual deadness, but he offers little on the broader questions of social and economic change. No one, in fact, has successfully documented or refuted ministerial arguments regarding the emergence of an alien society. David Hall contradicts Pope's assertion of congregational health by linking declension to declining ministerial authority (*Faithful Shepherd*, chap. 10). Yet Hall provides no quantitative data to explain or document that decline.

In Connecticut arguments for declension combined elements of both myth and social reality. The reality was a society undergoing rapid economic and demographic change, an evolution ably documented in Bushman's *Puritan to Yankee*. Myth related to the ministers' attack on spiritual deadness and worldliness. The latter were coded words reflecting the ministers' disgust with the aggressiveness and independence of the brethren and the ministers' desire to disrupt the laity's campaign for moral rebirth.

5. Hooker, *Survey*, p. 50.

6. Ibid., p. 46.

7. Ibid., p. 50.

8. Ibid., p. 47.

9. Ibid., p. 48–49.

10. I have been able to document covenant revisions or "renewals" in thirteen Connecticut or Connecticut Valley churches between 1670 and 1690 (for comparison, the Connecticut Assembly listed twenty-one towns in its tax levy for 1670; twenty-six in 1690). The unavailability of church records for many of Connecticut's churches during this period prevents a higher—and probably more accurate—total of covenant alterations. The covenants that have survived conform in content to the analysis that follows (see *Connecticut Court Records*, 2: 137, and 4: 42–43).

11. Northampton Church Records, Vol. 1, February 22, 1668.

12. Ibid.

13. Ibid.

14. Ibid.

15. Ibid.

16. Fitch, *An Explanation of Solemn Advice*, pp. 69–71.

17. *Hartford Catalogue*, p. 22. Of the signers only seventeen had

joined the church by 1707, excluding a few who were already members in 1695.

18. Council's Decision, Connecticut Archives, Ecclesiastical, Vol. 1, January 31, 1677.

19. Ibid.

20. Ibid.

21. Petition of Windsor Church to the General Court, Connecticut Archives, Ecclesiastical, Vol. 1, documents 66a-c.

22. Ibid.

23. Woodbridge sued for redress, and the Court eventually awarded him a 290-acre farm. See *Connecticut Court Records*, 3: 82.

24. Samuel Mather to Increase Mather, November 4, 1678, "Mather Papers," MHS, *Collections*, 4th ser., 8 (Boston, 1868), 381.

25. John Whiting to Increase Mather, February 27, 1678/79, Mather Papers, p. 464.

26. Not surprisingly, Increase called him a Presbyterian; see Walker, *Hartford*, p. 218.

27. Ibid., p. 217.

28. Stiles, *Windsor*, pp. 183–184. Mather's role in the affair was clarified in a letter to John Haynes regarding Foster. After advising Foster that Windsor was too "congregational," Mather reported to Haynes on the question of Foster's Presbyterianism, recounting an alleged conversation between himself and Foster. "His [Foster's] answer was that he believed he knew the reason of my proposal, for [?] had acquainted him with what yourself had written to Mr. Oakes and me, and upon that account he was not so free to express himselfe; only said that he never upon any occasion declared against the way Congregational. To be sure he is as large respecting the subject of Baptisme as the Synod of 62." Damning with feint praise, Mather concluded that if Windsor wanted Foster, he would not discourage it (Increase to John Haynes, 1679, Walker, *Hartford*, pp. 215–216).

29. Mather to Haynes, 1679, Walker, *Hartford*, pp. 217–218. Foster died a few months later during an epidemic.

30. John Whiting to Increase Mather, October 25, 1682, Mather Papers, p. 466.

31. *Connecticut Court Records*, 3: 104. See also Stiles, *Windsor*, pp. 188–189.

32. Windsor, Connecticut, Records of the First Congregational Church, membership lists.

33. John Lockwood, *Westfield and Its Historic Influences 1669–*

1719 (Springfield, 1922), pp. 180–181. The narrative of the founding of the church is based on Taylor's church record.

34. Ibid., pp. 111–113.

35. Ibid., pp. 114–117.

36. Hartford, Connecticut, Records of the First Church of Hartford, esp. Vol. 10, Accounts and Records, 1685–1772, Connecticut State Library. See also Wethersfield, Conn., Records of the First Congregational Church, 1697–1733, Connecticut State Library, Vol. 2, January 2, 1703.

37. Hartford Church Records, Vol. 1, May 10, July 10, 1703.

38. See the Wethersfield Church Records, esp. Vol. 2.

39. Ibid., January 2, 1703.

40. The influence of the "lay reformation" on admission practices was sizable. I have found seventeen churches turning to moral behavior as the standard for full membership between 1670 and 1725 (eleven before 1700; six more by 1725). During the same years twelve churches demanded evidence of saving grace (seven founded before 1700; five founded after that date). Probably five or six churches adopting moral behavior simply let the profession of religious experience fall into disuse. There were about thirty-five churches in the colony in 1725.

James P. Walsh in "The Pure Church in Eighteenth Century Connecticut" (unpublished Ph.D. dissertation, Columbia University, 1967), contends that the Great Awakening reversed the trend I have described and fostered a renewed emphasis on saving grace and churches of the demonstrably elect. This is an argument often applied to separatist groups in the Awakening, but his study is the first to apply it to a majority of all the Congregational churches in Connecticut (see his conclusion and appendices I and II, and my argument in Chap. 9, below).

41. Lockwood, *Westfield*, pp. 114–115.

42. Farmington, Connecticut, Records of the First Church of Christ, Connecticut State Library, Vol. 1, June 15, 1673.

43. Ibid.

44. Ibid.

45. Ibid.

46. Ibid., December 17, 1706.

47. Middletown, Connecticut, Records of the First Congregational Church, Connecticut State Library, Vol. 1, December 30 and January 17, 1668.

48. Ibid., June 2, 1672.

49. Silas Blake, *The Later History of the First Church of Christ, New London, Connecticut* (New London, 1900), pp. 29–35.

50. Caulkins, *New London*, p. 38. Like Northampton after 1672, several churches began automatically to admit children of the church to full membership at their majority.

51. See Wethersfield Church Records, Vol. 2, January 2, 1703.

52. Northampton Church Records, Vol. 1, November 5, 1672.

53. Entry dated "1690," Edward Taylor's Notebook, Massachusetts Historical Society; see also Solomon Stoddard, *The Doctrine of Instituted Churches Explained and Proved from the Word of God* (London, 1700), pp. 12, 18–22.

54. These estimates are based on membership lists contained in the records of each of the churches.

55. Pope, *Half-Way Covenant*, p. 125. My own survey of extant church records supports his conclusion.

56. Conclusion based on a survey of the half-way lists of twelve churches, 1670–1725.

57. See E. Brooks Holifield, "The Renaissance of Sacramental Piety in Colonial New England," *William and Mary Quarterly*, 3rd ser., 29 (1972), 33–48.

58. Caulkins, *New London*, p. 380.

59. Not many churches employed the half-way covenant according to the 1662 synod's dictates. A few of those were founded after the contention of the midcentury. Others—like Farmington (which adopted the covenant in 1708), Norwich, and New Haven—were in communities only mildly affected by dissension.

60. Northampton Church Records, Vol. 1, January 29 and February 16, 1668; November 5, 1672; December 9, 1714.

61. Middletown Church Records, Vol. 1, February 25, 1671.

62. Ibid., January 26, 1672.

63. Ibid., November 4, 1668.

64. Ibid., Vol. 1.

65. Woodbury, Connecticut, Records of the First Congregational Church, Connecticut State Library, Vol. 1, May 4, 1670. The Stratford Second Church was the Presbyterian faction from First Church which withdrew after a long struggle over several issues, especially membership requirements. The new church organized around a covenant but required no "public profession" for admission. Also, any professing Christian was baptized after owning the covenant, a practice disputed by First Church.

66. Ibid., July 11, 1708.

67. The attempt was partially successful, for only about thirty percent of half-way members, men and women, ever entered full communion. That was, however, a higher percentage than any other church.

68. This analysis of practices in Hartford is based on membership data in Vol. 10 of the Hartford Church Records and from similar data contained in the *Hartford Catalogue*, pp. xiii–xx, 3–47.

69. Pope, *Half-Way Covenant*, pp. 273 ff. My figures support his conclusion—to a point. Pope argues that the theme of declension, common to almost all ministerial writings of the late seventeenth century, was a myth not supported by statistical evidence of declining church membership. David Hall adds that, myth or fact, declining church membership and declension were ministerial obsessions (*Faithful Shepherd*, pp. 288–289). My response to their argument is threefold. First, the Connecticut minister's lament, initially, referred to the effects of midcentury dissension. It was contention and not waning piety which produced sharp membership decline. Second, the theme of declension indicated, eventually, the failure of the ministry's spiritual awakening, a failure magnified by awareness of the brethren's successes. That explained the continuation of declension arguments even when church membership was rising. Third, although a religious revival did take place in the last decades of the century, it was not a spiritual revival—as the ministry continually pointed out—but a lay-inspired reorganization of the church and expansion of its activities and influence into the community. Unlike the revival of the 1630's or the later Great Awakening, the late seventeenth-century reformation consciously neglected the spirit and concentrated, instead, upon behavior. The brethren tried to mold the church into a vehicle for moral consensus and proper behavior among members and nonmembers alike.

70. No one—not even Pope—argues that church growth stayed abreast of town growth. Precise population and church membership figures are lacking, but even a cursory examination of known figures indicates a sizable gap between church and town. A few examples will suffice. In 1700 Northampton's church, including both full and half-way members, included a little over a third of the total population; Waterbury's and New London's encompassed between a third and a half; Norwich's about a third; Lebanon's about a third; and Hartford's two churches about a third. These estimates are based on church records and population figures in local histories and Evarts B. Greene

and Virginia D. Harrington, *American Population before the Federal Census of 1790* (New York, 1932).

Considering the goals which underlay both clerical and lay reformations of the late seventeenth century, however, the disparity between church membership and town population may have little real meaning. First, neither laymen nor clergy revealed a desire to create churches encompassing everyone. Second, the ministry's fear of declining membership reflected a greater concern for the laity's refusal to respond to appeals for spiritual awakening. Third, all available evidence indicates that the brethren were content with the results of their own moral reformation.

7. THE POLITICS OF ECCLESIASTICAL DISRUPTION

1. Holifield, "Renaissance of Sacramental Piety," pp. 33–36.

2. For an exhaustive analysis of the nature and extent of early ministerial meetings in Massachusetts, see Scholz, "The Reverend Elders," chaps. 1–4.

3. Bushman, *Puritan to Yankee*, p. 150.

4. The development of the association movement in Massachusetts and Connecticut deserves greater attention from historians than it has received. The interested reader is invited to consult Williston Walker, *The Creeds and Platforms of Congregationalism* (New York, 1893; 2nd ed., Boston, 1960), pp. 463–495; Hall, *Faithful Shepherd*, pp. 218–226; Trumbull, *History of Connecticut*, 1: 406–409; Scholz, "The Reverend Elders," chap. 6; Miller, *From Colony to Province* (I have used the 1961 Beacon paperback edition) chaps. 14–16, for the substance of the preceding discussion.

5. Some of the more important treatments of Stoddard are Perry Miller, "Solomon Stoddard, 1643–1729," *Harvard Theological Review*, 34 (1941), 277–320, as well as his *From Colony to Province*; Morgan, *Visible Saints*; Pettit, *The Heart Prepared*; Pope, *The Half-Way Covenant*; Thomas A. Schafer, "Solomon Stoddard and the Theology of the Revival," in Stuart C. Henry, ed., *A Miscellany of American Christianity: Essays in Honor of H. Shelton Smith* (Durham, N. C., 1963), pp. 328–361; James P. Walsh, "Solomon Stoddard's Open Communion: A Reexamination," *New England Quarterly*, 43 (1970), 97–114; Middlekauff, *The Mathers*, chap. 7. Portions of chapters 7-9 are contained in Paul R. Lucas, "An Appeal to the Learned: The Mind of Solomon

Stoddard," *William and Mary Quarterly*, 3rd ser., 30 (1973), 257–292. Unless otherwise noted, facts concerning Stoddard's career and ministry are from Trumbull, *Northampton*.

6. See Samuel Sewall to Solomon Stoddard, December 10, 1728, "Letter Book of Samuel Sewall," MHS, *Collections*, 6th ser., 2 (Boston, 1888), 259.

7. William Williams, *The Death of a Prophet Lamented* (Boston, 1729), p. 24.

8. Ibid., Miller, "Solomon Stoddard," pp. 278–281.

9. Miller, "Solomon Stoddard," pp. 282–284.

10. See my "Appeal to the Learned," pp. 276–277.

11. For the role of the Bay clergy, especially Norton, in the political struggle in Massachusetts after the Restoration, see my article "Colony or Commonwealth: Massachusetts Bay, 1661-1666," *William and Mary Quarterly*, 3rd ser., 24 (1967), 88–107. See also the Petition of Boston Non-Freemen to the Massachusetts General Court, May 4, 1665, Massachusetts Archives, Vol. 106.

12. Holifield, *The Covenant Sealed*, pp. 117–133, 213–214. See John Humphrey, *An Humble Vindication of a Free Admission Unto the Lords Supper, Published for the Ease, support and Satisfaction of tender Consciences (otherwise remedies) in our mixt congregations as it was delivered at two sermons* (London, 1651), pp. 3–11, 53–59; and John Timson, *To Receive the Lords Supper, The Actual Right and Duty of all Church-Members of Years not Excommunicate* (London, 1655), pp. 134–143.

13. See my "Appeal to the Learned," pp. 257–261.

14. Stoddard, *Instituted Churches*, pp. 1–5, 22, 25–28. See also Increase and Cotton Mather's analysis of Stoddard's position, "A Defence of Evangelical Churches," intro. to John Quick, *The Young Mans Claim unto the Sacrament of the Lords-Supper. Or, the Examination of a Person approaching to the Table of the Lord* (Boston, 1700; original publication London, 1691).

15. In his chapter on Stoddard in *From Colony to Province*, Miller was correct in asserting that Stoddard differed from most New England divines in that his God was more Old Testament than New. Miller was wrong, however, in arguing that Stoddard upheld a capricious, irrational God. Stoddard's God was perhaps more terrible than the God of most of his colleagues, yet he was still bound by the "law" and, although above it, agreed to abide by it (the binding Covenant of Grace and Christ's atonement). Stoddard, *The Safety of Appearing at the Day of Judgement, In the Righteousness of Christ: Opened and*

Applied (Boston, 1687), p. 205. If anything, Stoddard's notion of God made the Deity a very rational being. Stoddard believed that God's plan for man was perfectly clear and understandable and represented an unbroken chain from creation to the present. Although all-powerful, God acted rationally, and man could easily interpret His plan as it was revealed in history. This was Stoddard's message in both *Safety of Appearing* and *Instituted Churches*.

16. Stoddard, *Instituted Churches*, pp. 5–6, 18–19, 22. Stoddard did not leave to chance the decision to seek membership. Although most ordinances existed only for visible saints, the "scandalous" were not ignored. They were to be impelled to reform and seek membership through another ordinance: enlightened preaching. Stoddard dwelt very little on preaching in his early treatises, although his Northampton revivals or "harvests" were common knowledge. From occasional remarks it is known, however, that he envisioned preaching as primarily an educative function designed to instruct the sinner in Christian doctrine and morality, thus qualifying him for church membership. Later he altered radically his conception of the preaching function, giving it a position of preeminence in the process of conversion. Simultaneously, he deemphasized the saving power of other ordinances, especially the Lord's Supper. See a more lengthy discussion of Stoddard's conception of preaching in Chap 9, below. See also Stoddard, *Instituted Churches*, pp. 22–25, and Stoddard, *The Inexcusableness of Neglecting the Worship of God, Under a Pretence of being in an Unconverted Condition* (Boston, 1708), p. 27.

17. Stoddard, *Instituted Churches*, pp. 7–8, 25–29.

18. Ibid., pp. 29–32.

19. Ibid., pp. 12, 18–22.

20. Edward Taylor's Notebook, entry dated "1690."

21. Ibid.

22. Northampton Church Records, Vol. 1, December 9, 1714.

23. According to the doctrine of the "seals," the Lord's Supper was a commemoration or seal of the covenant of grace between God and man. Therefore, it was often argued that admission to the Supper ought to be restricted to known regenerates.

24. Everett Emerson and Mason I. Lowance, eds., "Increase Mather's Confutation of Solomon Stoddard's Observations Respecting the Lord's Supper, 1680," *Proceedings of the American Antiquarian Society*, 33 (1973), 56.

25. Stoddard, *Safety of Appearing*, pp. 119–125, 175–180.

26. Mather, *Magnalia*, 1: 385–387. See also Increase's speech to the

synod in Boston on July 4, 1700, in Worthington C. Ford (ed.), "The Diary of Cotton Mather," MHS, *Collections*, 7th ser., 7 (Boston, 1911), 384-388. Increase Mather's fear of Stoddard is discussed in Miller, *Colony to Province*, pp. 226-248.

27. Westfield to Northampton, July 3, 1673, Taylor Notebook.

28. Northampton to Westfield, July 29, 1673, ibid.

29. Westfield to Northampton, August 21, 1673, ibid.

30. Edward Taylor, "A Particular church is God's House," Taylor Ms, Prince Collection, Boston Public Library.

31. Taylor to Stoddard, February 13, 1687/88, Taylor Notebook.

32. Ibid.

33. Stoddard to Taylor, June 4, 1688, Taylor Notebook.

34. Ibid.

35. Walker, *Creeds and Platforms*, pp. 414–415; Miller, *Colony to Province*, pp. 33–39.

36. Walker, *Creeds and Platforms*, p. 415.

37. Solomon Stoddard, *An Appeal to the Learned* (Boston, 1709), pp. 93–94.

38. Ibid. See also "Peter Thacher's Journal," in Walker, *Creeds and Platforms*, p. 419.

39. Walker, *Creeds and Platforms*, p. 419.

40. Stoddard, *An Appeal*, pp. 93–94.

41. Walker, *Creeds and Platforms*, p. 418.

42. Ibid., p. 433.

43. Miller describes the fencing between Stoddard and the Mathers in "Solomon Stoddard," pp. 302–305, and *Colony to Province*, chaps. 15–16.

44. Increase and Cotton Mather, "A Defence of Evangelical Churches," in Quick, *Young Man's Claim*, p. 22.

45. See, for example, Cotton Mather, *Ecclesiastes The Life of the Reverend and Excellent, Jonathan Mitchel* (Boston, 1697).

46. Cotton's *Magnalia* was an oblique attack on Presbyterian innovators, including Stoddard. His diary contained numerous references to Stoddard's activities in the 1690's as well as disparaging remarks about Presbyterians from either himself or father Increase. The diary also mentions several attempts by the Mathers to organize ministerial opposition to Presbyterians (see, for example, a copy of the Pronouncement of an Assembly of Ministers at Boston, May 1697, Records of the First Church of Wethersfield, Connecticut, Vol. 2, Connecticut State Library).

47. Mather, *Magnalia*, 1: 436–437.

48. For example, Thomas Parker, first minister of Newbury, Mass., was a Presbyterian and a critic of Bay Congregationalism. Mather, however, refused to give him a label. He noted Parker's "largeness in his principles about church government" (p. 483), but quickly added that the differences between Parker and his colleagues were "not so great as that between Theodus and Pollinis" (p. 483). Parker was remembered not for his Presbyterianism but for his "diligence," "charity," and his "immoderate studies" which brought a "miserable defluxion of rheum upon his eyes" (p. 482).

49. This is, of course, a rather liberal restatement of Mather's theme. Though it may be found in the life of every major clergyman, it is most obvious in the Fifth book "Acts and Monuments," an historical outline of the "Faith and Order" and analysis of the decisions of major synods, 2: 177–338. See also Perry Miller's comments on the significance of the *Magnalia* in "Solomon Stoddard," pp. 301–302.

8. THE STODDARD-MATHER DEBATE

1. The major treatises published during the Stoddard-Mather debate are listed in Miller's "Solomon Stoddard," pp. 303–304. Miller's article on Stoddard and his chapter entitled "Contention" in *Colony to Province* remain the most complete analyses of the debate.

2. Benjamin Colman, Simon Bradstreet, and Timothy Woodbridge, *Gospel Order Revived* (New York, 1700); Increase Mather, *Order of the Gospel* (Boston, 1700).

3. Although no Valley minister except Woodbridge published his views during the debate, a number expressed themselves in sermons to their congregations or in treatises which, for one reason or another, never appeared in print. In the northern portion of the Valley, for example, Edward Taylor of Westfield preached against Stoddard. Some of his sermons eventually appeared in print, several appearing with Mather's *Order of the Gospel*. In the Hartford area Samuel Mather of Windsor wrote a long treatise denouncing Stoddard. The manuscript, untitled and undated, is in the Connecticut Historical Society. Elsewhere in Connecticut, Gurdon Saltonstall of New London labored on Stoddard's behalf, although none of his thoughts were published. The Massachusetts Historical Society possesses a pro-Stoddard manuscript sermon given before the New London church in 1703.

4. There is considerable debate over whether the Brattle Street Church (1698) was intended to be a Presbyterian or an Anglican church or neither. Most scholars have argued for Anglicanism (see, for example, Clifford K. Shipton, *Sibley's Harvard Graduates*, 4, Cambridge, Mass., 1933, pp. 122–123). Miller, (*Colony to Province*, pp. 240–260) does not opt for either label. Instead he sees the church as the result of a conspiracy of wealthy Boston merchants who could no longer tolerate the stultifying qualities of the New England mind, as opposed to the protectors of orthodoxy, the Mathers. Miller believed that the founders of Brattle Street, including Benjamin Colman, were linked with Stoddard as the representative vanguard of a Yankee society which recognized that the "New England Way" no longer conformed to the demands of life in the bustling, acquisitive society of early eighteenth-century New England.

5. Mather, *Order of the Gospel*, p. 8. It was the same tactic, though in expanded form, that he had used earlier in trying to isolate Stoddard from other Presbyterians by forcing the Northampton cleric to admit and defend his converting ordinances.

The Heads of Agreement (1691) was the product of two years of meetings between English Congregationalists and Presbyterians after the Toleration Act (1689). Increase Mather, in England the whole time, played a vital role in formulating the document and thus emerged as the great champion of compromise. But English Presbyterians differed from their Scottish colleagues, who were more firmly wedded to synodical government, and it was the Scottish variety that found favor among New England's clergy. Hence, Mather tried to discredit New England's Presbyterians for not adhering to the Heads (see Miller, *Colony to Province*, pp. 216–225).

6. Mather, *Order of the Gospel*, p. 5.

7. Ibid., pp. 5-7.

8. Ibid.

9. Ibid., pp. 5–15.

10. Mather listed the following as "dangerous" opinions: (a) that the churches not inquire into the regeneration of applicants; (b) that particular church covenants were needless and unscriptural; (c) that nonmembers could vote in the selection of a minister; (d) that all professing Christians had a right to baptism; (e) that brethren had no voice in ecclesiastical councils; (f) that the minister's call stemmed from the imposition of "hands" rather than election by the members; (g) that persons could be installed as ministers without the consent of neighboring churches. *Order of the Gospel*, p. 8.

11. Ibid., p. 22.

12. Ibid., p. 8.

13. Quick, *Young Mans Claim.*

14. Increase and Cotton Mather, "Defence of Evangelical Churches," introduction to Quick, *Young Mans Claim*, pp. 9-11. Herein the elder Mather argued that his *Order of the Gospel* was to be construed as an answer to Stoddard and that he meant it as such. Yet it seems apparent from his argument in the "Defence" that much of what Stoddard wrote took him by surprise. Why else would he have appended a sixty-two page treatise to Quick's pamphlet if he had said all that was necessary in the *Order of the Gospel?*

15. Ibid., p. 10.

16. Ibid., pp. 24, 27.

17. Ibid., p. 26. In their debate at the Synod of 1679 Stoddard had tried to justify open communion with references to the practice of the Jewish church. Mather labeled it an absurd argument but saw nothing sinister in it because Stoddard himself drew no larger conclusions from it. See Emerson and Lowance, "Increase Mather's Confutation," pp. 47–49.

18. Mather, "Defence of Evangelical Churches," pp. 43–50, 59–60.

19. See above, Chap. 7, note 23.

20. Mather hints that Samuel Rutherford once flirted with the notion of "converting" ordinances.

21. Mather, "Defence of Evangelical Churches," pp. 43–46.

22. Ibid., pp. 30–31.

23. The authorship of this important piece remains in doubt. That Colman was the prime contributor seems to be generally accepted, but his co-authors are more difficult to identify. The American Antiquarian Society, Worcester, Massachusetts, possesses a copy that was Increase Mather's own. On the front Mather identified the authors as Colman, Simon Bradstreet, and "T" Woodbridge, suggesting Timothy Woodbridge of Hartford.

24. Miller assumed that *Gospel Order Revived* was written only to defend the Brattle Street Church and that Colman, the author, had the support of the merchant-founders of that church. Several manuscripts contained in the Colman Papers, MHS, indicate, however, that considerable disagreement existed between ministers and laymen over the correct form of church polity. One letter in particular suggests that the founders intended to form an Anglican church (J. Nelson to Benjamin Colman, May 20, 1699, Colman Papers, Vol. 1). Yet Colman was a Presbyterian, and several of his later letters suggest that he sought to

mold the church into a Presbyterian church but was frustrated by the Congregationalism of the land: see esp. Colman to Robert Wodrow, December 9, 1717, in Niel Caplan, ed., "Some Unpublished Letters of Benjamin Colman, 1717-1725," MHS, *Proceedings*, 77 (1965), 107. This would tend to lend credence to the supposition that the *Gospel Order Revived* was a purely ministerial undertaking, devoid of the conspiratorial aspects suggested by Miller (see above, note 4). It also indicates a possible explanation for the author's decision to turn the treatise into a general defense of New England Presbyterianism while ostensibly defending only the "innovations" of Brattle Street.

25. Colman, *Gospel Order Revived*, p. 39.

26. Ibid., p. ii.

27. Ibid.

28. Ibid., p. iii.

29. Ibid., p. iv.

30. Ibid., p. vi.

31. The preceding analysis is taken from the introduction to the *Gospel Order Revived*, esp. pp. v–viii.

32. Ibid., p. 7.

33. Ibid., p. 12.

34. Ibid., p. 21.

35. See ibid., pp. ii–viii, 11–27, for the essence of the authors' Presbyterianism.

36. I have searched the archives of both Connecticut and Massachusetts for evidence linking Connecticut clergymen or churches to Stoddard's views and found practically nothing.

37. Gurdon Saltonstall, "Sermon Preached before the First Church of New London," December 26, 1703, Sermons of Gurdon Saltonstall, MHS. Stephen Mix, Stoddard's son-in-law, requested in his will that all his daughters receive copies of Stoddard's works (see Adams and Stiles, *Windsor*, 1: 330–332), and partially endorsed Stoddard in his *Extraordinary Displays of the Divine Majesty and Power* (New London, Conn., 1728), p. 29.

38. Increase opposed the Association movement as it emerged in the Proposals of 1705 and the Saybrook Platform of 1708. This opposition probably explains why Increase was willing and eager to engage Stoddard in a debate which both knew would destroy ministerial unity and bring public attention to ministerial goals and plans (see Middlekauff, *The Mathers*, pp. 225–226).

39. The failure of the Proposals is discussed at various points in Miller, *Colony to Province*, esp. pp. 261–266.

40. Northampton Church Records, Vol. 1, December 9, 1714. Forbes Library, Northampton, Massachusetts.
41. Walker, *Creeds and Platforms*, p. 498.
42. *Connecticut Court Records*, 5: 51.
43. Ibid.
44. Walker, *Creeds and Platforms*, pp. 501–502. Walker's discussion of the synod and the events surrounding the Platform remains the best published account.
45. Ibid., pp. 498–502; *Connecticut Court Records*, 5: 51.
46. Ibid., p. 457.
47. Ibid.
48. The passage is from the Ezra Stiles MSS, Yale University Library, New Haven, Connecticut, and is quoted in Walker, *Creeds and Platforms*, p. 501.
49. Ibid., p. 505. The section of the Platform on church government is to be found on pp. 502–605.
50. Ibid., p. 87; *Connecticut Court Records*, 5: 5, 87.
51. Ibid.

9. FROM THE SAYBROOK PLATFORM TO
THE GREAT AWAKENING

1. Walker, *Creeds and Platforms*, pp. 502–506.
2. Bushman, *Puritan to Yankee*, p. 150. The Saybrook Synod also climaxed a two-decade campaign by the clergy to have ministers' salaries guaranteed, or at least protected, by statute. That campaign, never publicized by the clergy, surfaced in 1690 when the General Assembly created a committee "to lay a good foundation for the settlement of a pious, able ministry." There was considerable public opposition, however, and two years later the Assembly refused to adopt the committee's recommendations (*Connecticut Court Records*, 4: 28, 73).
The ministers persisted, and in May 1697 they won a significant, if short-lived, victory. The Assembly ordered each town to divide its minister's salary among the inhabitants according to the ability of each to pay. Moreover, the Assembly warned that anyone not paying the ministerial levy would be subject to immediate prosecution in the County Court. The towns reacted adversely. A year later part of the law was nullified when the Court learned that some towns were using it to place ministers on one-year contracts, renewable only after severe scrutiny of the minister's deportment and capabilities. A year later

more of the law was declared void when the ministers complained that the Assembly's attempts to set a value on the commodities (wheat, corn, chickens, etc.) used to pay them were so ineffective and inefficient that the ministers would be better off with no law at all (*Connecticut Court Records*, 4: 290, 209, 259, 267, 198–199). The Assembly then tried to make amends to the clergy for the mess caused by the 1697 law by declaring ministers exempt from the yearly tax rate (ibid., p. 187).

The ministers achieved more success in 1708 when the Assembly agreed to let ministers place their salary in the county "rate" or tax levy and have it collected accordingly. Like the opposition that greeted the Platform, this law proved very unpopular and it was repealed in 1710 (*Connecticut Court Records*, 4: 50, 180). A few years later the Assembly made yet another attempt to guarantee the ministers' maintenance by giving local tax collectors the right to confiscate and sell property for nonpayment of the minister's levy (see, for example, *Connecticut Court Records*, 4: 315). That law, too, generated considerable hostility, some of which is discussed by Bushman in his chapter 10. All in all, the ministers' attempts to protect their salaries from the whims of church members and nonmembers fell far short of the results desired.

3. For example, in February 1799 the Hartford North Association sent the following message to member churches:
This Association gives information to all whom it may concern, that the Constitution of the Churches in the State of Connecticut, founded on the common usage, and the confession of faith, heads of agreement, and articles of church discipline, adopted at the earliest period of the Settlement of this State, is not Congregational, but contains the essentials of the church of Scotland, or Presbyterian Church in America, particularly as it gives decisive power to Ecclesiastical Councils; and a Consociation consisting of Ministers and Messengers or a lay representation from the churches is possessed of substantially the same authority as a Presbytery (Walker, *Creeds and Platforms*, p. 514).

4. See Jones, *Congregational Commonwealth*, chap. 3.

5. In Fairfield County the ministry ignored the legalized structure of the associations and formed a Presbyterian synod. See Walker, *Creeds and Platforms*, p. 509, and Stratford, Connecticut, Records of the First Congregational Church, Connecticut State Library, 1: 5–8.

6. M. Louise Green, *The Development of Religious Liberty in Con-*

necticut (Boston, 1905), pp. 146–152; Walker, *Creeds and Platforms*, pp. 508–512. About a dozen churches eventually rejected the Platform in its entirety. Compounding the confusion over the Platform was the fact that some churches reached no decision. A survey of the extant church records of the eighteenth century reveals congregations periodically debating the Platform, some as late as the 1780's. For the associations such indecision was tantamount to rejection.

Bushman (*Puritan to Yankee*, p. 219) echoes other historians in assuming that the Saybrook Platform and its associations remained a powerful, viable force in eighteenth-century Connecticut until undercut by New Light/Old Light squabbling during and after the Great Awakening. My survey of the Platform's reception over seven decades is, admittedly, less than systematic, but the evidence from the first two decades of the eighteenth century is sufficient to convince me that the Platform and the associations never had a modicum of the power commonly attributed to them. At least one other historian of the period agrees (James P. Walsh, "The Pure Church in Eighteenth Century Connecticut," unpublished Ph.D. thesis, Columbia University, 1970, p. 42).

7. Bumsted, "Revivalism and Separatism in New England," pp. 591–592.

8. South Windsor, Connecticut (formerly East Windsor), Records of the First Congregational Church, Connecticut State Library, Vol. 1, "A History of the Church" (author unknown).

9. Hartford Church Records, Vol. 1, January 13, 1720.

10. Missing from the list of original churches were, for example, Westfield, West Springfield, and Northfield.

11. Hampshire Association to the Enfield Church, 1715, Ms., Forbes Library.

12. Ibid.

13. Hampshire Association to the Enfield Church, August 20, 1718, Gratz Collection, American Section, "American Colonial Clergy," Box 25, Historical Society of Pennsylvania, Philadelphia.

14. Stoddard, *Inexcusableness of Neglecting The Worship of God*, pp. 11–12, 16–17, 25–27. Cf. Stoddard's argument in *Instituted Churches*, p. 22, where he states emphatically that all ordinances, and especially the Lord's Supper, exist primarily for conversion.

15. Stoddard, *Inexcusableness of Neglecting The Worship of God*, preface.

16. Solomon Stoddard, *An Appeal to the Learned. Being A Vindica-*

tion of the Right of Visible Saints to the Lords Supper, Though they be destitute of a Saving Work of God's Spirit on their Hearts: Against the Exceptions of Mr. Increase Mather (Boston, 1709).

17. Stoddard's continuing concern for the unconverted as well as his fear of impending doom for New England is ably demonstrated in *The Efficacy of the fear of Hell, to restrain Men from Sin* (Boston, 1713), pp. 5–10. The elements of his new plan for reaching the unconverted were sketched in two sermons bound with *Efficacy*. These sermons, undated, were delivered during a revival in Northampton. One was entitled "Minister's had need have the Spirit of the Lord upon them, in order to the reviving of religion among the people." The other was "To Preach the Gospel to the Poor."

18. Appended to Stoddard, *The Presence of Christ with the Ministers of the Gospel* (Boston, 1718).

19. Stoddard, *An Examination*, pp. 1–3.

20. Ibid., pp. 1–2, 11.

21. Ibid., pp. 7, 14–15, 16.

22. Stoddard, *Safety of Appearing*, pp. 119–125; his argument should be compared with his *Guide to Christ* (Boston, 1714), preface, pp. 3-23, and *The Nature of Saving Conversion, and the Way wherein it is Wrought* (Boston, 1719), pp. 81–83, for obvious similarities.

23. This is the essence of *Guide to Christ*. Throughout the sacramental phase of his career Stoddard emphasized that preaching was meant primarily to edify those not able to qualify as visible saints, while other ordinances were to prepare and convert professing Christians. Thus in downgrading the converting power of some ordinances, he enlarged and enhanced the meaning and scope of gospel preaching. See, for example, *Inexcusableness of Neglecting The Worship of God*, p. 27.

24. Stoddard's argument, repeated often between 1713 and 1729, may be gleaned from several of his writings. In addition to *Guide to Christ* and *Efficacy*, see *Presence of Christ, The Defects of Preachers Reproved* (New London, Conn., 1724), and *The Duty of Gospel-Ministers to preserve a People from Corruption* (Boston, 1718). The most concise statement I have found of his position is the sermon "Minister's had need have the Spirit," given around 1712, printed with Stoddard's *Efficacy* and also appended to the 1816 edition of *Guide to Christ* (Northampton, Mass., 1816), pp. 157–175.

25. Stoddard, *Guide to Christ*, p. XXI. Cf. his argument in *The Falseness of the Hopes of Many Professors* . . . (Boston, 1708), p. 16.

26. Stoddard paraphrased Hooker when he wrote, "The word of

God is an hammer, and men must smite with strength to make the nail enter, or the rock to break. If the word of God be preached in a dull dead way, it is not like to have much efficacy." "Minister's had need have the Spirit," in *Guide to Christ*, p. 159. See also the sermon following, "To whom is the gospel to be preached?" pp. 163–169, 176–183. Other passages illustrating Stoddard's doctrine of minister and Word are quoted by Schafer, "Solomon Stoddard," passim.

27. Stoddard's evangelicalism was matched by that of his colleague at Hatfield, William Williams, in *The Great Salvation Revealed and Offered in the Gospel* (Boston, 1717). Like Stoddard, Williams based his treatise on Paul's letters, emphasized the role of minister and gospel in conversion, and issued a call for a ministerially inspired revival. Other examples of Williams' evangelicalism are found in *A Painful Minister The Peculiar Gift of the Lord of the Harvest* (Boston, 1717), *The Great Duty of Ministers To Advance the Kingdom of God* (Boston, 1726), and *The Honour of Christ.* In Connecticut one of the most ardent advocates of the new evangelicalism was Eliphalet Adams of New London. Adams' arguments closely paralleled those of Stoddard and Williams, exalting the power and authority of the minister because of his central position in the conversion process. Adams' commitment to Pauline theology was complete, his zeal for revival an obsession. See esp. *A Sermon Preached at Windham . . .* (New London, Conn., 1721), *The Work of Ministers, rightly to Divide the Word of Truth* (New London, Conn., 1725), and *Ministers Must take heed to their Ministry, to Fulfil it* (New London, Conn., 1726). There were also other treatises on the new evangelicalism published by ministers of lesser note. These include two by Jonathan Marsh of Windsor, *An Essay, To Prove the Thorough Reformation of a Sinning People is not to be Expected . . .* (New London, Conn., 1721), and *The Great Care and Concern of Men Under Gospel-Light* (New London, Conn., 1721); an ordination sermon by Isaac Chauncey of Hadley entitled, *The Faithful Evangelist, Or the True Shepherd* (Boston, 1725); also Samuel Whitman of Farmington, *Practical Godliness the Way to Prosperity* (New London, Conn., 1714); and John Woodward of Norwich, *Civil Rulers are God's Ministers, for the Peoples Good* (Boston, 1712).

28. The reference to the Hampshire County Weekly Lecture is from Warham Williams Journal, 1712, MHS. A Hartford County Weekly Lecture began soon after and is discussed in Walker, *Hartford*, pp. 268–270.

29. Holifield, *The Covenant Sealed*, pp. 228–229.

30. Adams, *Sermon at Windham*, pp. ii–iv.

31. See Bumsted, "Revivalism and Separatism," pp. 588–612.

32. See, for example, Bushman, *Puritan to Yankee*, chaps. 12–15; or C. C. Goen, *Revivalism and Separatism in New England: Strict Congregationalists and Separate Baptists in the Great Awakening* (New Haven, 1962). An exception to the pattern of disruption is noted and analyzed by James Walsh, "The Great Awakening in the First Congregational of Woodbury, Connecticut," *William and Mary Quarterly*, 3rd ser., 28 (1971), 543–562.

CONCLUSION

1. Bushman, *Puritan to Yankee*, preface.
2. Ibid., p. 288.
3. Ibid., preface.

INDEX